PATTERN-ORIENTED SOFTWARE ARCHITECTURE

Wiley Series in Software Design Patterns

The WILEY SERIES IN SOFTWARE DESIGN PATTERNS is designed to meet the needs of today's software architects, developers, programmers and managers interested in design patterns. Frank Buschmann, the Series Editor, as well as authors, shepherds and reviewers will work collaboratively within the patterns community to strive for high-quality, highly researched, thoroughly validated, classic works which document accepted and acknowledged design experience. Priority will be given to those titles that catalog software patterns and pattern languages with a practical, applied approach in domains such as:

- Distributed systems
- Real time systems
- Databases
- Business information systems
- Telecommunications
- Organizations
- Concurrency
- Networking

Books in the series will also cover conceptual areas of how to apply patterns, pattern language developments and architectural/component-based approaches to pattern-led software development.

TITLES PUBLISHED

- PATTERN-ORIENTED SOFTWARE ARCHITECTURE, Volume 1

Frank Buschmann, Regine Meunier, Hans Rohnert, Peter Sommerlad and Michael Stal

| 0 471 95869 7 | 476pp | 1996 | Hardback |

- PATTERN-ORIENTED SOFTWARE ARCHITECTURE, Volume 2

Douglas Schmidt, Michael Stal, Hans Rohnert and Frank Buschmann

| 0 471 60695 2 | 636pp | 2000 | Hardback |

- A PATTERN APPROACH TO INTERACTION DESIGN

Jan Borchers

| 0 471 49828 9 | 250pp | 2001 | Hardback |

- SERVER COMPONENT PATTERNS

Markus Völter, Alexander Shmid, Eberhard Wolff

| 0 471 84319 5 | 462pp | 2002 | Hardback |

- ARCHITECTING ENTERPRISE SOLUTIONS

Paul Dyson, Andy Longshaw

| 0 470 85612 2 | 384pp | 2004 | Hardback |

- PATTERN-ORIENTED SOFTWARE ARCHITECTURE, Volume 3

Michael Kircher, Prashant Jain

| 0 470 84525 2 | 312pp | 2004 | Hardback |

PATTERN-ORIENTED SOFTWARE ARCHITECTURE

Patterns for Resource Management

Volume 3

Michael Kircher,
Siemens AG Corporate Technology, Munich, Germany

Prashant Jain,
IBM Research Labs, Delhi, India

JOHN WILEY & SONS, LTD

Reprinted October 2005, March 2006, March 2008

Other Wiley Editorial Offices

John Wiley & Sons Inc., 111 River Street, Hoboken, NJ 07030, USA

Jossey-Bass, 989 Market Street, San Francisco, CA 94103-1741, USA

Wiley-VCH Verlag GmbH, Boschstr. 12, D-69469 Weinheim, Germany

John Wiley & Sons Australia Ltd, 33 Park Road, Milton, Queensland 4064, Australia

John Wiley & Sons (Asia) Pte Ltd, 2 Clementi Loop #02-01, Jin Xing Distripark, Singapore 129809

John Wiley & Sons (Canada) Ltd, 22 Worcester Road, Etobicoke, Ontario M9W 1L1

Wiley also publishes its books in a variety of electronic formats. Some content that appears in print
may not be available in electronic books.

British Library Cataloguing in Publication Data

A catalogue record for this book is available from the British Library

ISBN 978-0-470-84525-7 (hbk)

For Christa, my parents, and grandparents

Michael Kircher

For Ruchi, Aanya, and my parents

Prashant Jain

Table of Contents

Foreword by Frank Buschmann

I never thought this would happen: a new volume of the POSA series is published and nobody from the original 'Party of Five' is on the author list. Yet I am very proud that I was wrong! I am proud because this book shows that a new generation of smart software engineers has grown up and is actively contributing their experience to the patterns community. I am proud because the book demonstrates that the pattern idea is still thriving. And I am proud, of course, because our original POSA vision from 1996 is still inspiring patterns authors to build on our material and enhance, mature, and evolve it.

The topic chosen for this POSA volume is key for the success of almost every software system: resource management. This may appear obvious, but only a decade ago many developers thought resource management was of concern only in the embedded systems domain. In the desktop and enterprise spheres only a few developers paid attention to the topic. Why care about resources like memory, for example—if you run out of it, you can simply upgrade your machine. I must admit that in the earlier days of my career I had a similar perspective: resources were just 'there' and unlimited. How wrong I was! Fortunately I shot myself in the foot and quickly learned my lesson.

Today few developers ignore the importance of resource management. With the advent of component-based systems, application servers, and the growing complexity and size of the applications running on our computers, it is realized that managing resources carefully can make a significant difference to the quality of a software system. Resources such as memory, CPU power, threads, connections, and so on are limited even on the biggest servers. Yet these servers are expected to provide a high quality of service to all their users, even if they are accessed by zillions of users simultaneously. This conflict is only resolvable if the server's resources are managed explicitly and with care. However, the term 'resource' is not limited to low-level things like memory or connections. In today's networked computing world, resources can also include components and services that are used remotely by client applications. Multiple client applications often compete for access to these components and services. Ensuring that all clients are served sufficiently well is the subject of appropriate resource management.

However, acknowledging the importance of resource management and doing it well are two different things. Effective resource management is both difficult and challenging. If you do it well, your applications will be efficient, stable, scalable, predictable, and accessible. If you do it badly, your applications will at best provide very limited operational quality. At worst they will just fail—it is as simple as that. Allowing a container to do resource management is not always a solution, because many software systems cannot afford such infrastructures. Even if using a container is a feasible option, you need to understand how its resource management works to be able to build high quality systems. Many applications using containers fail simply because of lack of understanding.

How can you acquire this understanding? What sources can you mine for the challenges in resource management, the solutions to master these challenges, and the do's and don't associated with the solutions? One such source is the book you are holding, the third volume of the POSA series. It presents experiences and solutions in resource management gained over many years. All such experiences and solutions have proved their quality in active duty in countless well-known applications and middleware. Capturing these experiences and solutions as patterns makes them accessible to every software developer. Novices can learn about the fundamental concerns and solutions in resource management, while experts can cross-check and evaluate alternative solutions and read about details of a particular solution. I am unaware of any other literature on resource management that is equally comprehensive.

As said at the beginning: I am proud of this book. If you read it, you will know why.

Frank Buschmann
Siemens AG, Corporate Technology

Foreword by Steve Vinoski

If you've been a software developer for any appreciable length of time, you have almost certainly experienced what I call the 'stroll down computer memory lane'. This event occurs regularly when developers get together in a social setting, such as having lunch together. It starts out innocently enough, with one of the developers describing a recent run-in with an especially difficult problem. Not to be outdone, another developer chimes in with a story detailing the conquest of an even worse problem. From there, each new story attempts to outdo the last, until only the old-timers are left speaking about primitive machines that had to be programmed with punch cards or toggle switches and had only a few bytes of RAM. I am waiting for the day that during a stroll down computer memory lane, someone tries to convince me that back when he or she started programming, there were only zeros to program with, and no ones!

Developers are able to compare stories in the manner described above because programming inherently requires many trade-offs. Applications have to share computing resources with other applications. Memory space and disk storage are not infinite. CPUs can process only a certain number of instructions per second. Disk and device I/O can take a relatively long time. Establishing database connections and network connections can be expensive in terms of time and resources. Throughout the history of electronic computing, tremendous advances have been made in hardware, operating systems, middleware, and applications. Unfortunately, despite these advances, programming remains very much an art of choosing the right trade-offs to maximize the effectiveness of the overall computing solution.

All applications manage resources of some kind, such as memory, connections to networks or databases, or threads. However, there is a marked difference between applications that are written and tuned to manage resources well and those that aren't. Ignoring resource management is not a problem for simple applications that run only occasionally for brief periods of time, such as basic command-line utilities or configuration GUIs. However, a lack of focus on resource management is a recipe for failure when developing long-running applications that must be robust, high performance, and scalable, such as Web servers, application servers, and notification systems.

The patterns in this book are about resource management. Generally, resources can be acquired, managed, and released, and the patterns presented here specifically target those three areas. These are the primary areas that can have a profound influence on the overall performance, size, scalability, and durability of a running application. For example, many applications acquire memory from the heap. For an application like a Web or application server, every individual heap memory allocation made in the request-handling code path decreases the server's performance and scalability, due to the cost of invoking the heap manager and the cost of acquiring and releasing mutexes needed to protect the heap for concurrent access. Such an application might instead apply a pattern such as Partial Acquisition to eagerly acquire as many resources as possible before entering the request code path, and apply the Caching or Pooling patterns to keep the resources around for the next request, rather than releasing them and later reacquiring them. Even experienced developers can be pleasantly surprised by the degree to which applying the right combination of resource management patterns can positively impact the performance and scalability of an application.

This book continues with the POSA tradition of emphasizing practical solutions. I especially like the fact that each pattern in this book includes a fairly detailed section describing implementation issues, as well as a section that provides an extensive list of known applications of the pattern. In addition, there are two chapters describing detailed case studies that show not only how the patterns might be applied to real-world applications, but also how the patterns relate to each other within such applications. Patterns are, after all, descriptions of approaches that have been proven to work in real applications, and the fact that the authors have so effectively tied them back to their sources and influences ensures that the patterns maintain that important connection with the real world.

Software patterns generally help us decide what trade-offs to make in our architectures and designs, and where to make them. Programming is, after all, a human endeavor, and patterns raise the levels of abstraction and communication that teams use to socialize their architectures and designs. As a long-time middleware architect, designer, and implementer, I have at one time or another successfully applied each of the patterns that Prashant and Michael present here. Unfortunately, I did so before the approaches were captured as patterns, which means that my teammates and I spent many hours devising our own variations, implementing them, measuring them to determine their trade-offs, and refining and tuning them based on our measurements. Now, because Michael and Prashant have clearly and comprehensively documented these approaches as a pattern language, you and your teammates can more easily discuss them and understand what they're good for, determine the best circumstances under which to apply them, and understand the forces you need to concern yourselves with when implementing them.

Armed with the knowledge of these resource management patterns and good performance measurement tools, you'll be pleasantly surprised at how quickly and easily you can take an application with only mediocre performance and scalability and turn it into something that races along instead. With these kinds of skills, your stories at the next stroll down computer memory lane will impress even the old-timers.

Steve Vinoski
Chief Engineer, Product Innovation
IONA Technologies

About This Book

This is a book about patterns for resource management in software systems. The patterns provide solutions for problems that are typically encountered by software architects and developers when trying to provide an effective and efficient means of managing resources in a software system. Efficient management of resources is critical in the execution of any kind of software. From embedded software in a mobile device to software in a large enterprise server, it is important that resources, such as memory, threading, files, or network connections, are managed efficiently to allow the systems to function properly and effectively.

The first volume of the Pattern Oriented Software Architecture (POSA) series [POSA1] introduced a broad-spectrum of general-purpose patterns in software design and architecture. The second volume of the series [POSA2] narrowed the focus to fundamental patterns for building sophisticated concurrent and networked software systems and applications. This volume uses patterns to present techniques for implementing effective resource management in a system.

The patterns in this book are covered in detail and make use of several examples. As with the previous POSA volumes, the book provides directions to the readers on how to implement the patterns presented. Additionally, the volume presents a thorough introduction to resource management, and two case studies, in which the patterns are applied to two different domains. The patterns presented are independent of any implementation technique, such as .NET, Java or C++, even though the examples are given in Java and C++. The patterns are grouped by different areas of resource management, and hence address the complete lifecycle of resources: resource acquisition, resource lifecycle and resource release.

The patterns in the book provide an extensive coverage of the sphere of resource management. We began documenting these patterns several years ago based on our experiences of building many different software systems. Most of the patterns have been presented or workshopped at leading conferences. However, what we felt was missing was an effort to pull the patterns together in the form of a pattern language and present it in such a way that the pattern language can be applied to multiple domains.

The scope of resource management is vast. The challenges that are faced by system designers and developers dealing with the management of resources are constantly changing as new technologies emerge. We anticipate that additional patterns in resource management will be discovered and documented with time. The *Concluding Remarks* chapter of this book talks about what lies ahead in the effort to evolve the resource management pattern language.

Intended Audience

This book is for all software architects, designers, and developers. They can use the patterns described in the book to solve the challenges in resource management that every typical software system faces.

The book will also be useful to students of computer science, as it can provide them with a broad overview of the available best practices in resource management.

Structure of the Book

The book is divided into two parts. The first part provides an introduction to the topic of resource management and the patterns in resource management. The patterns presented in the first part have been grouped into three chapters, *Resource Acquisition*, *Resource Lifecycle*, and *Resource Release*, to correspond with the typical lifecycle of resources. The second part of the book applies the patterns to two case studies.

While the first part of the book looks at resource management from a problem domain perspective, the second part of the book does so from an application domain perspective. The patterns in this book are not isolated. In fact, throughout our coverage of resource management patterns, we make extensive references to other related and relevant patterns. For each such pattern, we have included thumbnail descriptions in the *Referenced Patterns* chapter.

The book contains many examples of the use of the patterns. While the patterns use individual examples, each case study chapter uses a single example in a particular domain to tie all the patterns together. This acts as a running example by presenting problems in that particular domain and uses the individual patterns together to address the problems presented. This approach allows us to prove the broad applicability of the patterns while still showing how they connect together.

The first chapter, *Introduction*, formally introduces the topic of resource management in software systems and defines its scope. The chapter describes why managing resources in software systems effectively and efficiently is challenging. It also introduces patterns and shows how they can be used to address the challenges of resource management.

Chapter 2, *Resource Acquisition*, describes patterns that address the forces affecting the acquisition of resources. Resources must be acquired before they can be used. However, acquisition of resources should not degrade system performance, nor should it produce any bottlenecks. For large resources or resources that become available only in parts, the adaptation of the resource acquisition strategy is essential.

Chapter 3, *Resource Lifecycle*, describes patterns that resolve forces affecting the lifecycle of resources. Resources can have very different lifecycles. For example, some resources are both heavily and frequently used, while others may only be used once. When a resource is no longer needed, it can be released. However, determining when to release a resource is not trivial. Explicit control of the lifecycle of a resource can be tedious and error-prone. To address this problem, automated resource management techniques are needed. In addition, in certain architectures such as distributed systems, multiple resources have to work together to achieve a higher common goal. As every resource can potentially be managed by its own thread of control, the collaboration and integration of multiple resources needs to be coordinated.

Chapter 4, *Resource Release*, describes patterns that deal with the efficient and effective release of resources. Resources no longer needed should be returned to the resource environment to optimize system performance and allow other users to acquire them. However, if a released resource needs to be used again by the same resource user, the resource must be re-acquired, impacting performance. The challenge is to find the right balance and to determine when to release resources. Furthermore, explicit invocation of resource management operations, such as the release of a resource, is tedious. How can the management effort be kept at a minimum while ensuring high efficiency and scalability?

In Chapter 5, *Guidelines for Applying Resource Management*, we present guidelines for applying resource management, which describe a recipe for applying the resource management pattern language to a particular domain effectively.

Chapter 6, *Case Study: Ad Hoc Networking*, shows how an ad hoc networking application can be built and its resource management requirements addressed using the patterns we describe.

Chapter 7, *Case Study: Mobile Network*, ties all the patterns into a pattern language, and uses that pattern language to address the requirements of a case study in the telecommunications domain.

In Chapter 8, *The Past, Present, and Future of Patterns*, Frank Buschmann continues the tradition of looking back at the forecasts about 'where patterns are going' made in the earlier POSA volume. He further analyzes where patterns are now, and makes predictions about the future of patterns.

Chapter 9, *Concluding Remarks*, completes the main content of the book. This chapter includes an analysis of what future work in the area of resource management might include.

Referenced Patterns documents all the patterns we reference as thumbnails, and *Notations* contains a key to all the notations that we use in this book.

For supplementary material, we encourage you to visit our Web site at `http://www.posa3.org`. The site contains all the source code that we present in the patterns, together with updates to the patterns themselves. The site also contains any additions to the resource management pattern language that have been made over time.

If you have any comments, constructive criticism, or suggestions for improvement, please send them to us via e-mail to authors@posa3.org.

Guide to the Reader

This book is constructed so that you can read it from cover to cover. If you know what you want to achieve, however, you may want to choose your own route through the book. In this case, the following hints can help you decide which topics to focus on and the order in which to read them:

- To see how individual patterns can be used in practice and how they work together, start with the problem and solution sections of the patterns, then continue with the case studies in Chapters 6 and 7.

- To get a feeling for the broad applicability of the pattern language, look for the abstracts and known uses of each pattern in Chapters 2 to 4.

- To see how the resource management pattern language fits into existing patterns work, especially those that touch on the area of resource management, refer to Section 1.5, *Related Work*.

We summarize the pattern language inside the front and back covers. Inside the front cover, we present a quick overview of the pattern language by listing the abstracts of all patterns. Inside the back cover, we present a pattern map illustrating the relationships between the patterns.

Acknowledgements

It is a pleasure for us to thank the many people who supported us in writing this book. Foremost, we would like to thank our shepherd, Charles Weir, and the reviewers of this book: Cor Baars, Frank Buschmann, Fabio Kon, Karl Pröse, Christa Schwanninger, Michael Stal, Christoph Stückjuergen, Bill Willis, and Egon Wuchner. Special thanks to the Silicon Valley Patterns Group, with outstanding contributions from Trace Bialik, Jeffrey Miller, Russ Rufer, and Wayne Vucenic. Collaborating on the Internet using Wiki to obtain feedback from the Silicon Valley Patterns Group proved to be very effective.

We wish to thank our EuroPLoP and PLoP shepherds who have extensively reviewed individual patterns: Pascal Costanza, Ed Fernandez, Alejandra Garrido, Bob Hanmer, Kevlin Henney, Irfan Pyarali, Terry Terunobu, John Vlissides, and Uwe Zdun. We also wish to thank the reviewers of individual chapters: Roland Grimminger, Kevlin Henney, Michael Klug, Douglas C. Schmidt, Peter Sommerlad, and Markus Völter. Kevlin also supported us by providing many of the chapter citations, reviewing the correct usage of UML in our diagrams, and giving recommendations on the use of white space.

We also wish to thank Kirthika Parameswaran, with whom we worked on the idea of implementing JinACE [KiJa04], a Jini-like [Sun04c] framework implemented using C++. Our work inspired us to dig deeper into the concept of ad hoc networking and ultimately discover the patterns behind it. We want to thank her for the brainstorming sessions via long e-mail exchanges.

We are grateful to Douglas C. Schmidt, who encouraged us to view our research on JinACE from a pattern language perspective. The patterns that subsequently emerged motivated us to start working on the resource management pattern language.

Further, we wish to thank the pattern team at Siemens AG, Corporate Technology: Martin Botzler, Frank Buschmann, Michael Stal, Karl Pröse, Christa Schwanninger, Dietmar Schütz, and Egon Wuchner.

For the wonderful support on this book, we would like to thank our contacts at John Wiley & Sons: Gaynor Redvers-Mutton, Juliet Booker and Jonathan Shipley. Steve Rickaby, our copy editor, did a great job in helping us polish the book. It was a pleasure working with him.

Finally, we wish to express our special thanks to Frank Buschmann. He not only served as a reviewer of the book, and contributor of the chapter on *The Past, Present, and Future of Patterns*, but also gave us inspiration and encouragement to help us complete the book.

About The Authors

Michael Kircher

Michael Kircher is currently working as Senior Software Engineer at Siemens AG Corporate Technology in Munich, Germany. His main fields of interest include distributed object computing, software architecture, patterns, eXtreme Programming, and management of knowledge workers in innovative environments. He has been involved as a consultant and developer in many projects, within various Siemens business areas, building software for distributed systems. Among those were the development of software for UMTS base stations, postal automation systems, and operation and maintenance software for industry and telecommunication systems.

During his studies he was a member of the research group lead by Douglas C. Schmidt, where he was involved in the development of the Real-Time CORBA implementation TAO (The ACE ORB). That was when he discovered the world of patterns. In the course of implementing an efficient multi-threaded dispatching mechanism for TAO, he co-authored his first pattern with Irfan Pyarali, Leader/Followers.

In recent years he has published at numerous conferences on topics such as patterns, software architecture for distributed systems, and eXtreme Programming. Together with Prashant, he organized several workshops on the topics covered by this book at conferences such as OOPSLA and EuroPLoP.

In his spare time Michael likes to combine family life with enjoying nature on foot and by bike. The best place for him to relax is in his custom-made hide, while watching wildlife accompanied by his hunting dog Ella.

Prashant Jain

Prashant Jain is currently working as a Technical Staff Member at IBM Research Labs in Delhi, India. His main fields of interest include distributed systems, e-commerce, software architecture, patterns and eXtreme programming. At IBM he has been doing research on emerging technologies in the area of e-commerce.

Prashant obtained his Masters degree in Computer Science from Washington University in St. Louis, U.S.A. It was there that he developed a keen interest in design patterns, and in 1996 co-authored his first pattern with his advisor, Douglas C. Schmidt. Since then he has been actively involved in the pattern community by means of authoring pattern submissions and organizing pattern workshops at conferences such as OOPSLA and EuroPLoP.

His passion for travel has seen Prashant living and working in countries that include India, Japan, the USA, and Germany. His professional experience includes working for companies such as Siemens AG, Fujitsu Network Communications Inc., and Kodak Health Imaging Systems Inc. He has also been actively involved in the Centre for Distributed Object Computing at Washington University.

In his spare time, Prashant enjoys travelling, dining out, watching movies and swimming. But his most cherished activity is engaging in logical conversations with his four-year old daughter Aanya, which often leave him speechless.

1 Introduction

> *"A common mistake that people make
> when trying to design something completely foolproof
> is to underestimate the ingenuity of complete fools."*
>
> *Douglas Adams*

A *resource* is an entity that is available in limited supply such that there exists a requestor, the *resource user*, that needs the entity to perform a function, and there exists a mechanism, the *resource provider*, that provides the entity on request. In the context of software systems, a resource can include, among other things, memory, synchronization primitives, file handles, network connections, security tokens, database sessions, and local as well as distributed services. A resource can be anything from a heavyweight object such as an application server component [VSW02] to a fine-grained lightweight object such as a file handle.

Determining what is a resource can sometimes be challenging. For example, in programming environments an image, such as a JPEG or

GIF file, is often referred to as a resource. In reality, however, there are no acquisition and release semantics defined for an image—instead, it is the data that makes up the image that constitutes a resource. Therefore a more accurate representation would be to treat the memory an image is using as a resource, which needs to be acquired when the image is loaded and released when the image is no longer needed.

There are numerous ways of categorizing resources. In the simplest, resources can be viewed as either *reusable* or *non-reusable*. Reusable resources typically are acquired from a resource provider, used and then released. Once the resources have been released they can be acquired and used again. An example of a reusable resource is memory that is allocated by and released to the operating system. Other examples of reusable resources include file handles and threads. Reusable resources are the most important form of resource, because the resource provider typically only has a limited number of resources, and therefore reusing resources that are not consumed makes logical sense. In contrast, non-reusable resources are consumed, and therefore once acquired are either not released, or their release is implicit. An example of a non-reusable resource is processing time in a computing grid [Grid04]—once the processing time is acquired and used, it is gone and cannot be returned.

A different method of categorizing resources is based on how the resources are accessed or used. A resource, once acquired, can be concurrently used either by multiple users or a single user. Examples of resources that are concurrently accessible by multiple users include services, queues, and databases. If a resource that can be concurrently accessed by multiple users has changeable state, then access to that resource needs to be synchronized. On the other hand, if a resource that can be concurrently accessed by multiple users does not have state, then no synchronization is needed. An example of a resource that does not need synchronization is a stateless session bean of a J2EE EJB [Sun04b] application server. On the other hand, a network communication socket is an example of a resource that needs synchronization. A resource that can be concurrently accessed by multiple users need not be acquired explicitly by each user. Instead, resource users can share references to the resource, such that a resource user initially acquires the resource reference and others just use it.

In contrast, if a resource can only be used by a single user, it is called an exclusive resource. An example of an exclusive resource is the processing time of a service. The processing time can be regarded as a non-reusable exclusive resource that is provided by the service, which is the resource provider. Resource users can acquire processing time from the service. The service itself can be regarded as another resource. Acquiring the service means acquiring the processing time.

Exclusive resources can be both reusable as well as non-reusable. However, if a resource is non-reusable, it is always exclusive, since it can only be used by a single resource user. Furthermore, if an exclusive resource is reusable, then it must be serially reusable—the resource is reused over time through the resource provider.

Putting resources into different categories is often neither so simple nor even meaningful. For example, in contrast to the processing time of a service, CPU time can also be regarded as an example of a valuable resource. On one hand one might regard CPU time as a non-reusable exclusive resource that is acquired by a thread, which is the resource user. However, in reality CPU time is not under the control of any application, but is instead under the control of the operating system. From an application perspective, the operating system assigns the CPU to a thread, so the thread does not really acquire the CPU as resource.

Resources often depend on other resources. For example, a file handle as a resource represents a file, which can again be thought of as a resource. Another example is a service that is provided by a component, which consists of thread and memory resources. These resource dependencies can be represented in the form of a graph across multiple layers of resource providers.

The following table summarizes the categorization of resources, giving one example per category:

	reusable	non-reusable
exclusive	memory	processing time
concurrent	read-only object	–

1.1   Overview of Resource Management

Resource management in software systems is the process of controlling the availability of resources to resource users. A resource user can be any entity that acquires, accesses, or releases resources. Resource management includes ensuring that the resources are available when needed, that their lifecycle is deterministic and that they are released in a timely manner to ensure the liveliness of the systems that use them.

Managing resources is hard; managing them efficiently is even harder. Very often the non-functional requirements of a piece of software, such as performance, scalability, flexibility, stability, security, and quality of service, depend heavily on efficient resource management. These non-functional requirements act as forces that influence the way the software is designed and implemented. While each force can be independently addressed when developing a system, it is trying to find a balance among several of these forces that makes it especially challenging. In striking a balance among such forces, several questions and issues need to be addressed. For example, is the performance of a system more critical than making the system flexible and easy to maintain? Similarly, is predictability of the response time of a system more important than its scalability? Is fast initial access to a service more important than the average access time?

Addressing several of these forces simultaneously is challenging. This is because resolving one of the forces often requires compromising some other aspect of the system. For example, flexibility often comes at the expense of system performance. Similarly, optimizing special use cases, such as initial access to a service, usually results in an increase in complexity and very often an increase in latency in handling the average use case. A strong dependency on efficient resource management is tightly coupled with the challenge to address these often conflicting forces. Addressing most of the forces has to do with the way resources are acquired, accessed, and managed in general.

The following major forces need to be considered when designing systems with efficient resource management:

- *Performance.* A system whose performance is critical has to exhibit many properties. Among these are low latency and high throughput. Since each action typically involves many resources, it is important to avoid unnecessary resource acquisitions, releases, and accesses that incur processing overhead and delay.

- *Scalability.* Large and complex systems typically have a large number of resource users that access the resources multiple times. In many cases, systems are designed with use cases in mind, defining, for example the number of users to be expected. Very often these use cases are expanded over time as new requirements are added. For example, a new requirement could demand support for more users and higher transfer volumes while having minimum impact on system performance. If a system is able to fulfill these requirements it is said to be scalable. The way resources are managed and the way their lifecycle is managed plays a key role in achieving this goal. Besides the synchronization overhead, the acquisition and release of resources accounts for the largest portion of CPU cycles [SMFG01]. Besides scaling up, it is important to consider scaling down. To scale down means that software that has been designed and developed for large systems has to adapt to smaller systems and run with less resources.

- *Predictability.* Predictability means the system behaving as it is expected to behave. In systems with real-time requirements, the maximum response time of individual operations must be predictable. To achieve predictability, a system must manage its resources with care. When optimizations are applied, they must not diminish service predictability in favor of performance or scalability.

- *Flexibility.* A common requirement among systems is ease of configuration and customization. This implies that it should be possible to change the system configuration at the time of compilation, initialization, or run-time. Systems that are truly flexible leave this freedom to their users. In terms of resource management, therefore, the mechanics of acquisition, release and lifecycle control of resources need to be flexible, while still preserving performance, reliability, and scalability requirements.

- *Stability.* An important requirement of software systems is that frequent resource acquisition and release should not make the system unstable. Resource allocation and management must be done in a manner that leads to efficient use of resources and avoids scenarios of resource starvation that can lead to system instability. If multiple resources interact, or are involved as a group in any action, it has to be ensured that the system does not end up in an inconsistent state due to the failure of one or more resources.

- *Consistency.* All resource acquisition, access, and release must leave a software system in a consistent state. In particular, any inter-dependencies among resources must be well-managed to ensure system consistency.

Therefore, as can be seen, most of these forces are interdependent, and hence it is difficult to tackle one without influencing others. This is what makes resource management so hard and why it is important to address these issues in a well-structured way.

1.2   Scope of Resource Management

Resource management is an important aspect of almost every domain, ranging from small, embedded applications [NoWe00] to large enterprise systems [Fowl02], and even grid computing [BBL02]. Any system can benefit from efficient resource management regardless of the type of resources, or the availability of resources. For example, applications for small and embedded devices typically have limited resources, so the need for good resource management is obvious. The primary limiting factors are CPU performance, the available memory and the small bandwidth of networks and buses. Typical embedded applications include software for mobile phones and handheld devices.

Similarly, large enterprise systems run software for telecommunication switching and e-business applications. Such systems typically base their applications on top of frameworks and server-side component systems. In such systems, efficient resource management is essential to guarantee scalability, since adding additional hardware must be avoided to save cost.

It is common for the need for resource management to be discovered late in the development lifecycle, at the time of system integration and testing, when system analysis and performance analysis are performed. However, making changes to system design by that stage is difficult and costly. It is therefore important to address challenges in resource management early in the lifecycle of a software system.

Resources are acquired from some kind of resource provider. For example, memory is acquired from the operating system. Since acquisition is typically an expensive operation, the lifecycle of the acquired resource must be properly controlled to minimize additional overhead. Since an unused resource can also be considered an overhead, it is therefore important to control their timely release.

While it is important to address the primary forces of a software system that influence resource acquisition, access, and release, it is equally important to find solutions that are simple. Solutions that incur more overhead than benefit are not useful. Effective resource management should therefore result in simple programming models for the application developer. For example, introducing a level of transparency in the way resources are managed can help simplify the developer's task.

Most modern applications are built in the form of a layered [POSA1] architecture. Typically, an OS abstraction layer forms the lowest layer, followed by a middleware layer [POSA2] [VKZ04], a component or basic services layer [VSW02], and finally the actual application logic layer.

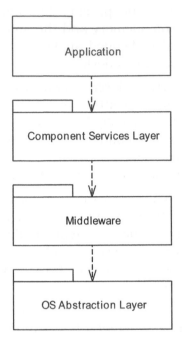

Resource management is not restricted to any of these layers. Instead, it is applicable at all levels of abstraction. For example, OS resources such as file handles and memory need to be handled with care by the OS abstraction layer. Similarly, the middleware layer has to manage many types of resource, such as connections and threads.

Resource management is important not only in local systems, but also in distributed systems. Distributed systems are much more complex to manage, since remote communication is unreliable. As a result, managing resources that are distributed across process boundaries becomes even more difficult.

1.3   Use of Patterns

Patterns help capture best practice in solving problems in almost every domain. Patterns have been applied to areas ranging from the architecture of buildings [Alex79] to the architecture of software systems and to teaching [Peda04]. In this book we specifically look at patterns applied to software architecture.

Patterns in software architecture can show how one or several design principles can be applied in a concrete situation to find an optimal solution. As described in [POSA1], the application of design principles finds its manifestation through many *enabling techniques*, such as abstraction, encapsulation and modularization. Using patterns can help to identify and document some of the design principles that are above the level of single classes and instances. These identified abstractions can then facilitate reuse of successful software architectures and designs. By reusing successful software architectures, common mistakes and pitfalls in software design can be avoided. For a more in-depth understanding of what a pattern is, as well as a history of patterns, please refer to [POSA1] and [POSA2].

As described earlier, efficient resource management inherently affects the design and development of any kind of software. In a multi-tier system, resource management is important at every tier of the system and even across tiers. It is essential that resource management is implemented properly from a system perspective.

The design techniques that must be used when implementing resource management in a system depend largely on the domain, the system constraints, and the system requirements. Patterns abstract from a particular domain and are driven by system requirements and constraints. They therefore provide the most effective means of describing the design techniques appropriate for use in a given system. One of the fundamental elements of a pattern is the context in which the pattern is applicable. This can be used to identify systems in which a particular resource management strategy should be used.

Another key element of a pattern is a set of forces that the pattern helps to address. In the context of resource management, this can be used to identify parts of a system where one or more patterns can be applied.

1.4   Patterns in Resource Management

At the beginning of this chapter we listed several forces that correspond to a set of non-functional requirements for typical software systems. Since these forces affect resource management, resolving them can lead to significant benefits for software systems. This book presents a pattern language for resource management that resolves these forces. In the context of this book, a resource includes everything defined earlier in this chapter. While each pattern presented in here is self-contained, the patterns together form a cohesive pattern language that can help software developers and designers to address some of the challenges of resource management. The following is a synopsis of the patterns presented in the book and the forces they resolve.

- *Performance.* The Eager Acquisition (53) pattern helps to speed up initial resource access, and thus the response time of the overall system. The Caching (83) pattern increases performance by avoiding expensive re-acquisition of regularly used resources. The Pooling (97) pattern can improve the performance of an application, as it helps reduce the time spent in costly release and re-acquisition of resources.

- *Scalability.* The Leasing (149) and Evictor (168) patterns help to free unused resources, reducing the risk of resource starvation and thereby increasing system scalability and stability. The Coordinator (111) pattern provides a solution that is scalable with the number of participants in the system. The Caching (83) and the Pooling (97) patterns help to avoid expensive resource acquisition and release, benefitting system scalability. Similarly, the Lazy Acquisition (38) and Partial Acquisition (66) patterns ensure that resources are acquired only when they are actually needed, thus reducing the number of resources required at a specific point in time. The Resource Lifecycle Manager (128) pattern supports scalability by managing the lifecycle of resources, and ensuring that an optimal number of resources are maintained.

- *Predictability.* The Eager Acquisition (53) pattern avoids expensive resource acquisitions at run time. It increases the predictability of a system by ensuring that the response time for resource acquisition and access is fairly constant. By a similar argument, the Pooling (97) pattern also improves performance, provided that resources are acquired from the resource pool.

- *Flexibility.* The Lookup (21) pattern decouples resource providers from resource users. This decoupling helps to make the overall system much more flexible. The Partial Acquisition (66) and Lazy Acquisition (38) patterns allow for flexibility at a different level, allowing for flexible exchange of acquisition strategies.

- *Stability.* The Lazy Acquisition (38) and Eager Acquisition (53) patterns reduce the resource consumption at any given time. The patterns help to minimize resource consumption, ensuring system stability. The Pooling (97) pattern helps to increase system stability by avoiding regular low-level acquisition and release of resources. The Evictor (168) pattern reduces the probability of resource exhaustion and thus increases the stability of an application. The Leasing (149) pattern helps to increase system reliability and stability by reducing the wastage of unused resources, and by ensuring that resource users do not access invalid resources. The Resource Lifecycle Manager (128) pattern can ensure that a resource is allocated to a user only when a sufficient amount of resources are available. This can help make the system more stable by avoiding situations in which a user may cause resource starvation by acquiring resources from the system directly.

- *Consistency.* The Coordinator (111) pattern helps to ensure consistency among local as well as distributed resources.

Note that the patterns described above have been grouped based on the forces they address. The chapters that describe the patterns in detail group the patterns based on the various stages of resource management, namely resource acquisition, resource lifecycle, and resource release. We return to the grouping of patterns based on forces when we cover the two case studies.

The following figure shows the relationship between the non-functional requirements and the resource management patterns presented in this book.

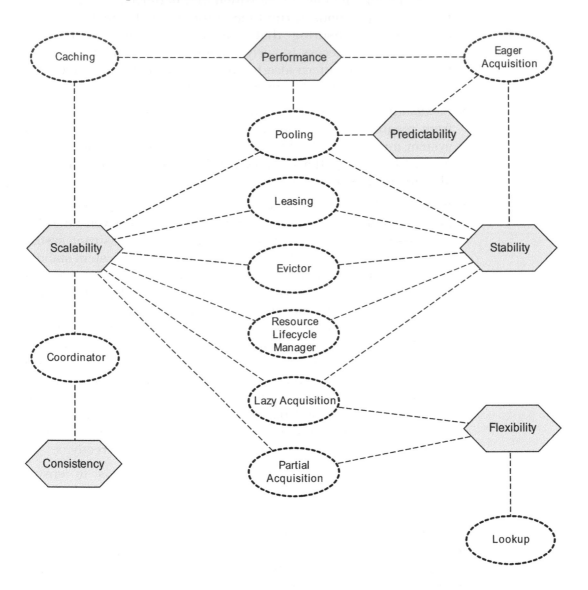

1.5   Related Work

Patterns in software architecture are not islands, and are interconnected by their contexts. Every pattern has an initial context and a resulting context. The resulting context of one pattern forms the initial context of another pattern. As a result, describing a pattern typically involves referencing several other patterns. Such referenced patterns can be looked on as fitting closely with the pattern being described when trying to solve a particular problem. Looking at this from another perspective, patterns can be summarized as systems of patterns [POSA1] that describe a specific problem domain in software development.

Patterns in general do not apply to only one industry such as telecommunications or to one domain such as embedded systems. In addition, patterns can be applied to many areas that share the same core context, the context of the pattern.

The widespread interest of software designers and developers in patterns started with the book, *Design Patterns – Elements of Reusable Object-Oriented Software* [GoF95] by Erich Gamma, Richard Helm, Ralph Johnson and John Vlissides (the 'Gang of Four'). Their book describes best practices in developing flexible software using object orientation and frameworks. A year later, the book *Pattern Oriented Software Architecture – A System of Patterns* [POSA1] was published as the first book in POSA series. POSA1 documents basic architectural patterns and gives recommendations for designing and building software frameworks and applications. Both GoF95 and POSA1 center around patterns for software architectures, but neither touch the area of resource management.

As pattern work is ongoing, conferences such as PLoP and EuroPLoP, organized by the Hillside Group [Hill04], provide an active forum for sharing new patterns in the community. The Pattern Language of Program Design (PLoPD) [PLoPD1] [PLoPD2] [PLoPD3] [PLoPD4] books summarize the published material. For an extensive list of published patterns up to the year 2000, refer to *The Pattern Almanac* [Risi00], written by Linda Rising.

Existing pattern literature that focuses on specific problem domains only touches the edges of resource management. Some of the most relevant work is listed below. For individual related patterns, refer to the *See Also* sections of the patterns in this book.

- *Concurrent and networked objects. Pattern-Oriented Software Architecture – Patterns for Concurrent and Networked Objects* [POSA2] documents patterns found in concurrent and network-oriented applications and middleware. The contained concurrency patterns, such as Active Object, Monitor Object, Half-Sync/Half-Async, Leader/Followers, and Thread-Specific Storage, describe how to deal with concurrent access to resources, such as objects and event sources, efficiently and effectively. Since POSA2 provides an extensive coverage of the area of concurrency patterns, we do not cover concurrency issues in resource management in this book. Another excellent book that covers concurrency patterns, specific to Java, is *Concurrent Network Programming* [Lea99] by Doug Lea. For patterns specific to real-time systems, we recommend *Doing Hard Time* [Doug02] by Bruce P. Douglass.

- *Remote communication.* The pattern language described in *Remoting Patterns* [VKZ04] builds on POSA2, by describing how to build distributed object infrastructures. It describes the constituent parts of common middleware technologies, such as CORBA [OMG04a], Web Services [W3C04], and .NET Remoting [Ramm02]. The remote objects managed by those distributed object infrastructures are resources. Therefore, several of the patterns presented in this book, such as Lookup (21), Lazy Acquisition (38), Pooling (97), and Leasing (149), recur in that pattern language, but are specialized for remote objects.

- *Component infrastructures. Server Component Patterns* [VSW02] contains a pattern language for today's component infrastructures, such as EJB [Sun04b] and COM+ [Ewal01]. The patterns build on those described in POSA2 and *Remoting Patterns* [VKZ04]. Components are resources that are managed by the component infrastructures. So *Server Component Patterns* contains Naming and Instance Pooling, which are specializations of Lookup (21) and Pooling (97) in our pattern language. Further, the Managed Resource pattern is an application of the Resource Lifecycle Manager (128) pattern in our pattern language.

- *Fault tolerance.* Fault tolerance helps to ensure the consistency and stability of a system and is therefore related to patterns in resource management. Fault tolerance techniques, such as those described by [Lapr85] and [ALR01] are common practice in today's high-reliability systems. A coverage of the techniques as patterns has been provided by Titos Saridakis [Sari02]. His patterns can be categorized into error detection, recovery, and masking. The individual patterns from those three areas can be combined to build a specific fault-tolerant solution. Fault tolerance techniques help to ensure the stability of a system by detecting failed or defective resources and providing a means to recover from such errors or mask them.

- *Small systems with limited memory.* Charles Weir and James Noble describe patterns for efficient memory management in small/ embedded systems in *Small Memory Software* [NoWe00]. As memory is a typical resource in resource management, several patterns are similar. For example, Paging in [NoWe00] is a specialization of Caching (83), while Variable Allocation, Fixed Allocation, and Pooled Allocation are specializations of Lazy Acquisition (38), Eager Acquisition (53), and Pooling (97) respectively. The Garbage Collector [JoLi96] pattern is related to the Evictor pattern (168). The overlap is natural and not redundant, as [NoWe00] gives detailed guidance on applying the concepts to memory, whereas our book gives a more general guidance.

- *Enterprise systems.* Martin Fowler's book *Patterns of Enterprise Application Architecture* [Fowl02] presents patterns that are most commonly used in today's enterprise systems. The performance and scalability forces are also important for enterprise systems. Therefore, the book describes, among many other patterns, two that help to address these forces: Lazy Load and Data Transfer Object, which are related to Lazy Acquisition (38) and Caching (83) respectively.

A book that complements Fowler's book well is *Enterprise Integration Patterns* [HoWo03], with its patterns that describe how to design, build and deploy messaging solutions in enterprise applications.

Enterprise Solution Patterns Using Microsoft .NET [TMQH+03] documents best practices in building enterprise systems using the

.NET technology [Rich02]. The Page Cache pattern documented in [TMQH+03] is directly related to Caching (83).

Another excellent book on the topic of enterprise solutions is *Architecting Enterprise Solutions: Patterns for High-Capability Internet-based Systems* [DyLo04] by Paul Dyson and Andrew Longshaw. The authors give architectural and practical guidance on how to build large-scale enterprise solutions. The associations between the patterns and the non-functional characteristics, which they address, are especially valuable. Their patterns Resource Pooling and Local Cache are directly related to the patterns in this book.

Documenting patterns only in the context of a specific application domain limits the applicability of the patterns to that domain unnecessarily. In many cases application domains can learn from each other. For example, software development projects in the real-time and embedded domain are increasingly making extensive use of best practices and technologies from the enterprise domain. This is proving to be especially successful, as the real-time domain is benefitting greatly from greater levels of abstraction that are achievable with the higher performance of today's CPUs. Various workshops and discussions on patterns for distributed real-time and embedded systems at conferences such as OOPSLA (Conference on Object-Oriented Programming Systems, Languages, and Applications) over the past several years have confirmed this.

1.6 Pattern Form

All the patterns presented in this book are self-contained and follow the POSA1 pattern form. This form allows us to present both the essence and the key details of a pattern. Our goal is to serve readers who just want an overview of the fundamental ideas of individual patterns, as well as those who want to know how the patterns work together in depth.

Each section in the POSA form sets the stage for the subsequent sections. The *Example* section introduces the *Context*, *Problem*, and

Solution sections, which summarize a pattern's essence. The *Solution* section precedes the *Structure* and *Dynamics* sections, which present more detailed information about how a pattern works, preparing readers for the *Implementation* section.

The *Example Resolved, Variants, Known Uses, Consequences* and *See Also* sections complete each pattern description. We include extensive cross-references to help you to understand the relationships between the patterns presented here and other published patterns.

The *Implementation* section of each pattern description provides detailed steps to follow in order to implement the pattern, together with sample code for each pattern. If you want an overview of all the patterns first, you may therefore want to skip the *Implementation* sections on your initial pass through the book, and come back to them when you need to know the implementation details of a particular pattern. In the diagrams that explain the structure and behavior of our patterns we have tried to follow standard UML [Fowl03] whenever possible.

The *Structure* section of the patterns makes use of Class-Responsibility-Collaborators (CRC) cards [BeCu89]. CRC cards help to identify and specify objects or the components of an application in an informal way, especially in the early phases of software development. A CRC card describes a component, an object, or a class of objects. The card consists of three fields that describe the name of the component, its responsibilities, and the names of other collaborating components.

The *Variants* section of the patterns describes related patterns, which are derived from the current pattern by extending or changing the problem and/or the solution.

The *Specialization* section of the patterns documents how a specialized form of the pattern can be used to address specific problems or settings. Since a pattern, in general, abstracts from such specifics, this section helps to describe cases in which a specialized form of the pattern can be applied.

2 Resource Acquisition

"I find that a great part of the information I have was acquired by looking up something and finding something else on the way."

Franklin P. Adams

The lifecycle of a resource begins with its acquisition. How and when resources are acquired can play a critical role in the functioning of a software system. By optimizing the time it takes to acquire resources, system performance can be significantly improved.

Before a resource can be acquired, the most fundamental problem to be solved is how to find a resource. The Lookup (21) pattern addresses this problem and describes how resources can be made available by resource providers, and how these resources can be found by resource users.

Once a resource has been found, it can be acquired. The timing of resource acquisition is important, and is mainly addressed by Lazy Acquisition (38) and Eager Acquisition (53). While Lazy Acquisition defers acquisition of resources to the latest possible point in time, Eager Acquisition instead strives to acquire resources as early as possible. Both extremes are important and are heavily dependent on the use of the resources.

If resources that are acquired are not used immediately it can lead to their wastage. Lazy Acquisition addresses this problem and consequently leads to better system scalability. On the other hand, some systems have real-time constraints and stringent requirements for the timing of resource acquisition. Eager Acquisition addresses this problem, and consequently leads to better system performance and predictability.

A resource of large or unknown size may not be needed completely, and therefore it might be sufficient to acquire only part of the resource. The Partial Acquisition (81) pattern describes how the acquisition of a resource can be partitioned into steps to allow only part of the resource to be acquired. Partial Acquisition can serve as a bridge between Lazy Acquisition and Eager Acquisition. The first step of Partial Acquisition typically acquires part of the resource eagerly, while subsequent steps defer further resource acquisition to a later stage.

The Lookup pattern can be used with both reusable and non-reusable resources. Furthermore, it can support both concurrently accessible resources and exclusive resources. This is because Lookup only focuses on providing access to resources, and does not deal with how the resources are actually used.

Lazy Acquisition, Eager Acquisition and Partial Acquisition can also be used with both reusable and non-reusable resources. However, if a reusable resource is concurrently accessible, the three patterns can provide certain optimizations such that the resource is only acquired once and can then be shared by the concurrent users. Such an optimization requires special handling in the case of Partial Acquisition. This is because the amount of a resource that is partially acquired can vary among the concurrent users.

Lookup

The *Lookup* pattern describes how to find and access resources, whether local or distributed, by using a lookup service as a mediating instance.

Example   Consider a system that consists of several services implemented as remote objects using CORBA [OMG04a]. To access one of the distributed services, a client typically needs to obtain a reference to the object that provides the service. An object reference identifies the remote object that will receive the request. Object references can be passed around in the system as parameters to operations, as well as the results of requests. A client can therefore obtain a reference to a remote object in the system from another object. However, how can a client acquire an initial reference to an object that the client wants to access?

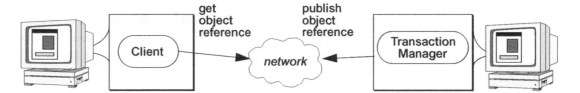

For example, in a system that provides a distributed transaction service, a client may want to obtain a reference to the transaction manager so that it can participate in distributed transactions. How can a server make the transaction manager object reference that it created widely available? How can a client obtain the transaction manager object reference without having a reference to any other object?

Context   Systems where resource users need to find and access local and distributed resources.

Problem   Resource providers may offer one or more resources to resource users. Over time additional resources may be added or existing resources may be removed by the resource provider. One way the resource provider can publish the availability of existing resources to interested resource users is by periodically sending a broadcast message. Such messages need to be sent on a periodic basis to ensure that new resource users joining the system become aware of available resources. Conversely, a resource user could send a broadcast message requesting all available resource providers to respond. Once the resource user receives replies from all available resource providers, it can then choose the resource(s) it needs. However, both of these approaches can be quite costly and inefficient, since they generate lots of messages, which proliferate across the network in the case of a distributed system. To address this problem of allowing resource providers to publish resources and for resource users to find these resources in an efficient and inexpensive manner requires the resolution of the following *forces*:

- *Availability.* A resource user should be able to find out on demand what resources are available in its environment.

- *Bootstrapping.* A resource user should be able to obtain an initial reference to a resource provider that offers the resource.

- *Location independence.* A resource user should be able to acquire a resource from a resource provider independent of the location of the resource provider. Similarly, a resource provider should be able to provide resources to resource users without having knowledge of the location of the resource users.

- *Simplicity.* The solution should not burden a resource user when finding resources. Similarly, the solution should not burden a resource provider providing the resources.

Solution   Provide a lookup service that allows resource providers to make resources available to resource users. The resource provider advertises resources via the lookup service along with properties that describe the resources that the resource providers provide. Allow resource users to first find the advertised resources using the properties, then retrieve the resources, and finally use the resources.

For resources that need to be acquired before they can be used, the resource providers register references to themselves together with properties that describe the resources that the resource providers provide. Allow resource users to retrieve these registered references from the resource providers and use them to acquire the available resources from the referenced resource providers.

For resources, such as concurrently reusable services, that do not need to be first acquired and can instead be accessed directly, the resource providers register references to the resources together with properties that describe the resources. Allow resource users to directly access the resources without first interacting with the resource providers.

The lookup service serves as a central point of communication between resource users and resource providers. It allows resource users to access resource providers when resources need to be explicitly acquired from the resource providers. In addition, the lookup service allows resource users to directly access resources that do not need to be acquired from resource providers. In both cases, the resource users need not know about the location of the resource providers. Similarly, the resource providers don't need to know the location of the resource users that want to acquire and access the resources that they provide.

Structure   The following participants form the structure of the Lookup pattern:

- A *resource user* uses a resource.

- A *resource* is an entity such as a service that provides some type of functionality.

- A *resource provider* offers resources and advertises them via the lookup service.

- A *lookup service* provides the capability for resource providers to advertise resources via references to themselves, and for resource users to find these references.

The following CRC cards describe the responsibilities and collaborations of the participants.

Class Resource User	*Collaborator* • Resource • Lookup Service • Resource Provider	*Class* Resource	*Collaborator*
Responsibility • Searches for a resource. • Uses a resource.		*Responsibility* • Provides some type of functionality.	

Class Resource Provider	*Collaborator* • Resource • Lookup Service	*Class* Lookup Service	*Collaborator*
Responsibility • Provides resources to resource users. • Advertises resources together with their properties via the lookup service.		*Responsibility* • Allows resource providers to advertise resources. • Allows resource users to find advertised resources. • Associates properties with resources.	

The following class diagram illustrates the structure of the Lookup pattern.

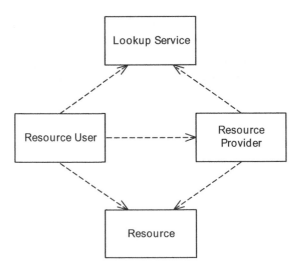

The resource user depends on all three other participants: the lookup service to find the resource provider, the resource provider to acquire the resource, and the resource to actually access it.

Dynamics   There are three sets of interactions in the Lookup pattern.

Scenario I. In the first interaction, a resource provider advertises a resource with the lookup service. It is assumed that the resource provider already knows the access point of the lookup service. For the interactions necessary when the resource provider has no access point to the lookup service, refer to Scenario III. On advertisement of the resource, the resource provider registers a reference to itself with the lookup service, together with some properties that are descriptive of the type of resources that the resource provider provides.

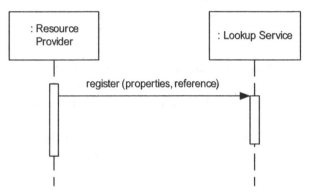

Scenario II. In the second scenario, a resource user finds a resource provider using a lookup service, and includes the following interactions:

• The resource user queries the lookup service for the desired resource using one or more properties, such as resource description, interface type, and location.

• The lookup service responds with the reference to the resource provider, which provides the desired resource.

• The resource user uses the reference of the resource provider to acquire and access the resource.

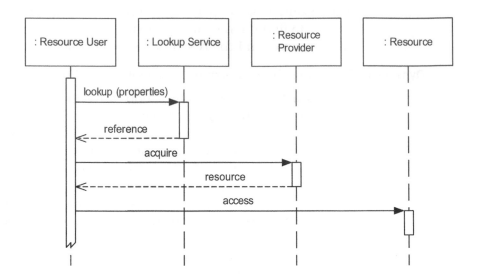

Scenario III. In distributed systems the access point of the lookup service might not be known to the resource user and the resource provider. In such cases the access point might be configured via the runtime environment of the application, or the application might use a bootstrapping protocol to find the access point. The bootstrapping protocol may be a broadcast, multicast or a combination of several unicast messages.

The necessary steps are:

- The resource provider or resource user searches for a lookup service via a bootstrapping protocol.

- The lookup service responds announcing its access point.

The following sequence diagram shows these interactions, which are valid for the resource provider as well as the resource user. In the diagram, the resource provider uses broadcast as a bootstrapping protocol.

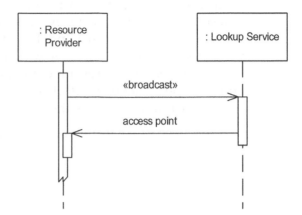

Implementation   There are four steps involved in implementing the Lookup pattern:

1   *Determine the interface for a lookup service.* A lookup service should facilitate advertisement and lookup of resources, either directly or through their resource providers. It should provide an interface that allows resource providers to register and unregister references. The reference is associated with properties that describe the resource offered. The lookup service keeps a list of the registered references and their associated properties. These properties can be used by the lookup service to select one or more resources or resource providers based on queries sent by the resource user. In the simplest case, the properties may just contain the name or type of a single resource that the resource provider provides. Queries from resource users on the lookup service return either a valid reference, or an error code when no matching resource could be found.

Different policies can be defined for the lookup service. For example, the lookup service may support bindings with duplicate names or properties. The lookup service should also provide an interface that allows resource users to retrieve a list of all available resource providers. The search criteria used by the resource users can be a simple query-by-name, or a more complex query mechanism as described in implementation step 5, *Determine a query language.*

2   *Determine whether to register resource references or resource provider references.* Depending on the kind of resource and its acquisition strategy, either the reference to the resource provider or the reference

to the resource is registered with the lookup service. If a resource must first be acquired explicitly by a resource user, then the reference of the resource provider providing that resource should be registered with the lookup service, together with properties that describe the resource provided by the resource provider. It may be advantageous to require explicit acquisition of a resource to control the type of resource user that can access the resource.

When a resource provider provides multiple resources, the reference of a resource provider can be such that it identifies the resource as well. This can be useful in enabling the resource provider to associate acquisition requests with desired resources. See the *Multi-faceted Resource Provider* variant for details.

On the other hand, if resources need not be explicitly acquired and can be directly accessed by resource users, then references to the resources along with properties describing them can be registered with the lookup service. For example, in the case of concurrently reusable resources, resources can be made available directly to resource users by registering references to the resources with the lookup service. Examples of such resources include read-only objects and Web Services [W3C04]. Such resources either do not have any synchronization issues, or can synchronize access themselves.

3   *Implement the lookup service.* Internally, the lookup service can be implemented in many different ways. For example, the lookup service may keep the registered references and their meta information in some kind of a tree data structure, helpful when complex dependencies must be modelled, or in a simple hash map. For non-critical and heavily changing resource advertisements, the information may be stored transiently, while for critical advertisements the associations should be made persistent, with an appropriate backend persistency mechanism.

➥   For example, the CORBA implementation Orbix [Iona04] uses the COS Persistent State Service to persist the name bindings in its Naming Service, which is an implementation of the lookup service. Other CORBA implementations such as TAO [Schm98] [OCI04] persist the bindings using memory-mapped files.   ❑

4   *Provide the lookup service access point.* To communicate with the lookup service, an access point is necessary, such as a Java

reference, a C++ pointer or reference, or a distributed object reference, which typically includes information such as the host name and the port number where the lookup service is running. This information can be published to resource providers and resource users by several means, such as writing to a file that can be accessed by resource providers and resource users, or through well-defined environment variables.

➡   For example, a lot of CORBA implementations publish the access point of the Naming Service using property or configuration files, which can be accessed by clients.   ❏

If an access point is not published by the lookup service, it will be necessary to design a bootstrapping protocol that can allow resource providers and resource users to obtain the access point. Such a bootstrapping protocol is typically designed using a broadcast or a multicast protocol. The resource provider or user sends an initial request for a reference to a lookup service using the bootstrapping protocol. On receiving the request, typically one or more lookup services send a reply back to the requestor, passing their access points. The resource provider can then contact the lookup service to publish its reference. Similarly, a resource user can contact the lookup services to obtain references to registered resource providers.

➡   In CORBA, a client or server can acquire the access point of a Naming Service using the `resolve_initial_references()` call on the ORB. Internally, the ORB may use a broadcast protocol to acquire the access point of the Naming Service, such as an object reference.   ❏

5   *Determine a query language.* The lookup service may optionally support a query language that allows resource users to search for resources using complex queries. For example, a query language could be based on a property sheet that describes the type of resource in which a resource user is interested. When using the lookup service to query a resource, the resource user may submit a list of properties that should be satisfied by the requested resource. The lookup service can then compare the list of properties submitted by the resource user against the properties of the available resources. If a match is found, the reference to the corresponding resource or resource provider is returned to the resource user.

➥   The CORBA Trading Service [OMG04f] is a lookup service that allows properties to be specified corresponding to a resource that is registered with it. Resource providers are server applications that register CORBA objects with it. The object references will point to the server application, but will also identify the CORBA object as a resource. A client, as resource user, can build an arbitrarily complex query using a criterion that is matched against the properties of the registered CORBA objects. The client is returned a reference to the CORBA object in the server application.   ❏

Example Resolved

Consider the example in which a client wants to obtain an initial reference to a transaction manager in a distributed CORBA environment. Using the Lookup pattern, a lookup service should be implemented. Most CORBA implementations provide such a lookup service, either in the form of a Naming Service, a Trading Service, or both. These services are accessible via the Internet Inter-ORB Protocol (IIOP) and provide well-defined CORBA interfaces.

In our example, the server that creates a transaction manager is a resource provider. The server should first obtain a reference to the Naming Service, then use it to register the reference of the created transaction manager. The reference contains the access point of the server, and it identifies the registered resource in the server. The C++ code below shows how a server can obtain the reference to the Naming Service and then register the transaction manager with it.

```
// First initialize the ORB
CORBA::ORB_var orb = CORBA::ORB_init(argc, argv);

// Create a transaction manager
TransactionMgr_Impl *transactionMgrServant =
  new TransactionMgr_Impl;

// Get the CORBA object reference of it.
TransactionMgr_var transactionMgr =
  transactionMgrServant->_this();

// Get reference to the initial naming context
CORBA::Object_var obj =
  orb->resolve_initial_references("NameService");

// Cast the reference from CORBA::Object
CosNaming::NamingContext_var name_service =
  CosNaming::NamingContext::_narrow(obj);
```

```
// Create the name with which the transaction manager will be bound
CosNaming::Name name;
name.length(1);
name[0].id = CORBA::string_dup("Transactions");

// Register transactionMgr object reference in the
// Naming Service at the root context
name_service->bind(name, transactionMgr);
```

Once the transaction manager has been registered with the Naming Service, a client can obtain its object reference from the Naming Service. The C++ code below shows how a client can do this.

```
// First initialize the ORB
CORBA::ORB_var orb = CORBA::ORB_init(argc, argv);

// Get reference to the initial naming context
CORBA::Object_var obj =
    orb->resolve_initial_references("NameService");

// Cast the reference from CORBA::Object
CosNaming::NamingContext_var name_service =
    CosNaming::NamingContext::_narrow(obj);

// Create the name with which the transactionMgr
// is bound in the Naming Service
CosNaming::Name name;
name.length(1);
name[0].id = CORBA::string_dup("Transactions");

// Resolve transactionMgr from the Naming Service
CORBA::Object_var obj = name_service->resolve(name);

// Cast the reference from CORBA::Object
TransactionMgr_var transactionMgr =
    TransactionMgr::_narrow(obj);
```

Once the initial reference to the transaction manager has been obtained by the client, the client can then use it to invoke operations, as well as to obtain references to other CORBA objects and services.

Variants *Self-registering Resources.* The participants, resource provider and resource, can be implemented by the same software artifact. In this case, since there is no distinction between a resource and a resource provider, the reference that is registered with the lookup service will be that of the resource. For example, a resource such as a distributed service can directly register with the lookup service, providing a reference to itself.

Multi-faceted Resource Provider. When a resource provider offers more than one resource that needs to be acquired, the registered reference of the resource provider can also identify the resource. The resource provider registers a unique reference to itself for each resource that it advertises in the lookup service. The reference that is registered with the lookup service would correspond to the resource provider, but would indirectly refer to a unique resource provided by that resource provider.

Resource Registrar. A separate entity can be responsible for registering references with the lookup service other than the one that actually provides the resources. That is, the resource providers need not be the one that register references with the lookup service; this responsibility can be handled by a separate entity called a resource registrar.

Federated Lookup. Several instances of the lookup service can be used together to build a federation of lookup services. The instances of lookup services in a federation cooperate to provide resource users with a wider spectrum of resources. The Half-Object Plus Protocol [Mesz95] pattern describes how to separate lookup service instances while still keeping them synchronized.

A federated lookup service can be configured to forward requests to other lookup services if it cannot fulfill the requests itself. This widens the scope of queries and allows a resource user to gain access to additional resources it was not able to reach before. The lookup services in a federation can be in the same or different location domains.

Replicated Lookup. The lookup service can be used to build fault-tolerant systems. Replication is a well-known concept in providing fault tolerance and can be applied at two levels using lookup service:

- Firstly, the lookup service itself can be replicated. Multiple instances of a lookup service can serve to provide both load balancing and fault tolerance. The Proxy [GoF95] pattern can be used to hide the selection of a lookup service from the client. For example, several ORB implementations provide smart proxies [HoWo03] on the client side that can be used to hide the selection of a particular lookup service from among the replicated instances of all the lookup services.

- Secondly, both the resources and the resource providers whose reference are registered with a lookup service can also be replicated. A lookup service can be extended to support multiple registrations of resource providers for the same list of properties, such as the same name in the case of the CORBA Naming Service. The lookup service can be configured with various strategies [GoF95] to allow dispatch of the appropriate resource provider upon request from a resource user. For example, a lookup service could use a round-robin strategy to alternate between multiple instances of a transaction manager that are registered with it using the same list of properties. This type of replication is used by Borland [Borl04] to extend the scalability of their CORBA implementation, Visibroker.

Consequences   There are several **benefits** of using the Lookup pattern:

- *Availability*. Using the lookup service, a resource user can find out on demand what resources are available in its environment. Note that a resource or its corresponding resource provider may no longer be available, but its reference may not have been removed from the lookup service. See the *Dangling References* liability for further details.

- *Bootstrapping*. The lookup service allows a resource user to obtain initial resources. In distributed systems a bootstrapping protocol allows the resource user to find the lookup service and then use it to find other distributed services.

- *Location independence*. The lookup service provides location transparency by shielding the location of the resource providers from the resource users. Similarly, the pattern shields the location of the resource users from the resource providers.

- *Configuration simplicity*. Distributed systems based on a lookup service need little or no manual configuration. No files need to be shared or transferred in order to distribute, find and access remote objects. The use of a bootstrapping protocol is a key feature for ad hoc networking scenarios, in which the environment changes regularly and cannot be predetermined.

- *Property-based selection*. Resources can be chosen based on properties. This allows for fine-grained matching of user needs with resource advertisements.

There are some **liabilities** of using the Lookup pattern:

- *Single point of failure.* One consequence of the Lookup pattern is the danger of a single point of failure. If an instance of a lookup service crashes, the system can lose the registered references along with the associated properties. Once the lookup service is restarted, the resource providers would need to re-register the resources with it unless the lookup service has persistent state. This can be both tedious and error-prone, since it requires resource providers to detect that the lookup service has crashed and then restarted. In addition, a lookup service can also act as a bottleneck, affecting system performance. A better solution, therefore, is to introduce replication of the lookup service, as discussed in the *Variants* section.

- *Dangling references.* Another consequence of the Lookup pattern is the danger of dangling references. The registered references in the lookup service can become outdated as a result of the corresponding resource providers being terminated or moved. In this case the Leasing (149) pattern, as applied in Jini [Sun04c], can help, by forcing the resource providers to prolong the 'lease' on their references regularly if they do not want their entries removed automatically.

- *Unwanted replication.* Problems can occur when similar resources with the same properties are advertised but replication is not wanted. Depending on the implementation of the lookup service, multiple instances of the same resource may be registered erroneously, or one resource provider may overwrite the registration of a previous resource provider. Enforcing that at least one of the properties is unique can avoid this problem.

Known Uses   **CORBA** [OMG04a]. The Common Object Services Naming Service and Trading Service implements lookup services. Whereas the query language of the Naming Service is quite simple, using just names, the query language of the Trading Service is powerful and supports complex queries for components.

LDAP [HoSm97]. The Lightweight Directory Access Protocol (LDAP), defines a network protocol and information model for accessing information directories. An LDAP server allows the storage of almost any kind of information in the form of text, binary data, public key certificates, URLs, and references. Often LDAP servers are protected by permissions, as they contain critical information that must be secured from unauthorized access. LDAP clients can query the information stored on LDAP servers. Large organizations typically centralize their user databases of e-mail, Web and file sharing servers using LDAP directories.

JNDI [Sun04f]. The Java Naming and Directory Interface (JNDI) is an interface in Java that provides naming and directory functionality to applications. Using JNDI, Java applications can store and retrieve named Java objects of any type. In addition, JNDI provides querying functionality by allowing resource users to look up Java objects using their attributes. Using JNDI also allows integration with existing naming and directory services such as the CORBA Naming Service, RMI registry [Sun04g], and LDAP.

Jini [Sun04c]. Jini supports ad hoc networking by allowing services to join a network without requiring any pre-planning, installation, or human intervention, and by allowing users to discover devices on the network. Jini services are registered with Jini's lookup service, and these services are accessed by users using Jini's discovery protocol. To increase network reliability, the Jini lookup service regularly broadcasts its availability to potential clients.

COM+ [Ewal01]. The Windows Registry is a lookup service that allows resource users to retrieve registered components based on keys. A key can be either a ProgId, a GUID (Global Unique IDentifier) or the name and version of a component. The registry allows then to retrieve the associated components.

UDDI. The Universal Description, Discovery, and Integration protocol (UDDI) [UDDI04] is a key building block of Web Services [W3C04]. The UDDI allows publishers of Web Services to advertise their service and clients to search for a matching Web Service. The advertisements contain service descriptions and point to detailed technical specifications that define the interfaces to the services.

Peer-to-peer networks. Peer-to-Peer (P2P) networking technologies, such as JXTA [JXTA04], support advertisement and discovery of peers and resources. Resources in the context of P2P are often files and services

DNS [Tane02]. The Domain Name Service (DNS) is responsible for the coordination and mapping of domain names to and from IP addresses. It consists of a hierarchy of name servers that host the mapping. It is therefore a good example of how a federated lookup works. Clients query any nearby name server, sending a UDP packet containing a name. If the nearby name server can resolve it, it returns the IP address. If not, it queries the next name server in the hierarchy using a well-defined protocol.

Grid computing [BBL02] [Grid04] [JAP02]. Grid computing is about the sharing and aggregation of distributed resources such as processing time, storage, and information. A grid consists of multiple computers linked to form one virtual system. Grid computing uses the Lookup pattern to find distributed resources. Depending on the project, the role of the lookup service in the system is often referred to as 'resource broker', 'resource manager', or 'discovery service'.

Eclipse plug-in registry [IBM04b]. Eclipse is an open, extensible IDE that provides a universal tool platform. Its extensibility is based on a plug-in architecture. Eclipse includes a plug-in registry that implements the Lookup pattern. The plug-in registry holds a list of all discovered plug-ins, extension points, and extensions and allows clients to locate these by their identity. The plug-in registry itself can be found by clients through several framework classes.

Telephone directory service. The Lookup pattern has a real-world known use case in the form of telephone directory services. A person X may want to obtain the phone number of person Y. Assuming person Y has registered his/her phone number with a lookup service, in this case a telephone directory service, person X can then call this directory service and obtain the phone number of person Y. The telephone directory service will have a well-known phone number, for example 411 or a Web site [ATT04], thus allowing person X to contact it.

Receptionist [TwAl83]. A receptionist at a company can be considered as a real-life example of the Lookup pattern. The receptionist manages the contact information in the form of the phone numbers of all the employees of the company. When a caller wishes to contact an employee, they first speak to the receptionist, who then provides the 'reference' of the person being sought. Similarly, if a new person joins the company or an existing employee leaves, their contact information is typically updated by the receptionist to handle future queries.

See Also The Activator [Stal00] pattern registers activated components with a lookup service to provide resource users with access to them. In many cases the references retrieved from a lookup service are actually references to factories, implementing the Abstract Factory [GoF95] pattern. This decouples the location of components from their activation.

The Sponsor-Selector [Wall97] pattern decouples the responsibilities of resource selection from resource recommendation and hands these responsibilities to two participants, the selector and the sponsor respectively. Sponsor-Selector can be used in Lookup to improve the finding of a resource that matches the resource user's demand. The role of the sponsor would coincide with the resource provider, while the lookup service would be the selector.

The Service Locator pattern [ACM01] encapsulates the complexity of JNDI lookups for EJB [Sun04b] home objects and the creation of business objects.

Credits We would like to thank our EuroPLoP 2000 shepherd, Bob Hanmer, for his feedback and valuable comments. We would also like to thank everyone at the writer's workshop at St. Martin, Austria during our Siemens retreat 2000, Frank Buschmann, Karl Pröse, Douglas C. Schmidt, Dietmar Schütz, and Christa Schwanninger, as well as the people of the writer's workshop at EuroPLoP 2000, Alexandre Duret-Lutz, Peter Gassmann, Thierry Geraud, Matthias Jung, Pavel Hruby, Nuno Meira, James Noble, and Charles Weir, for their valuable comments and suggestions.

Lazy Acquisition

The *Lazy Acquisition* pattern defers resource acquisitions to the latest possible time during system execution in order to optimize resource use.

Example   Consider a medical Picture Archiving and Communication System (PACS) that provides storage of patient data. The data includes both patient details such as address information as well as medical history. In addition, the data can include digitized images originating from various sources, such as X-rays and computer tomography scanners. In addition to supporting different sources of patient data, the PACS system must provide efficient access to the data. Such data is typically accessed by physicians and radiologists for diagnosis and treatment purposes.

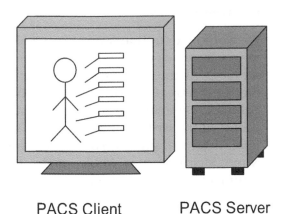

PACS Client   PACS Server

A PACS system is typically built using a three-tier architecture. The middle tier of the system maintains business objects that represent the patient data. Since the data must be persisted, these business objects and the data they contain are mapped to some persistent store, typically a database. When a physician queries for a particular patient, the data is fetched and the corresponding business object is created. This business object is delivered to the presentation layer of the system, which extracts the relevant information and presents it to the physician. The time it takes to fetch the relevant patient data and create the business objects is proportional to the size of the patient data. For a patient with a long medical history and several digitized images corresponding to various medical examinations, fetching all the data and creating the corresponding business object can take a lot of time. Since high performance is a typical non-functional requirement of such systems, a delay in fetching patient records can be a big problem.

How can the PACS system be designed so that retrieval of patient information is quick regardless of the number of images in the patient's record?

Context A system with restricted resources that must satisfy high demands, such as throughput and availability.

Problem Limited resource availability is a constraint faced by all software systems. In addition, if the available resources are not managed properly, it can lead to bottlenecks in the system and can have a significant impact on system performance and stability. To ensure that resources are available when they are needed, most systems acquire the resources at start-up time. However, early acquisition of resources can result in high acquisition overheads, and can also lead to wastage of resources, especially if the resources are not needed immediately.

Systems that have to acquire and manage expensive resources need a way of reducing the initial cost of acquiring the resources. If these systems were to acquire all resources up front, a lot of overhead would be incurred and a lot of resources would be consumed unnecessarily.

To address these problems requires resolution of the following *forces*:

- *Availability.* Acquisition of resources should be controlled such that it minimizes the possibility of resource shortage and ensures that a sufficient number of resources are available when needed.

- *Stability.* Resource shortage can lead to system instability, and therefore resources should be acquired in a way that has minimum impact on the stability of the system.

- *Quick system start-up.* Acquisition of resources at system start-up should be done in a way that optimizes the system start-up time.

- *Transparency*. The solution should be transparent to the resource user.

Solution Acquire resources at the latest possible time. The resource is not acquired until it becomes unavoidable to do so. When the initial request for a resource is made by the resource user, a resource proxy is created and returned. When the resource user tries to access the resource, the resource proxy acquires the actual resource and then redirects the access request of the resource user to the resource. The resource user is therefore dependent on the resource proxy, but as this provides the same interface as the resource, whether the resource proxy or the resource is accessed is transparent to the resource user.

By using a proxy to represent resources that are potentially expensive to acquire, the overall cost of acquiring a set of resources can be minimized. In addition, by not acquiring a large number of resources up front, the total number of resources that need to be managed simultaneously is also minimized.

Structure The following participants form the structure of the Eager Acquisition pattern:

- A *resource user* acquires and uses resources.

- A *resource* is an entity such as a connection or memory.

- A *resource proxy* intercepts resource acquisitions by the resource user and hands the lazily acquired resources to the resource user.

- A *resource provider* manages and provides several resources.

The following CRC cards describe the responsibilities and collaborations of the participants.

Class **Resource User**	Collaborator • Resource Proxy	Class **Resource**	Collaborator
Responsibility • Acquires and uses a resource.		Responsibility • Is acquired and used through the resource proxy.	
Class **Resource Proxy**	Collaborator • Resource • Resource Provider	Class **Resource Provider**	Collaborator • Resource
Responsibility • Pretends to be the resource. • Provides the same interface as the resource. • Makes the actual resource available from the resource provider.		Responsibility • Manages and provides resources to resource proxies.	

The following class diagram illustrates the structure of the Lazy Acquisition pattern.

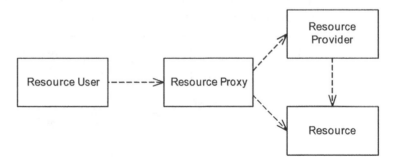

The class diagram shows that the resource user depends on the resource proxy. Since the resource proxy provides the same interface as the resource, whether the resource proxy or the resource is accessed is transparent to the user.

Dynamics   **Scenario I.** In this scenario, the resource provider not only provides resources, but also acts as a factory for creating resource proxies.

When the resource user tries to acquire a resource from the resource provider, the resource provider creates and returns a resource proxy to the resource user, instead of the actual resource.

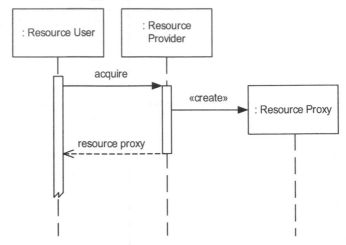

Scenario II. The key dynamics of Lazy Acquisition is the acquisition of the resource by the resource proxy on the first access by the resource user. Initially, the resource proxy does not own the resource. Only at first access is the actual resource acquired. All subsequent access to the resource are forwarded by the resource proxy to the actual resource. The resource user does not notice the level of indirection provided by the resource proxy.

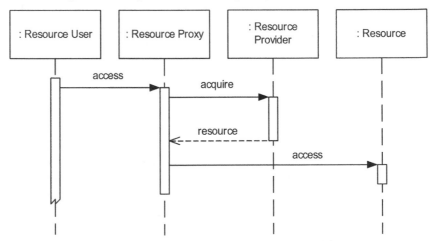

Implementation The implementation of this pattern is described by the following steps:

1 *Identify resources that need to be acquired lazily.* Using profiling and system analysis, identify resources with one or more of the following properties:

   • Resources that are expensive to acquire,

   • Resources that are available only in limited number, and

   • Resources that remain unused for a long time after acquisition.

   Review each identified resource and its use, and decide whether through the lazy acquisition of the resource overall resource availability, system stability, and system start-up can be improved. Apply the following implementation steps to each of the identified resources.

2 *Define the resource proxy interface.* For every resource that needs to be acquired lazily, define a resource proxy as Virtual Proxy [GoF95] [POSA1] whose interface is identical to that of the resource.

➡
```
interface Resource {
    public void method1 ();
    public void method2 ();
}

public class ResourceProxy implements Resource {
    public void method1 () {
        // ...
    }
    public void method2 () {
        // ...
    }
}                                                                ❑
```

3 *Implement the resource proxy.* Implement the resource proxy such that it hides the lazy acquisition of the resource. The resource proxy will acquire the resource only when the resource is actually accessed by the resource user. Once the actual resource has been acquired, the resource proxy should use delegation to handle all resource access requests. Depending upon the resource, the resource proxy may also be responsible for initializing the resource after acquiring it.

```
➥     public class ResourceProxy implements Resource {
          public void method1 () {
              if (!acquired)
                  acquireResource ();
              resource.method1 ();
          }
          public void method2 () {
              if (!acquired)
                  acquireResource ();
              resource.method2 ();
          }
          private void acquireResource () {
              // ...
              acquired = true;
          }
          private boolean acquired = false;
      }                                                           ❏
```

4   *Define the acquisition strategy.* Define the strategy by which the
    resource is actually obtained from the resource provider by the
    resource proxy. The Strategy [GoF95] pattern can be applied to
    configure different types of strategy. A simple strategy could be to
    delay acquisition of the resource until the resource is accessed by the
    resource user. An alternative strategy could be to acquire the
    resource based on some state machine. For example, the
    instantiation of a component might trigger the resource proxy of
    another existing component to acquire its corresponding resources.
    In addition, the resource proxy may also provide the ability to switch
    off lazy acquisition entirely, in which case the resource will be
    acquired immediately.

    ➥   The acquireResource() method in the code sample below can be
    used by resource users to trigger the explicit acquisition of the
    resource by the resource proxy.

```
      public class ResourceProxy implements Resource {
          // ...
          void acquireResource () {
              resource = new ResourceX ();
          }
          ResourceX resource;
      }                                                           ❏
```

    Configure the resource acquisition strategy in the resource proxy,
    which acquires the resource.

5   *Implement a proper resource release strategy for the lazily acquired
    resources.* If the resources are not to be released by the resource user

explicitly, then use either the Evictor (168) pattern or Leasing (149) pattern for automatically releasing the resources. For this, the lazily acquired resource needs either to implement the EvictionInterface, or be registered with a lease provider, respectively.

Example Resolved

Consider the example of a medical Picture Archiving and Communication System (PACS). In order to solve the problem of quick retrieval of patient information, use the Lazy Acquisition pattern.

When a request is made to fetch all the information for a particular patient, create a query that does not fetch any image data. For each image in the patient record, create an image proxy in the business object that is returned. The presentation layer will process the business object and present all the information. For all the image proxies that it encounters, it will create links in the presentation that is generated. When an image corresponding to such a link needs to be viewed, it can then be fetched (lazily) from the file system. Images are stored on the file system directly, as storing images with their large amounts of binary data in a database is typically inefficient.

Using this solution optimizes fetching of textual patient data, which is typically not large. This can provide the physician with a good summary of the patient's medical history. If the physician wishes to view any image from the patient's record, that can be fetched lazily and on demand.

The sample code below shows the class PatientManager, which queries the database for the patient record. It fetches all data except the images.

```
public class PatientManager {
    public static PatientRecord getPatientRecord (String patientId) {
        return dbWrapper.getRecordWithoutImages (patientId);
    }
}
```

The returned PatientRecord holds a list of MedicalExams, which in turn reference an image each. The class MedicalExam cannot differentiate between a regularly loaded image and a lazily loaded image, as the interface to it is the same.

```
interface PatientRecord
{
    String getName ();
    String getAddress ();
```

```
    List getMedicalExams ();
}

interface MedicalExam
{
  Date getDate ();
  // Get the digitized image for this exam
  Image getImage ();
}

interface Image
{
  byte [] getData ();
}
```

The Image interface can be implemented using various strategies. The ImageProxy class below implements the lazy acquisition of the image by loading it from the file system only when actually accessed.

```
public class ImageProxy implements Image
{
  ImageProxy (FileSystem aFileSystem, int anImageId) {
    fileSystem = aFileSystem;
    imageId = anImageId;
  }

  public byte [] getData () {
    if (data == null) {
      // Fetch the image lazily using the stored ID
      data = fileSystem.getImage (imageId);
    }
    return data;
  }

  byte data[];
  FileSystem fileSystem;
  int imageId;
}
```

Note that the ImageProxy needs to have information about how to retrieve the lazily-acquired image from the file system.

Specializations   Some specialized patterns derived from Lazy Acquisition are:

Lazy Instantiation [BiWa04b]. Defer the instantiation of objects/ components until the instance is accessed by a user. As object instantiation is very often linked with dynamic memory allocation, and memory allocations are typically very expensive, lazy instantiation saves cost up front, especially for objects that are not accessed. However, using lazy instantiation can incur a dramatic overhead in situations in which a burst of users concurrently access objects, leading to a high-demand situation.

Lazy Loading. Defer the loading of a shared library until the program elements contained in that library are accessed. The Component Configurator Pattern [POSA2] can be used to implement this. Lazy Loading is often combined with Lazy Instantiation, since objects need to be instantiated when loaded. Lazy Load [Fowl02] describes how to defer loading the state of an object from the database until a client is actually interested in that object.

Lazy State [MoOh97]. Defer the initialization of the state of an object until the state is accessed. Lazy State is often used in situations in which a large volume of state information is accessed rarely. This pattern becomes even more powerful in combination with Flyweight [GoF95], or Memento [GoF95]. In networks of objects, the Lazy Propagator [FeTi97] describes how dependent objects can determine when they are affected by state changes and therefore need to update their state

Lazy Evaluation [Pryc02]. Lazy evaluation means that an expression is not evaluated until the expression's result is needed for the evaluation of another expression. Lazy evaluation of parameters allows functions to be partially evaluated, resulting in higher-order functions that can then be applied to the remaining parameters. Using lazy evaluation can significantly improve the performance of the evaluation, as unnecessary computations are avoided. In programming languages such as Java or C++, evaluation of sub-conditions in a Boolean expression is done using lazy evaluation, in the form of short-circuiting operators such as '&&'.

Lazy Initialization [Beck97]. Initialize the parts of your program the first time they are accessed. This pattern has the benefit of avoiding overhead in certain situations, but has the liability of increasing the chance of accessing uninitialized parts of the program.

Variable Allocation [NoWe00]. Allocate and deallocate variable-sized objects as and when you need them. This specialization applies Lazy Acquisition specifically to memory allocations and deallocations.

Variants *Semi-Lazy Acquisition.* Instead of acquiring a resource lazily as late as possible or at the beginning, the resource can also be acquired at three additional times. The idea is that you don't obtain the resource in the beginning but you also don't wait until the resource is actually needed—you load the resource some time in between. An example could be a network management system in which a topology tree of the network needs to be built.

There are three options:

- Build it when the application starts.
  - *For*: the tree is available as soon as the application is initialized.
  - *Against*: slow start-up time.
- Build it when the user requests it.
  - *For*: fast start-up time.
  - *Against*: the user has to wait for the tree to be constructed.
- Build it after the application has started and before the user requests it.
  - *For*: fast start-up time and tree is available when needed.

The last option is commonly used in network management systems.

Consequences   There are several **benefits** of using the Lazy Acquisition pattern:

- *Availability*. Using Lazy Acquisition ensures that not all resources are acquired up front. This helps to minimize the possibility that the system will run short of resources, or will acquire resources when they are not needed.

- *Stability*. Using Lazy Acquisition ensures that resources are acquired only when needed. This avoids needless acquisition of resources up front, thus reducing the possibility of resource exhaustion and making the system more stable.

- *Optimal system start-up*. Using Lazy Acquisition ensures that resources that are not needed immediately are acquired at a later stage. This helps to optimize system start-up time.

- *Transparency*. Using Lazy Acquisition is transparent to the resource user. The resource proxy hides the actual acquisition of the resource from the resource user.

There are some **liabilities** of using the Lazy Acquisition pattern:

- *Space overhead.* The pattern incurs a slight space overhead, as additional memory is required for proxies resulting from the indirection.

- *Time overhead.* The execution of the lazy acquisitions can introduce a significant time delay when a resource is acquired, and also overhead during regular program execution, due to the additional level of indirection. For real-time systems such behavior might not be acceptable.

- *Predictability.* The behavior of a lazy acquisition system can become unpredictable. If multiple parts of a system defer resource acquisition as late as possible, it can lead to bursts when all parts of the system attempt to acquire resources at the same time.

Known Uses **Singleton**. Singletons [GoF95], objects that exist uniquely in a system, are usually instantiated using lazy instantiation. In some cases Singletons are accessed by several threads. The Double-Checked Locking [POSA2] idiom can be used to avoid race conditions between threads during instantiation.

Haskell [Thom99]. The Haskell language, like other functional programming languages, allows lazy evaluation of expressions. Haskell only evaluates as much of a program as is required to get the answer. Using this demand-driven evaluation, data structures in Haskell are evaluated just enough to deliver the answer, and parts of them may not be evaluated at all.

Java 2 platform, Enterprise Edition (J2EE) [Sun04b]. Enterprise JavaBeans (EJB) containers in J2EE application servers [Iona04] host many different components simultaneously. To avoid resource exhaustion, they need to ensure that only components that are actually used by clients are active, while others should be inactive. A typical solution is the application of Lazy Loading and Lazy Instantiation for the components and their state. This saves valuable resources and assures scalability. Also, Java Server Pages (JSPs) are typically compiled into servlets by many J2EE application servers only when they are actually accessed, rather than when they are deployed.

Ad hoc networking [Sun04c] [UPnP04]. In ad hoc networking only temporal relationships between devices and their components exist, so that it becomes too expensive to hold on to resources that are not actually needed currently. This means that components need to be loaded, instantiated, destroyed, and unloaded regularly. Ad hoc networking frameworks therefore need to offer mechanisms such as lazy loading and lazy instantiation. It is also possible to run lazy discovery of devices—the application will not be notified until the discovered device list changes from the last discovery run by the underlying framework [IrDA04].

Operating systems. A common behavior of operating systems is to defer the complete loading of application libraries until they are actually needed. For example, on most Unix systems such as Solaris [Sun04h] and Linux, an environment variable called LD_BIND_NOW can be used to specify whether or not the shared objects (.so files) should be loaded using a lazy model. Under a lazy loading model, any dependencies that are labeled for lazy loading will be loaded only when explicitly referenced. By taking advantage of a function call's lazy binding, the loading of a dependency is delayed until it is first referenced. This has the additional advantage that objects that are never referenced will never be loaded.

.NET Remoting [Ramm02]. In .NET Remoting so-called 'singleton remote objects' are objects that can be used by multiple clients, but only one instance of the respective object type can exist at the same time in the server. Those singleton remote objects are only instantiated on first access, even though clients might obtain references to them before the first access.

COM+ [Ewal01]. Just-in-Time (JIT) activation is an automatic service provided by COM+ that can help to use server resources more efficiently, particularly when scaling up your application to do high-volume transactions. When a component is configured as being 'JIT activated', COM+ will at times deactivate an instance of it while a client still holds an active reference to the object. The next time the client calls a method on the object, which it still believes to be active, COM+ will reactivate the object transparently to the client, just in time. JIT activation is supported for COM+ and .NET based applications. .NET applications have to set configuration attributes of the .NET System.EnterpriseServices package.

JIT compilation. JIT compilation is heavily used in today's Java virtual machines (JVM). The compilation of the regular Java byte code into fast machine-specific assembler code is done just-in-time. One of the virtual machines that supports this feature is the IBM J9 JVM [IBM02]. The opposite of JIT compilation is ahead-of-time (AOT) compilation.

Java [Sun04a]. JVM implementations optimize Java class loading typically by loading the classes when the code of that class is to be first executed. This behavior is clearly following the Lazy Loading pattern.

Manufacturing [VBW97]. Just-in-Time manufacturing, as used in many industries such as the automobile industry, follows the same pattern. Parts of an assembly are manufactured as they are needed. This saves the cost of fixed storage.

Eclipse plug-in [IBM04b]. Eclipse is a universal tool platform—an open extensible IDE for anything and nothing in particular. Its extensibility is based on a plug-in architecture that allows every user to become a contributor of plug-ins. While the plug-in declarations that determine the visualization of the plug-ins' features are loaded eagerly, the actual logic, which is contained in Java archives (JAR), is loaded lazily on first use of any of the plug-in's functionality.

Heap compression. The research by [GKVI+03] employs a special garbage collector for the Java programming language that allows a heap smaller than the application's footprint to be used, by compressing temporarily unused objects in the heap. When such an object is accessed again, it lazily uncompresses portions of the object, thereby allocating the necessary memory.

FrameMaker [Adob04]. The desktop publishing program FrameMaker does not open and read referenced graphic files until the page containing the graphic is first displayed. The graphic is then rendered on the screen, and the rendered image is stored in temporary storage. When the page is displayed again, Framemaker checks for any updates to the referenced file. If no changes have been made to that file, it reuses the rendered image from temporary storage.

See Also The Eager Acquisition (53) pattern can be conceived as the opposite of Lazy Acquisition. Eager Acquisition describes the concept of acquiring resources up front to avoid acquisition overheads at the first access by clients.

Since both Lazy Acquisition and Eager Acquisition can be suboptimal in some use cases, the Pooling (97) pattern combines both into one pattern to optimize resource usage.

The Lazy Optimization [Auer96] pattern can help to tune performance once the program is running correctly and the system design reflects the best understanding of how the program should be structured.

The Thread-Specific Storage [POSA2] pattern uses a proxy to shield the creation of keys that identify the associated thread-specific object uniquely in each thread's object set. If the proxy does not yet have an associated key when accessed, it asks the key factory to create a new key.

Credits   Thanks to Frank Buschmann and Markus Völter for their valuable comments on earlier versions of this pattern. Special thanks to our EuroPLoP 2002 shepherd, Kevlin Henney, and the writer's workshop participants Eduardo Fernandez, Titos Saridakis, Peter Sommerlad, and Egon Wuchner.

Our copy-editor Steve Rickaby provided us with the nice known use for FrameMaker. FrameMaker was used for the whole of the writing and production of this book.

Eager Acquisition

The *Eager Acquisition* pattern describes how run-time acquisition of resources can be made predictable and fast by eagerly acquiring and initializing resources before their actual use.

Example   Consider an embedded telecommunication application with soft real-time constraints, such as predictability and low latency in execution of operations. Assume the application is deployed on a commercial off-the-shelf (COTS) operating system such as Linux, primarily for cost as well as portability reasons.

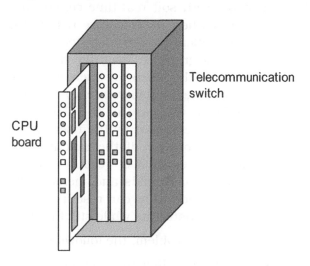

In most operating systems, operations such as dynamic memory allocation can be very expensive. The time it takes for memory allocations via operations such as new() or malloc() depends on the implementation of the operations. In most operating systems, including Real-Time Operating Systems (RTOS), the time it takes to execute dynamic memory allocations varies.

The main reasons for this are:

- Memory allocations are protected by synchronization primitives.

- Memory management, such as compaction of smaller memory segments to larger ones, consumes time.

If memory compaction is not done often enough, memory allocations can easily cause memory fragmentation. However, most operating systems, including some RTOS such as VxWorks [Wind04], do not provide such memory management, which can leave an application susceptible to memory fragmentation.

Context   A system that must satisfy high predictability and performance in resource acquisition time.

Problem   Systems with soft real-time constraints need to be stringent about how and when they acquire resources. Examples of such systems include critical industrial systems, highly scalable Web applications, or even the graphical user interface (GUI) of a desktop application. In each case, the users of such systems make certain assumptions about the predictability, latency, and performance of the system. For example, in the case of the GUI of a desktop application, a fast response is expected by the user and any delay in response can be irritating. However, if the execution of any user-initiated request results in expensive resource acquisition, such as dynamic acquisition of threads and memory, it can result in unpredictable time overheads. How can resources be acquired in systems with soft real-time constraints while still fulfilling the constraints?

To solve the problem, the following *forces* must be resolved:

- *Performance.* Resource acquisition by resource users must be fast.

- *Predictability.* Resource acquisition by resource users must be predictable—it should take the same amount of time each time a resource is acquired.

- *Initialization overhead.* Resource initialization at application run time needs to be avoided.

- *Stability.* Resource exhaustion at run time needs to be avoided.

- *Fairness.* The solution must be fair with respect to other resource users trying to acquire resources.

Solution   Eagerly acquire a number of resources before their actual use. At a time before resource use, optimally at start-up, the resources are acquired from the resource provider by a provider proxy. The resources are then kept in an efficient container. Requests for resource acquisition from resource users are intercepted by the provider proxy, which accesses the container and returns the requested resource.

The time at which the resources are acquired can be configured using different strategies. These strategies should take into account different factors, such as when the resources will be actually used, the number of resources, their dependencies, and how long it takes to acquire the resources. Options are to acquire at system start-up, or at a dedicated, possibly calculated, time after system start-up. Regardless of what strategy is used, the goal is to ensure that the resources are acquired and available before they are actually used.

Structure   The following participants form the structure of the Eager Acquisition pattern:

- A *resource user* acquires and uses resources.

- A *resource* is an entity such as memory or a thread.

- A *provider proxy* intercepts resource acquisitions by the user and hands the eagerly-acquired resources to the resource user in constant time.

- A *resource provider* provides and manages several resources.

The following CRC cards describe the responsibilities and collaborations of the participants.

Class **Resource User**	*Collaborator* • Resource • Provider Proxy	*Class* **Resource**	*Collaborator*
Responsibility • Acquires and uses resources.		*Responsibility* • Is acquired from the resource provider by the provider proxy and used by the resource user.	

Class **Provider Proxy**	*Collaborator* • Resource • Resource Provider	*Class* **Resource Provider**	*Collaborator* • Resource
Responsibility • Provides the same interface as the resource provider. • Intercepts resource acquisitions by the resource user and hands back eagerly-acquired resources in constant time.		*Responsibility* • Manages and provides resources to resource users.	

The following class diagram visualizes the structure of the Eager Acquisition pattern.

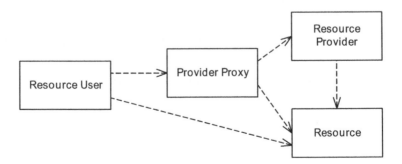

The resource user does not acquire the resource directly from the resource provider, but acquires it via the provider proxy.

Dynamics   **Scenario I.** The resource user creates a provider proxy, which it later uses to acquire the resource. The resource is acquired by the provider proxy before its use. At the latest, the resource is acquired when the resource user actually tries to acquire it.

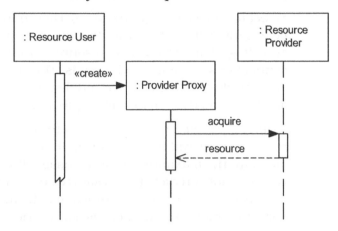

Scenario II. The resource user acquires a resource, but is intercepted by the provider proxy. The following sequence diagram shows how the resource user acquires the resource.

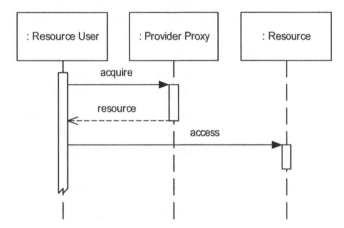

The provider proxy intercepts the acquisition request and returns an eagerly-acquired resource. The resource user can now access and use the resource.

Implementation   Five steps are involved in implementing the Eager Acquisition pattern.

1   *Select resources to acquire eagerly.* Determine the kind of resources to be eagerly acquired in order to guarantee predictable behavior of the overall system. Determine resources that are expensive, such as connections, memory, and threads. The acquisition of such resources is most likely to introduce unpredictability, and therefore they serve as ideal candidates for eager acquisition.

2   *Estimate resource usage.* Estimate the amount of resources a resource user will acquire during its lifetime. Perform test runs and measure the maximum resource usage, if it is not known up front. If you cannot predict the resource use, make it a configuration parameter, so it can be tuned easily after deployment. Provide operator information, such as log entries, for the actual resource utilization of eagerly acquired resources.

3   *Implement the provider proxy.* A provider proxy is responsible for the transparent integration of the Eager Acquisition pattern. It can be included in an actual design in several ways, for example by using a Virtual Proxy [GoF95] [POSA1] or Interceptor [POSA2]. A provider proxy can be obtained from an Abstract Factory [GoF95] by the resource user. When transparency is not required, the resource user acquires the resource directly from the resource provider, in which case a provider proxy is not required.

4   *Implement a container.* Implement a container, such as a hash map, to hold the eagerly-acquired resources. The container should allow predictable lookups. For example, a hash map can provide lookup in constant time.

5   *Determine a timing strategy.* Decide on a strategy, depending on when the provider proxy eagerly acquires the resources:

   • *At system start-up.* Implement a hook so that the code for the eager acquisition is executed at start-up time. The advantage of acquiring resources at system start-up is that the run time behavior of the system is not influenced, although it must be possible to predict the resource usage.

   • *Proactively during run time.* Use Reflection [POSA1] to detect system state that might lead to a need for resource acquisition by the resource user in the future. Proactive behavior has the advantage of being able to address acquisition requirements more closely. However, the cost of proactive behavior is higher complexity and execution overhead for continuous system monitoring.

6 *Determine initialization semantics.* Decide on how to initialize acquired resources to avoid initialization overhead. For some resources, a complete initialization on acquisition by the provider proxy is impossible. In such cases the initialization overhead during run time should be taken into account.

Example Resolved

Consider the embedded telecommunication application described earlier. To make the application predictable, three options exist:

- Implement the application objects as global variables, which is basically eager instantiation of objects.

- Put the objects on the stack, avoiding dynamic memory allocation altogether.

- Implement a memory pool that eagerly acquires memory from the operating system up front, after system start-up but before the first time dynamic memory allocation is needed. The memory pool is used by application objects to acquire their memory.

The first option has the disadvantage of losing control over initialization and release of memory. Further, many developers consider this design to be a poor one because of the high coupling it introduces into a system. Class static variables allow the location of definition to be more visible, but still have some of the same coupling problems, as well as issues regarding timing of initialization and release of memory. Using class static variables also hard-wires the number of instances of a class, which reduces the adaptability of a piece of software, as well as its ability to accommodate runtime/load-time variability.

The second option, working only with objects allocated on the stack, demands large stack sizes. Additionally, the lifecycle of the objects would have to map the call stack, otherwise objects could go out of scope while still being used.

The third option is much more flexible regarding the initialization of application objects, but has some restrictions. As described earlier, synchronization overhead and compaction of variable-sized memory blocks are the main reasons for poor predictability of memory acquisition time. The memory pool can only become more predictable than the operating system if it is able to avoid synchronization and management of variable-sized memory allocations.

To avoid synchronization overhead, memory pools need either to be dedicated to a thread, or to internalize thread-specific issues using, for instance, Thread-Specific Storage [POSA2]. For details, see also the Thread-Local Memory Pool [Somm02] pattern.

The following C++ class implements a simple memory pool for fixed-size blocks of memory without synchronization. It is expected to be used only by a single thread. The memory it provides is acquired eagerly in its constructor. For support of multiple block sizes, the memory pool internal management of blocks would need to be extended, or separate memory pools, one for each block size, would need to be instantiated.

```cpp
class Memory_Pool {
public:
  Memory_Pool (std::size_t block_size, std::size_t num_blocks)
  : memory_block_ (::operator new (block_size * num_blocks)),
    block_size_ (block_size),
    num_blocks_ (num_blocks)
  {
    for (std::size_t i = 0; i < num_blocks; i++)
    {
      void *block = static_cast<char*>(memory_block_) +
          i*block_size;
      free_list_.push_back (block);
    }
  }

  void *acquire (size_t size)
  {
    if (size > block_size_ || free_list_.empty())
    {
      // if attempts are made to acquire blocks larger
      // than the supported size, or the pool is exhausted,
      // throw bad_alloc
      throw std::bad_alloc ();
    }
    else
    {
      void *acquired_block = free_list_.front ();
      free_list_.pop_front ();
      return acquired_block;
    }
  }
```

```
void release (void *block)
{
    free_list_.push_back (block);
}


private:
    void *memory_block_;
    std::size_t block_size_;
    std::size_t num_blocks_;
    std::list<void *> free_list_;
};
```

An instance of the Memory_Pool class should be created for each thread that is spawned and needs to allocate memory dynamically. The eager acquisition of the memory blocks in the constructor, as well as acquisition of block-size memory in the acquire() method, can throw a bad_alloc exception.

```
const std::size_t block_size = 1024;
const std::size_t num_blocks = 32;
// Assume My_Struct is a complex data structure
struct My_Struct {
    int member;
    // ...
};

int main (int argc, char *argv[])
{
    try
    {
        Memory_Pool memory_pool (block_size, num_blocks);

        // ...

        My_Struct *my_struct =
            (My_Struct *) memory_pool.acquire (sizeof(My_Struct));

        my_struct->member = 42;
        // ...
    }
    catch (std::bad_alloc &)
    {
        std::cerr << "Error in allocating memory" << std::endl;
        return 1;
    }
    return 0;
}
```

The `acquire()` method uses the memory that has been eagerly acquired in the constructor of `Memory_Pool`. Ideally, the constructor should allocate enough memory initially so that all subsequent requests by `acquire()` can be fulfilled. However, in case there is insufficient memory to service a request by the `acquire()` method, additional memory would need to be acquired from the operating system. Therefore, `acquire()` would need to handle such cases as well. Of course, implementing acquisition only is not sufficient, and we also need to implement a proper disposal method [Henn03].

The above code only works for structures that are really just C-like. For real classes, the memory pool must be better integrated with the new and `delete` operators, such as:

```
void *operator new(std::size_t size, Memory_Pool &pool)
{
    return pool.acquire(size);
}
```

This would allow the struct above to be allocated as:

```
My_Struct *my_struct_a = new(memory_pool) My_Struct;
```

The price of optimization in this particular case is that for deletion, the traditional new/delete symmetry needs to be broken. Therefore, destroy the object explicitly and return its memory to the pool explicitly:

```
my_struct->~My_Struct();
memory_pool.release(my_struct);
```

For a more detailed discussion on how to integrate custom memory management techniques, see [Meye98].

Even though the above implementation makes certain assumptions and imposes some restrictions, it has the advantage of increased predictability of dynamic memory acquisitions. Furthermore, memory fragmentation is avoided, by allocating only fixed-size blocks. For alternative implementations, see the memory pool implementations of ACE [Schm02] [Schm03a] and Boost [Boos04].

Specializations   The following are some specializations of the Eager Acquisition pattern:

Eager Instantiation. In this case objects are instantiated eagerly and managed in a container. When the application, as resource user, requests new objects, new instances can be handed back from the list.

Eager Loading. Eager Loading applies eager acquisition to the loading of libraries, such as shared objects on Unix platforms, or dynamically linked libraries on Win32. The libraries are loaded up front, in contrast to Lazy Acquisition (38).

Variants   *Static Allocation.* Static Allocation, which is also known as Fixed Allocation [NoWe00], or Pre-Allocation, applies Eager Acquisition to the allocation of memory. Fixed Allocation is especially useful in embedded and real-time systems. In such systems memory fragmentation and predictability of the system behavior are more important than dynamic memory allocations.

Proactive Resource Allocation [Cros02]. Resource acquisitions can be made up front based on indications derived from resource usage by reflection techniques instead of purely basing it on estimations.

Consequences   There are several **benefits** of using the Eager Acquisition pattern:

- *Predictability.* The availability of resources is predictable, as requests for resource acquisitions from the user are intercepted and served instantly. Variation in delay in resource acquisition, incurred by the operating system, for example, is avoided.

- *Performance.* As resources are already available when needed, they can be acquired within a short and constant time.

- *Flexibility.* Customization of the resource acquisition strategy can easily be applied. Interception of resource acquisition from the user allows for strategized acquisition of resources by the provider proxy. This is very helpful in avoiding side effects such as memory fragmentation.

- *Transparency.* As the resources are eagerly acquired from the resource provider without requiring any user involvement, the solution is transparent to the user.

There are some **liabilities** of using the Eager Acquisition pattern:

- *Management responsibility.* Management of eagerly-acquired resources becomes an important aspect, as not all resources might immediately be associated with a resource user, and therefore need to be organized. Caching (83) and Pooling (97) patterns can be used to provide possible management solutions.

- *Static configuration.* The system becomes more static, as the number of resources has to be estimated up front. Overly-eager acquisitions must be avoided to guarantee fairness among resource users and to avoid resource exhaustion.

- *Over-acquisition.* Too many resources might be acquired up front by a subsystem that might not need all of them. This can lead to unnecessary resource exhaustion. However, properly tuned resource acquisition strategies can help to address this problem. Pooling (97) can also be used to keep a limit on the number of resources that are eagerly acquired.

- *Slow system start-up.* If many resources are acquired and initialized at system start-up, a possibly long delay due to eager acquisitions is incurred by the system. If resources are not eagerly acquired at system start-up, but later, there is still an overhead associated with it.

Known Uses   **Ahead-of-time compilation** [Hope02] [NewM04] is commonly used by Java virtual machines to avoid compilation overheads during execution.

Pooling (97). Pooling solutions, such as connection or thread pools typically pre-acquire a number of resources, such as network connections, or threads, to serve initial requests quickly.

Application servers [Sun04b]. In general, a servlet container of an application server offers no guarantee about when servlets are loaded or the order in which they are loaded. However, an element called <load-on-startup> can be specified for a servlet in the deployment descriptor, causing the container to load that servlet at start-up.

NodeB [Siem03]. In the software of the Siemens UMTS base station ´NodeB' the connections to various system parts are eagerly acquired at system start-up. This avoids unpredictable resource acquisition errors and delays during system run time.

Hamster [EvCa01]. A real-world known use is a hamster. It acquires as many fruits as possible before eating them in its burrow. The hamster stores the food in its cheek pouch. Unfortunately, no numbers are available regarding its estimations about how much it acquires eagerly.

Eclipse plug-in [IBM04b]. Eclipse is a universal tool platform—an open extensible IDE for anything and nothing in particular. Its extensibility is based on a plug-in architecture that allows every user to become a contributor of plug-ins. While the plug-in declarations that determine the visualization are loaded eagerly, the actual logic, which is contained in Java archives (JAR), is loaded lazily on first use of the any of the plug-in's functionality.

See Also   The opposite of Eager Acquisition is Lazy Acquisition (38), which allocates resources just in time, at the moment the resources are actually used.

The Pooling pattern (97) combines the advantages of Eager Acquisition and Lazy Acquisition into one pattern.

The Caching (83) pattern can be used to manage eagerly-acquired resources.

Credits   Thanks to the patterns team at Siemens AG Corporate Technology, to the EuroPLoP 2002 shepherd Alejandra Garrido, and the participants of the writer's workshop, Eduardo Fernandez, Titos Saridakis, Peter Sommerlad, and Egon Wuchner, for their valuable comments and feedback. Further, we are grateful to Andrey Nechypurenko and Kevlin Henney for their suggestions on the example source code of this pattern.

Partial Acquisition

The *Partial Acquisition* pattern describes how to optimize resource management by breaking up acquisition of a resource into multiple stages. Each stage acquires part of the resource, dependent upon system constraints such as available memory and the availability of other resources.

Example   Consider a network management system that is responsible for managing several network elements. These network elements are typically represented in a topology tree. A topology tree provides a virtual hierarchical representation of the key elements of the network infrastructure. The network management system allows a user to view such a tree, as well as get details about one or more network elements. Depending on the type of the network element, its details may correspond to a large amount of data. For example, the details of a complex network element may include information about its state as well as the state of its components.

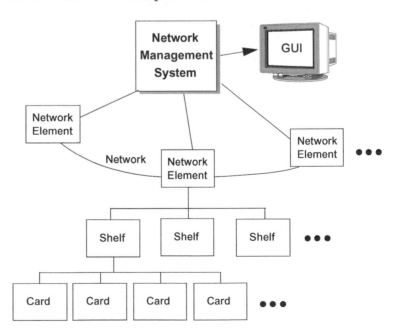

The topology tree is typically constructed at application start-up or when the application is restarting and recovering from a failure. In the first case, the details of all the network elements, along with their components and subcomponents, are usually fetched from the physical network elements. In the latter case, this information can be obtained from a persistent store as well as from the physical network elements. However, in either case obtaining all this information can have a big impact on the time it takes for the application to start up or recover. This is because completely creating or recovering a network element would require creating or recovering all its components. In addition, since each component can in turn be comprised of additional subcomponents, creating or recovering a component would in turn require creating or recovering all its subcomponents. Therefore the size of the resulting hierarchical topology tree, as well as the time it takes to create or recover all its elements, can be hard to predict.

Context Systems that need to acquire resources efficiently. The resources are characterized by either large or unknown size.

Problem Highly robust and scalable systems must acquire resources efficiently. A resource can include local as well as remote resources. Eager acquisition (53) of resources can be essential to satisfy resource availability and accessibility constraints. However, if these systems were to acquire all resources up front, a lot of overhead would be incurred and a lot of resources would be consumed unnecessarily. On the other hand, it may not be possible to lazily acquire all the resources, since some of the resources may be required immediately at application start-up or recovery. To address these conflicting requirements of resource acquisition requires resolution of the following *forces*:

- *Availability.* Acquisition of resources should be influenced by parameters such as available system memory, CPU load, and availability of other resources.

- *Flexibility.* The solution should work equally well for resources of fixed size and for resources of unknown or unpredictable size.

- *Scalability.* The solution should be scalable with the size of the resources.

- *Performance*. The acquisition of resources should have a minimal impact on system performance.

Solution   Split the acquisition of a resource into two or more stages. In each stage, acquire part of the resource. The amount of resources to acquire at each stage should be configured using one or more strategies. For example, the amount of resources to acquire at each stage can be governed by a strategy that takes into account available buffer space and required response time, as well as availability of dependent resources. Once a resource has been partially acquired, the resource user may start using it on the assumption that there is no need to have the entire resource available before it can be used.

Patterns such as Eager Acquisition (53) and Lazy Acquisition (38) can be used to determine when to execute one or more stages to partially acquire a resource. However, the Partial Acquisition pattern determines in how many stages a resource should be acquired, together with the proportion of the resource that should be acquired in each stage.

Structure   The following participants form the structure of the Partial Acquisition pattern:

- A *resource user* acquires and uses resources.

- A *resource* is an entity such as audio/video content. A resource is acquired in multiple stages.

- A *resource provider* manages and provides several resources.

The following CRC cards describe the responsibilities and collaborations of the participants.

Class Resource User	Collaborator • Resource
Responsibility • Acquires and uses resources.	

Class Resource	Collaborator

Responsibility
 • Is acquired from the
   resource provider and
   used by the resource
   user.	

Class Resource Provider	Collaborator • Resource

Responsibility
 • Manages and
   provides resources to
   resource users.	

The dependencies between the participants are shown in the following class diagram.

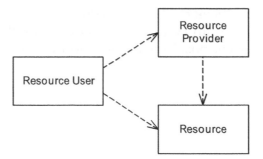

Dynamics   **Scenario I.** The sequence diagram below shows how the resource user partially acquires a resource in a series of acquisition steps. When all parts have been acquired, it accesses the resource.

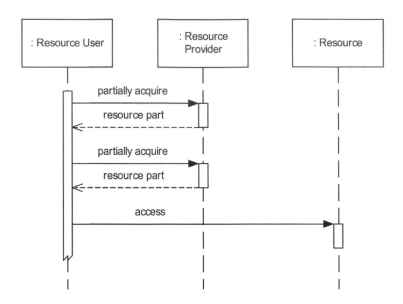

Scenario II. In some cases the resource user might not know when the next part of the resource is ready to be acquired. For example, a resource can be created incrementally, such as the arrival of network packets of a message stream. In such cases the user might not want to block on the acquisition, but be informed about the occurrence of such an event. The Reactor [POSA2] pattern is very useful for such scenarios. Here is how it works dynamically.

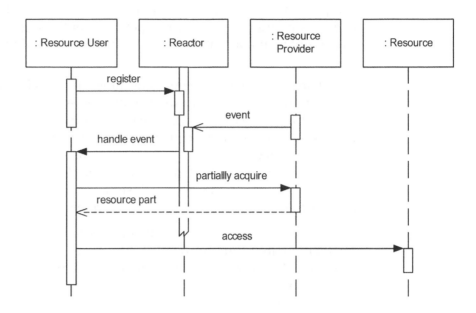

The reactor is triggered by some event from the resource provider about the availability of (parts of) the resource. The reactor in turn dispatches this event to the resource user, which in turn performs a partial acquisition. For more details, refer to [POSA2].

Implementation   There are six steps involved in implementing the Partial Acquisition pattern.

1   *Determine the number of stages.* The number of stages in which a resource should be acquired depends on system constraints such as available memory and CPU, as well as other factors such as timing constraints and the availability of dependent resources. For a resource of unknown or unpredictable size it may not be possible to determine the number of stages that it would take to acquire the entire resource. In this case, the number of stages would not have an upper bound, and a new stage would be executed until the resource has been completely acquired.

➡   In the case of the network management system in our example, the number of stages could correspond to the number of hierarchy levels in the topology tree. At each stage, an entire level of the hierarchy can be constructed by obtaining the details of the components of that level. If a level in the hierarchy is complex and contains a large number of components, obtaining the details of all the components of that level can be further divided into two or more stages.   ❑

2   *Select an acquisition strategy.* Determine when each stage of resource acquisition should be executed. Patterns such as Lazy Acquisition (38) and Eager Acquisition (53) can be used to control when one or more stages of resource acquisition should be executed. For example, Eager Acquisition can be used to acquire an initial part of the resource. The remaining parts can then be acquired using Lazy Acquisition, or can be acquired some time in between, after the system has started but before a user requests them.

➥   In the case of the network management system, Eager Acquisition (53) can be used to fetch the details of the network elements, but not of its internal components. The details of the components and sub-components of a network element can be fetched using Lazy Acquisition (38) when the user selects the network element in the GUI and tries to view the details of its components.   ❑

3   *Determine how much to acquire.* Configure strategies to determine how much to acquire partially at each stage. Different strategies can be configured to determine how much of a resource should be acquired in each stage. If the size of a resource is deterministic then a simple strategy can evenly distribute the amount of the resource to acquire at each stage among all the stages of resource acquisition. A more complex strategy would take into account available system resources. Thus, for example, if sufficient memory is available, such a strategy would acquire a large part of the resource in a single stage. At a later stage, if system memory is low, the strategy would acquire a smaller part of the resource.

Such an adaptive strategy can also be used if the size of the resource to be acquired is unknown or unpredictable. Additional strategies can be configured that make use of other parameters such as required response time. If there are no system constraints, another strategy could be used to acquire greedily as much of the resource as is available. Such a strategy would ensure that the entire resource is acquired in the shortest possible time. A good understanding of the application semantics is necessary to determine the appropriate strategies that should be used.

4 *Introduce a buffer* (optional). Determine whether the partially-acquired resource should be buffered. Buffering a resource can be useful if the size of the resource is unknown, or if the entire resource needs to be consolidated in one place before being used. If a resource needs to be buffered, the amount of buffer space to allocate should be determined to ensure the entire resource can fit. For a resource of unknown or unpredictable size, a buffer size should be allocated that is within the system constraints (such as available memory) but sufficiently large to handle the upper bound on the size of the resources in the system.

5 *Implement an acquisition trigger.* Set up a mechanism that is responsible for executing each stage of resource acquisition. Such a mechanism would then be responsible for acquiring different parts of a resource in multiple stages. Patterns such as Reactor [POSA2] can be used to implement such a mechanism. For example, a reactor can be used to acquire parts of a resource as they become available. An alternative mechanism can be set up that acquires parts of the resource proactively [POSA2].

6 *Handle error conditions and partial failures.* Error conditions and partial failures are characteristic of distributed systems. When using Partial Acquisition, it is possible that an error occurs after one or more stages have completed. As a result, part of a resource may have been acquired, but the attempt to acquire the subsequent parts of the resource would fail. Depending upon the application semantics, such a partial failure may or may not be acceptable. For example, if the resource being acquired in multiple stages is the contents of a file, then a partial failure would make inconsistent the data that has already been acquired successfully.

➥ On the other hand, in the case of the network management system in our example, the failure to obtain the details of one of the subcomponents will not have an impact on the details of the remaining components acquired successfully. A partial failure could still make the details of successfully acquired components available to the user.

One possible way to handle partial failures is to use the Coordinator (111) pattern. This pattern can help to ensure that either all stages of resource acquisition are completed, or none are. ❏

Consider the example of a network management system that is
responsible for managing a network of several network elements. The
network elements themselves consist internally of many components,
such as their CPU board, the connection switch, and the memory.
Loading the details of those components can take a long time. Using
the Partial Acquisition pattern, the acquisition of the details of the
network elements, along with their components, can be split into
multiple stages. In the initial stage only the details of the network
elements will be fetched from the physical network and a database.
The details of the components of the network elements will not be
fetched.

The topology manager of the network management system provides
details about the network element and its components to the
visualization subsystem, so that they can be displayed. The topology
manager retrieves the information from the database or from the
physical network elements, depending on the kind of data, static
configuration or current operating parameters. The Java code below
shows how a TopologyManager can defer fetching the details of the
components of a network element to a later stage.

```
public class TopologyManager
{
    // Retrieves the details for a specific network element.

    public Details getDetailsForNE (String neId) {
        Details details = new Details();

        // Fetch NE details either from physical network
        // element or from database ...

        // ... but defer fetching details of NE subcomponents
        // until later. Create a request to be inserted into
        // the Active Object message queue by the Scheduler.

        FetchNEComponents request =
            new FetchNEComponents (neId);

        // Now insert the request into the Scheduler so that
        // it can be processed at a later stage.
        scheduler.insert (request);

        return details;
    }
    private Scheduler scheduler;
}
```

The actual retrieval of network element components is done asynchronously by an Active Object [POSA2]. For this, requests are queued with the `Scheduler`, which runs in the active object's thread. The requests will fetch the network element's components when triggered by the `Scheduler`.

```
public class Scheduler implements Runnable {

    public Scheduler (int numThreads, ThreadManager tm) {
        // Spawn off numThreads to be managed by
        // ThreadManager. The threads would dequeue
        // MQRequest objects from the message queue and
        // invoke the call() method on each one
        // ...
    }

    // Insert request into Message Queue
    public void insert (Request request) {
        queue.insert (request);
    }

    public void run() {
        // Run the event loop
        // ...
    }

    private MessageQueue queue;
}
```

The main logic for retrieving the details of the components of the network element is contained in the `FetchNEComponents` class. It implements the `Request` interface, so that it can be scheduled by the `Scheduler`.

```
public interface Request {
    public void call ();
    public boolean canRun ();
}
```

The `Scheduler` will invoke `canRun()` to check if the `Request` can be executed. If it returns `true` it invokes `call()`, else it reschedules the request.

```
public class FetchNEComponents implements Request {
    public FetchNEComponents (String neId) {
        // Cache necessary information
    }

    // Hook method that gets called by the Scheduler.
    public void call () {
```

```
        // Fetch NE subcomponents using Partial Acquisition
    }

    // Hook method that gets called by the Scheduler to
    // determine if this request is ready to be processed.
    public boolean canRun () {
        // ...
        return true;
    }
}
```

The interactions between the classes are illustrated in the following
sequence diagram. When the user selects a network element, the
topology manager creates a request that acquires the shelf and card
information step by step. At each step the retrieved information is
handed to the user interface for visualization. On the selection of a
shelf of the same network element by the user, the details are
returned quickly, as they have been fetched in the background.

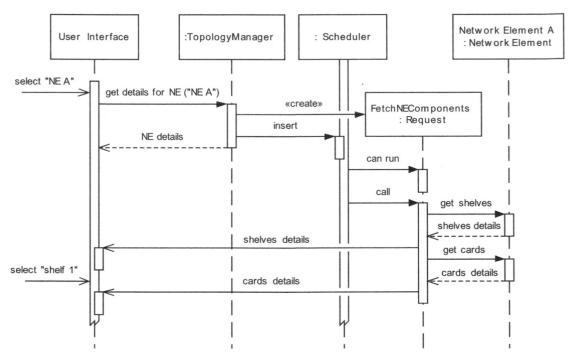

Using Partial Acquisition, the topological tree is therefore constructed
in multiple stages. The result is a significant increase in performance
when accessing network elements. The first request for details of a

network element, which is usually done at start-up, triggers the partial acquisition of the details of the components of the network element and makes them available by the time the user requests them. In addition, further logic can also be added such that the partial acquisition of the details of a network element can trigger the retrieval of the neighboring network elements. To integrate Partial Acquisition transparently, an Interceptor [POSA2] can be used (see *Variants*).

Variants *Transparent Partial Acquisition.* An interceptor can be introduced that would intercept a resource user's requests for resource acquisition and, using configured strategies, acquire an initial part of a resource. It would then acquire the remaining parts of the resource in additional stages transparent to the resource user. For instance, in the motivating example, an interceptor can be used to intercept requests and only fetch the network elements. The interceptor would not fetch the subcomponents immediately, as they can be fetched at a later stage transparent to the resource user.

Consequences There are several **benefits** of using the Partial Acquisition pattern:

- *Reactive behavior.* The Partial Acquisition pattern allows acquisition of resources that become available slowly or partially. If this partial acquisition is not done, the resource user would have to wait an undefined time before the resource became completely available.

- *Scalability.* The Partial Acquisition pattern allows the size of the resource being acquired to be scalable. The number of stages in which a resource is acquired can be configured depending upon the size of the resource being acquired.

- *Configurability.* The Partial Acquisition pattern can be configured with one or more strategies to determine in how many stages to acquire a resource, as well as how much of the resource to acquire at each stage.

There are some **liabilities** of using the Partial Acquisition pattern:

- *Complexity.* User algorithms that handle the resources need to be prepared to handle only partially-acquired resources. This can add a certain level of complexity to applications. In addition, using the Partial Acquisition pattern results in error handling becoming more complex. If one stage fails, an error-handling strategy must assure that the complete activity is restarted or corrected. On the other hand, error handling also becomes more robust. If a stage acquisition fails, the same stage can be reloaded without the necessity for a complete acquisition restart.

- *Overhead*. The Partial Acquisition pattern requires a resource to be acquired in more than one stage. This can result in an overhead of additional calls being made to acquire different parts of the same resource.

Known Uses **Incremental image loading**. Most modern Web browsers such as Netscape [Nets04], Internet Explorer [Micr04], or Mozilla [Mozi04] implement Partial Acquisition by supporting incremental loading of images. The browsers first download the text content of a Web page and at the same time create markers where the images of the page will be displayed. The browsers then download and display the images incrementally, during which the user can read the text content of the page.

Socket input [Stev03]. Reading from a socket also typically makes use of the Partial Acquisition pattern. Since data is typically not completely available at the socket, multiple read operations are performed. Each read operation partially acquires data from the socket and stores it in a buffer. Once all the read operations complete, the buffer contains the final result.

Data-driven protocol-compliant applications. Data-driven applications that adhere to specific protocols also make use of the Partial Acquisition pattern. Typically such applications follow a particular protocol to obtain data in two or more stages. For example, an application handling CORBA IIOP (Internet Inter-ORB Protocol) [OMG04a] requests typically reads the IIOP header in the first step to determine the size of the request body. It then reads the contents of the body in one or more steps. Note that such applications therefore use partially-acquired resources. In the case of an application handling an IIOP request, the application makes uses of the IIOP header obtained in the first stage.

Heap compression. The research by [GKVI+03] employs a special garbage collector for the Java programming language that allows the use of a heap smaller than the application's footprint. The technique compresses temporarily unused objects in the heap. When a compressed object is accessed again, only a part of the object is uncompressed, resulting in partial allocation of the memory. The remaining parts of the object are uncompressed in subsequent stages, as and when required.

Audio/Video streaming [Aust02]. When decoding audio and video streams the streams are acquired in parts. For videos, the algorithms typically acquire one or several frames at once, which are decoded, buffered, and displayed.

See Also
The Reactor [POSA2] pattern is designed to demultiplex and dispatch events efficiently. In the case of I/O operations it allows multiple resources that are acquired partially to be served reactively. Buffering can be used to keep partially-acquired resources in each stage. This can be especially useful if the size of the resource being acquired is unknown.

Credits
Thanks to the patterns team at Siemens AG Corporate Technology, to our PLoP 2002 shepherd, Terry Terunobu, and the writer's workshop participants Angelo Corsaro, Joseph K. Cross, Christopher D. Gill, Joseph P. Loyall, Douglas C. Schmidt, and Lonnie R. Welch, for their valuable feedback and comments.

3 Resource Lifecycle

*"Seek not, my soul, the life of the immortals;
but enjoy to the full the resources
that are within thy reach."*

Pindar

Once a resource has been acquired, its lifecycle must be managed effectively and efficiently. Managing a resource involves making it available to users, handling inter-resource dependencies, acquiring any dependent resources if necessary, and finally releasing resources that are no longer needed.

The Caching (83) pattern describes how the lifecycle of frequently-accessed resources can be managed to reduce the cost of re-acquisition and release of these resources, while maintaining the identity of the resources. It is a very common pattern that is used in a large number of highly-scalable enterprise solutions. In contrast to the Caching pattern, the Pooling (97) pattern optimizes acquisition and release of resources, while not maintaining the identity of the resources. Pooling is therefore preferable for stateless resources, as they require little or no initialization. Similar to Caching, Pooling is also used widely and includes examples such as pooling of components in component platforms and pooling of threads in distributed applications. Both Caching and Pooling are only applicable to reusable resources. Both patterns typically apply to exclusive reusable resources that are used serially by users. However, in some cases it may make sense to use Caching or Pooling for concurrently-accessible reusable resources. In such cases, both Caching and Pooling are oblivious of whether the resources are concurrently accessible or not, since resource access only takes place once the resources have been fetched from the cache or the pool.

Two or more entities, such as acquired resources, resource users, or resource providers, can interact with each other and produce changes to a software system. In such a situation, the entities are considered to be active and capable of participating in interactions that result in changes. Given such entities, it is important that any changes that are produced keep the system in a consistent state. The Coordinator (111) pattern ensures that in a task involving multiple entities, the system state remains consistent and thus overall stability is maintained.

The Resource Lifecycle Manager (128) pattern manages all the resources of a software system, thereby freeing both the resources to be managed, as well as their resource users, from the task of proper resource management. The Resource Lifecycle Manager is responsible for managing the lifecycle of all types of resource, including both reusable and non-reusable resources.

Caching

The *Caching* pattern describes how to avoid expensive re-acquisition of resources by not releasing the resources immediately after their use. The resources retain their identity, are kept in some fast-access storage, and are re-used to avoid having to acquire them again.

Example   Consider a network management system that needs to monitor the state of many network elements. The network management system is typically implemented as a three-tier system. End-users interact with the system using the presentation layer, typically a GUI. The middle-tier, comprising the business logic, interacts with the persistence layer, and is also responsible for communicating with the physical network elements. Because a typical network may consist of thousands of network elements, it is very expensive to set up persistent connections between the middle tier, the application server, and all the network elements. On the other hand, an end-user can select any of the network elements using the GUI to obtain details of the network element. The network management system must be responsive to the user request, and hence should provide low latency between user selection of a network element and the visualization of its properties.

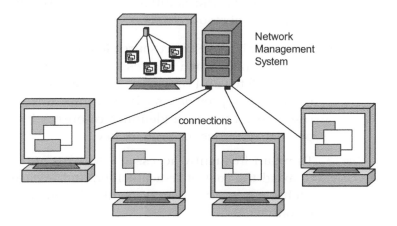

Establishing a new network connection for every network element selected by the user and destroying it after use incurs overhead in the form of CPU cycles inside the application server. In addition, the average time to access a network element can be too large.

Context   Systems that repeatedly access the same set of resources and need to optimize for performance.

Problem   Repetitious acquisition, initialization, and release of the same resource causes unnecessary overhead. In situations in which the same component or multiple components of a system access the same resource, repetitious acquisition and initialization incurs cost in terms of CPU cycles and overall system performance. The cost of acquisition, access, and release of frequently used resources should be reduced to improve performance.

To address the problem the following *forces* need to be resolved:

- *Performance.* The cost of repetitious resource acquisition, initialization, and release must be minimized.

- *Complexity.* The solution should not make acquisition and release of resources more complex and cumbersome. In addition, the solution should not add unnecessary levels of indirection to the access of resources.

- *Availability.* The solution should allow resources to be accessible even when the resource providers are temporarily unavailable.

- *Scalability.* The solution should be scalable with regard to the number of resources.

Solution   Temporarily store the resource in a fast-access buffer called a cache. Subsequently, when the resource is to be accessed again, use the cache to fetch and return the resource instead of re-acquiring it from the resource provider, such as an operating system that is hosting resources. The cache identifies resources by their identity, such as pointer, reference, or primary key.

To retain frequently-accessed resources and not release them helps to avoid the cost of re-acquisition and release of resources. Using a cache eases the management of components that access the resources.

When resources in a cache are no longer needed, they are released. The cache implementation determines how and when to evict resources that are no longer needed. This behavior can be controlled by strategies.

Structure The following participants form the structure of the Caching pattern:

- A *resource user* uses a resource.

- A *resource* is an entity such as a connection.

- A *resource cache* buffers resources that resource users release.

- A *resource provider* owns and manages several resources.

The following CRC cards show how the participants interact with each other

Class **Resource User**	*Collaborator*
Responsibility • Initially acquires the resource from the resource provider. • Uses the resource. • Releases unused resources to the resource cache. • Acquires cached resources from the resource cache.	• Resource • Resource Provider • Resource Cache

Class **Resource**	*Collaborator*
Responsibility • Is acquired from the resource provider and used by the resource user.	

Class **Resource Cache**	*Collaborator*
Responsibility • Buffers resources. • Eventually evicts resources.	• Resource • Resource Provider

Class **Resource Provider**	*Collaborator*
Responsibility • Owns and manages several resources.	• Resource

The following class diagram illustrates the structure of the Caching pattern.

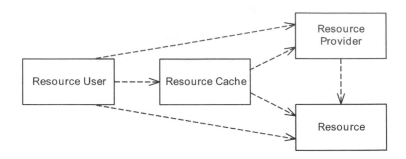

The resource provider, for example an operating system, hosts the resources that are initially acquired by the resource user. The resource user then accesses the resource. When no longer needed, the resource is released to the cache. The resource user uses the cache to acquire resources that it needs to access again. Acquisition of a resource from the cache is cheaper with respect to CPU utilization and latency compared to acquisition from the resource provider.

Dynamics   The following figure shows how the resource user acquires a resource from the resource provider. The resource is then accessed by the user. After the resource has been used it is put into a cache instead of releasing it to the resource provider.

When the resource user needs to access the same resource again, it uses the cache to retrieve it.

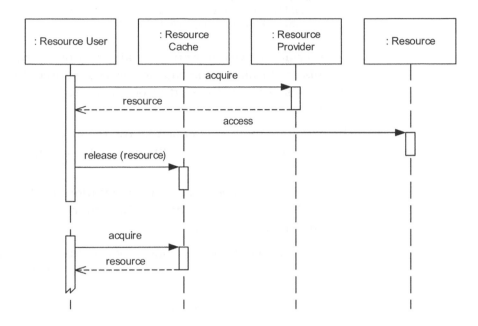

Implementation To implement the Caching pattern, the following steps should be followed:

1   *Select resources.* Select resources that benefit from caching. These are typically resources that are expensive to acquire and are used frequently. Caching is very often introduced as an optimization technique after identification of performance bottlenecks.

   In distributed systems two forms of caching can exist: client-side and server-side caching. Client-side caching is useful to save the bandwidth and time it takes to transmit server data repeatedly to the client. On the other hand, server-side caching is useful when many client requests lead to repeated acquisitions and release of the same resource in the server.

2   *Determine a caching interface.* When resources are released and re-acquired from the cache directly by the resource user, a proper interface must be designed. This interface needs to offer a release() and an acquire() method.

```
public interface Cache {
    public void release (Resource resource);
    public Resource acquire (Identity id);
}
```

The interface above relies on the availability of a separate resource ID, but this might not be the case for every resource. In some cases the ID of a resource might need to be calculated from properties of the resource.[1]   ❑

The release() method is called by the resource user when it releases the resource to the cache, instead of releasing it to the resource provider.

3   *Implement the cache.* The implementation of the acquire() and release() methods of the Cache interface provides the key functionality of the cache.

➡   The following code snippet shows the implementation of the release() method that is called on resource release by the resource user.

```
public class CacheImpl implements Cache {
    public void release (Resource resource) {
        String id = resource.getId ();
        map.put (id, resource);
    }
    // ...

    HashMap map;
}
```
                                                                    ❑

The release() method adds the resource to the map so that a later call on acquire can find it via its ID. For optimization reasons it is advisable to use a hash map, since that can perform look-up in almost constant time. The Comparand pattern [CoHa01] gives some ideas of how to perform comparisons between IDs. Depending on the kind of resource, the ID of the resource has to be determined first. In the case of our example, the resource can identify itself.

The acquire() method of the cache implementation should be responsible for looking up the resource from the map based on the ID. As a variant, when acquisition of the resource from the cache fails, which means that the resource with the required identity has not

---

1. We do not discuss this issue in detail since it is beyond the scope of the book.

been found, the cache itself can acquire the resource from the resource provider. For more details, please refer to the Transparent Cache variant in the *Variants* section

➡ The following piece of code shows an implementation of the acquire() method.

```
public class CacheImpl implements Cache {
    public Resource acquire (Identity id) {
        Resource resource = map.get (id);
        if (resource == null)
            throw new ResourceNotFound ();
        return resource;
    }
}                                                    ❏
```

4   *Determine how to integrate the cache* (optional). If the cache has to be integrated transparently, use an Interceptor [POSA2] or a Cache Proxy [POSA1]. Introducing an Interceptor or a Cache Proxy reduces the complexity of releasing resources explicitly to and re-acquiring resources from the cache by making the operations transparent. See the *Transparent Cache* variant in the *Variants* section for information on how to make the operations transparent. However, even with this approach, the level of indirection as a result of the look-up in the cache cannot be avoided.

5   *Decide on an eviction strategy.* The resources stored in the cache require storage space. When not used for a long time, it becomes inefficient to hold on to those resources. Therefore use an Evictor (168) to remove resources that are no longer being used. The integration of the Evictor can be done in multiple ways. For example, an Evictor can be invoked in the context of the release() method, or can be invoked by a timer at regular intervals. Of course, this behavior influences overall predictability. In addition, the Evictor can be configured with different strategies, such as Least Recently Used (LRU), Least Frequently Used (LFU), and other domain-specific strategies. The Strategy [GoF95] pattern can be used for this.

6   *Ensure consistency.* Many resources have states associated with them that must be properly initialized on resource creation. In addition, when resources are accessed using write operations, consistency needs to be ensured between the original resource and the resource in the cache that is mirroring it. When the original changes, callbacks are used to tell the mirror to update its copy. When the mirror

changes, most caches apply a strategy called 'write-through'. Using this strategy, changes to the mirror are applied both to the original and to the mirror directly. This functionality is typically implemented by an entity called a Synchronizer. Thus the Synchronizer becomes an important participant of the pattern. Some caches further optimize this functionality by introducing more complex logic for keeping the original and its mirror in the cache consistent.

Use a Strategy [GoF95] to decide on when to synchronize. In some cases only special operations, such as write operations, need to be synchronized immediately, whereas in other cases a periodic update might be advisable. Also, synchronization might be triggered by external events, such as updates of the original by other resource users.

➡   In our motivating example, if the physical data at the network element changes, the memory representation of the network element that is cached must change. Similarly, if the user changes a setting of a network element, the change must be reflected at the physical network element.   ❏

Example Resolved   Consider the network management system that needs to monitor the state of many network elements. The middle tier of the network management system will use the Caching pattern to implement a cache of connections to the network elements. On user access of a specific network element, the connection to the network element is acquired. When the connection is no longer needed, it is added to the cache. Later, when a new request for the connection arrives, the connection is acquired from the cache, thus avoiding high acquisition cost.

Subsequent connections to other network elements will then be established when the user first accesses them. When the user switches context to another network element, the connection is put back into the connection cache. If a user accesses the same network element, the connection will be reused. No delay will occur on the first access of the reused connections.

Variants   *Transparent Cache.* When the cache must be integrated transparently, the cache can use Lazy Acquisition (38) to acquire the resources that the client requests. This is only possible if the cache has knowledge of how to acquire and initialize such resources. By lazily acquiring resources initially, the resource user can remain oblivious of the existence of the cache.

Read-Ahead Cache. In a situation in which repetitious Partial Acquisition (66) is used to acquire resources, the system can be designed efficiently if a read-ahead cache is used. The read-ahead cache can acquire resources before they are actually used, ensuring that the resources are available when needed.

Cached Pool. A combination of a cache and a pool can be used to provide a sophisticated resource management solution. When a resource needs to be released from the cache, instead of returning it to the resource provider, it can be put into a pool. The cache therefore serves as an intermediate storage for the resource. The cache is configured with a timeout—once the time expires, the resource loses its identity and goes into the pool. The advantage is a small optimization—if the same resource is required and the resource has not yet been returned to the pool, you avoid the cost of initialization (the virtue of caching).

Layered Cache. In complex systems, the Caching pattern is often applied at several levels. For example, the Websphere Application Server (WAS) [IBM04a] applies caching at multiple levels. WAS provides the ability to cache the results of EJB methods actively. Storing commands in a cache for reuse by subsequent callers allows requests to be handled in the business logic tier rather than in the data tier, where processing is more expensive. WAS also provides a prepared statement cache that can be configured with the backend database for dynamic/static SQL statement processing. Depending on application data access patterns, the WAS prepared statement cache can improve application performance. To increase the performance of JNDI operations, WAS employs caching to reduce the number of remote calls to the name server for lookup operations. Finally, WAS provides data access beans that offer caching of database query results.

Consequences   Caching adds some performance overhead due to an additional level of indirection, but overall there is a performance gain, since resources are acquired faster.

There are several **benefits** of using the Caching pattern:

- *Performance.* Fast access to frequently used resources is an explicit benefit of caching. Unlike Pooling (97), caching ensures that the resources maintain their identities. Therefore, when the same resource needs to be accessed again, the resource need not be acquired or fetched from somewhere—it is already available.

- *Scalability.* Avoiding resource acquisition and release is an implicit benefit of caching. Caching by its nature is implemented by keeping frequently-used resources. Therefore, just like Pooling, Caching helps to avoid the cost of resource acquisition and release. This especially pays off in frequent usage, therefore improving scalability.

- *Usage complexity.* Caching ensures that the complexity of acquiring and releasing resources from a resource user perspective does not increase, apart from the additional step required to check the availability of the resource in the cache.

- *Availability.* Caching resources increases availability of resources whose resource providers are temporarily unavailable, since the cached resources are still available.

- *Stability.* Since Caching reduces the number of releases and re-acquisitions of resources, it reduces the chance of memory fragmentation leading to greater system stability. This is similar to Pooling.

There are some **liabilities** of using the Caching pattern:

- *Synchronization complexity.* Depending on the type of resource, complexity increases, because consistency between the state of the cached resource and the original data, which the resource is representing, needs to be ensured. This complexity becomes even worse in clustered environments, which in some extreme cases might render the pattern useless.

- *Durability.* Changes to the cached resource can be lost when the system crashes. However, this problem can be avoided if a synchronized cache is used.

- *Footprint.* The run-time footprint of the system is increased, as possibly unused resources are cached. However, if an Evictor (168) is used, the number of such unused cached resources can be minimized.

Caches are not a good idea if the application requires data to be always available on the expensive-to-access resources. For example, interrupt-driven I/O intensive applications as well as embedded systems often have no hardware memory caches.

A general note on optimizations: Caching should be applied carefully when other means, such as optimizing the acquisition of the resource itself, cannot be further improved. Caching can introduce some implementation complexity, complicating the maintenance of the overall solution, and increase the overall resource consumption, for example of memory, because cached resources are not released. Therefore consider the trade-off between performance, resource consumption, and complexity before applying Caching.

Known Uses   **Hardware cache** [Smit82]. Almost every central processing unit (CPU) has a hardware memory cache associated with it. The cache not only reduces mean memory access time, but also helps reduce bus traffic. Cache memory is typically faster than RAM by a factor of at least two.

Caching in file systems and distributed file systems [NW088] [Smit85]. Distributed file systems use Caching on the server side to avoid reading file blocks from disk all the time. The most frequently-used files are kept in the server's memory for quick access. File systems also use caching of file blocks on the client side to avoid network traffic and the latency incurred when the data has to be fetched from the server.

Data transfer object [Fowl02]. Middleware technologies such as CORBA [OMG04a] and Java RMI [Sun04g] allow the remote transfer of objects, as opposed to pure remote method invocation on a remote object. The remote object is actually transferred by value between the client and the server when methods are invoked on them locally. This is done to minimize the number of expensive remote method invocations. The object is held locally in a cache and represents the actual remote object. Though this approach improves performance, synchronization between the local copy and the remote original of the object must be implemented by the user.

Web proxy [Squi04]. A Web proxy is a proxy server located between a Web browser and Web servers. The Web proxy is accessed by the Web browser every time a Web page is accessed from any Web server in the World Wide Web. The Web proxy caches a Web page that is fetched by a browser from a Web server, and returns it when a subsequent request is sent for the same page. As a result, a Web proxy helps to reduce the number of Web page requests sent over the Internet by keeping frequently requested Web pages in its local cache.

Web browsers. Most popular Web browsers such as Netscape [Nets04] and Internet Explorer [Micr04] cache frequently-accessed Web pages. If a user accesses the same page, the browsers fetch the contents of the page from cache, thus avoiding the expensive retrieval of the contents from the Web site. Timestamps are used to determine how long to maintain the pages in cache and when to evict them.

Paging [Tane01] [NoWe00]. Modern operating systems keep pages in memory to avoid expensive reads from swap space on disk. The pages that are kept in memory can be regarded as being kept in a cache. Only when a page is not found in the cache does the operating system fetch it from disk.

File cache [KiSa92]. File caches improve performance and allow the files and directories of a mounted network drive to be available locally when off-line without a network connection. The files and directories are cached and synchronized against the original when connection is made to the network. Latest versions of the Microsoft operating system support file caches through a feature known as 'Offline Files'.

.NET [Rich02]. The .NET data sets can be viewed as in-memory databases. They are instantiated locally and filled by a SQL query on the database with one or more tables, using an `SqlDataAdapter`. From then on, clients can access the data in object-oriented fashion. The changes will only be reflected in the original database after the `SqlDataAdapter` is used to update them explicitly. Consistency with changes in the original data source is not automatically ensured.

Enterprise JavaBeans (EJB) [Sun04b]. Entity Beans of EJB represent database information in the middle tier, the application server. This avoids expensive data retrieval (resource acquisition) from the database.

Object cache [Orac03] [Shif04]. An object cache applies the pattern to the paradigm of object orientation. In this case, the resources are objects that have a certain cost associated with them when created and initialized. The object cache allows such expensive operations to be avoided when the resource's use allows for caching.

Data cache [RoDe90] [Newp04]. A data cache applies the pattern to data. Data is viewed as a resource that is in some cases hard to acquire. For example, such data could include a complex and expensive calculation, or some information that needs to be retrieved from secondary storage. This pattern allows fetched data to be reused to avoid expensive re-acquisition of data when it is needed again.

iMerge [Luce03]. The iMerge EMS is an element management system for the iMerge VoIP (Voice over Internet Protocol) hardware system, which uses SNMP as its communication interface. It uses Caching to optimize visualization and provisioning of lines between network elements.

See Also   The Pooling (97) pattern is similar to Caching, but has a major difference. The main idea behind Pooling is reuse of a resource that does not have an identity. It helps to avoid the cost of re-acquisition and release of resources. A resource is typically without any identity. The Caching pattern is different than the Pooling pattern, since Caching maintains the identity of a resource in memory. The difference allows Pooling to acquire resources transparently, whereas Caching expects the resource user to acquire the resource.

The Eager Acquisition (53) pattern typically uses Caching to manage eagerly-acquired resources.

An Evictor (168) can be used for eviction of cached data.

The Resource Lifecycle Manager (128) pattern can use Caching internally to provide fast access to stateful resources.

A Cache Proxy [POSA1] can be used to hide caching effects. Smart Proxies [HoWo03] in TAO [Schm98] [OCI04] intercepting remote invocations are especially designed for this.

The Cache Management [Gran98] pattern focuses on how to combine a cache with the Manager [Somm98] pattern, where the Manager pattern centralizes access, creation and destruction of objects. The description is more specific to objects and database connections, both in the context of Java.

The Page Cache [TMQH+03] pattern is a specialized cache for improving response times when dynamically-generated Web pages are accessed. A page cache is associated with a Web server, which uses it to store accessed pages indexed by their URL. When the same URL is requested, the Web server queries the cache and returns the cached page instead of dynamically generating its content again.

Credits   Thanks to Ralph Cabrera for sharing his experience on Caching with us and for providing the iMerge known use. Special thanks to Pascal Costanza, our EuroPLoP 2003 shepherd, for his excellent comments. Our acknowledgements further include the writer's workshop participants, Frank Buschmann, Kevlin Henney, Wolfgang Herzner, Klaus Marquart, Allan O'Callaghan, and Markus Völter.

Pooling

The *Pooling* pattern describes how expensive acquisition and release of resources can be avoided by recycling resources that are no longer needed. Once the resources are recycled and pooled, they lose their identity and state.

Example Consider a simple Web-based e-commerce application that allows users to select and order one or more items. Assume that the solution is implemented in Java using a three-tier architecture. The clients consist of Web browsers that communicate with a Java servlet engine such as Tomcat. The business logic is implemented by one or more Java servlets that execute in the Java servlet engine. The servlets themselves connect to a database using a Java Database Connection (JDBC) interface. The following figure shows such a set-up with two servlets executing in the servlet engine and connecting to a database.

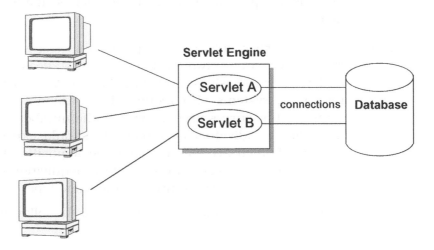

Most of the Web pages of the catalog are dynamically generated and depend on the database for their contents. For example, to obtain a list of available items in the catalog along with their pricing, a servlet connects to the database and executes a query. The servlet uses the results of the query to generate the HTML page that is displayed to the user. Similarly, if a user makes a purchase and enters payment details via an HTML form, the servlet connects to the database and updates it.

To execute SQL statements on the database, a servlet needs to obtain a connection to it. A trivial implementation would create a connection to the database for every request of the servlet. Such a solution can be very inefficient, since it incurs a delay in creating a connection to the database for every user request. In addition, such a solution is expensive, since it results in potentially thousands of connections being created within a short time period.

An optimization could be to store a connection in the session context of the servlet engine. This would allow reuse of a connection within session. Multiple requests from a user belonging to the same session would use the same connection to the database. However, an on-line catalog can potentially be accessed by hundreds of users simultaneously. So even with this solution a large number of database connections would be needed to meet the requirements.

Context   Systems that continuously acquire and release resources of the same or similar type, and have to fulfill high scalability and efficiency demands.

Problem   Many systems require fast and predictable access to resources. Such resources include network connections, instances of objects, threads, and memory. Besides providing fast and predictable access to resources, systems also require the solution to scale across the number of resources used, as well as the number of resource users. In addition, individual user requests should experience very little variation in their access time. Thus the acquisition time for resource A should not vary significantly from the acquisition time for resource B, where A and B are resources of the same type.

To solve the above-mentioned problems, the following *forces* need to be resolved:

- *Scalability.* Released resources should be reused to avoid the overhead of re-acquisition.

- *Performance.* Wastage of CPU cycles in repetitious acquisition and release of resources should be avoided.

- *Predictability.* The acquisition time of a resource by a resource user should be predictable even though direct acquisition of the resource from the resource provider can be unpredictable.

- *Simplicity.* The solution should be simple to minimize application complexity.

- *Stability.* Repetitious acquisition and release of resources can also increase the risk of system instability. For example, repetitious acquisition and release of memory can lead to memory fragmentation on operating systems without sophisticated memory management. The solution should minimize system instability.

Patterns such as Eager Acquisition (53) and Lazy Acquisition (38) resolve only a subset of these forces. For example, Eager Acquisition allows for predictable resource acquisition, whereas Lazy Acquisition focuses more on avoiding unnecessary acquisition of resources.

In summary, how can resource acquisition and access be made efficient while ensuring that predictability and stability are not compromised?

Solution   Manage multiple instances of one type of resource in a pool. This pool of resources allows for reuse when resource users release resources they no longer need. The released resources are then put back into the pool.

To increase efficiency, the resource pool eagerly acquires a fixed number of resources after creation. If the demand exceeds the available resources in the pool, it lazily acquires more resources. To free unused resources several alternatives exist, such as those documented by Evictor (168) or Leasing (149).

When a resource is released and put back into the pool, it should be made to lose its identity by the resource user or the pool, depending on the strategy used. Later, before the resource is reused, it needs to be re-initialized. If a resource is an object, providing a separate initialization interface can be useful. The resource identity, in many cases a pointer or a reference, is not used for identification by the resource user or the pool.

Structure   The following participants form the structure of the Pooling pattern:

- A *resource user* acquires and uses resources.

- A *resource* is an entity such as memory or a thread.

- A *resource pool* manages resources and gives them to resource users in response to acquisition requests.

- A *resource provider*, such as an operating system, owns and manages resources.

The following CRC cards describe the responsibilities and collaborations of the participants.

Class **Resource User**	*Collaborator* • Resource • Resource Pool
Responsibility • Acquires and uses resources. • Releases unused resources to the resource pool.	

Class **Resource**	*Collaborator*
Responsibility • Represents a reusable entity, such as memory or a thread. • Is acquired from the resource provider by the pool and used by the resource user.	

Class **Resource Pool**	*Collaborator* • Resource • Resource Provider
Responsibility • Acquires resources up front, if necessary. • Recycles unused resources returned by resource users.	

Class **Resource Provider**	*Collaborator* • Resource
Responsibility • Owns and manages several resources.	

The structure of the pattern is shown by the following class diagram.

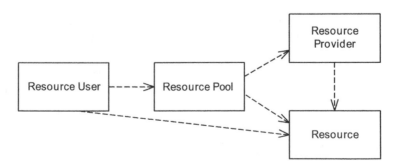

The resource user only depends on the resource pool and the actual resources. Resources are acquired by the pool from the resource provider.

Dynamics   The interactions between the participants are shown in the following sketch.

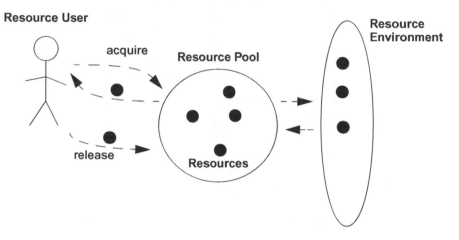

The interaction between the participants varies slightly depending on whether the resource pool eagerly acquires resources up front or not.

Assuming the pool does acquire the resources up front, subsequent acquisition requests from resource users are served from those resources. Resource users release resources to the resource pool when no longer needed. The resources are then recycled by the pool and returned on new acquisition requests.

A slightly more complex situation is described in the following sequence diagram, in which an acquisition request by a user leads to the acquisition of a resource from the resource provider. Acquisition on demand is done because no pre-acquired resources are available. The resource user accesses and uses the resource. When no longer needed, the user releases the resource back to the resource pool. The resource pool uses statistical data about resource usage to determine when to evict the resources from the pool. The statistical data includes use characteristics, such as last use and frequency of use. The second part of the figure shows a scenario in which the resource

pool decides to evict the resource based on statistical data after it has
been released by the resource user.

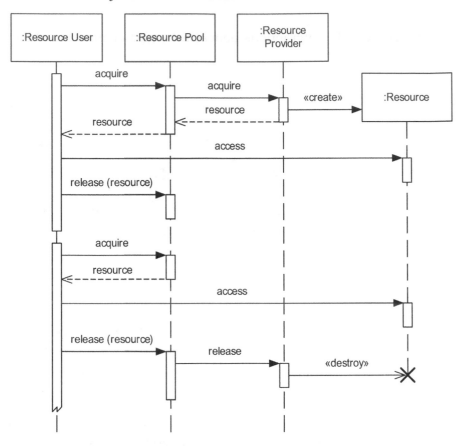

Implementation   Eight steps are involved in implementing the Pooling pattern.

1   *Select resources.* Identify resources that would benefit from being
    pooled in a resource pool. Simplify resource management by grouping
    resources into separate pools by their types. Grouping resources of
    different types into the same pool can complicate their management,
    as it makes multiple sub-pools and ad hoc lookups necessary.

2   *Determine the maximum size of the pool.* To avoid resource
    exhaustion, define the maximum number of resources that are
    maintained by the resource pool. The maximum number of resources
    available in the resource pool equals the number of eagerly-acquired
    resources plus the number of resources acquired on-demand, for

details refer to Lazy Acquisition (38). The maximum number of resources is typically set at initialization time of the pool, but it is also possible to base it on configurable parameters such as the current system load.

3   *Determine the number of resources to acquire eagerly.* To minimize resource acquisition time at run-time, it is recommended to eagerly acquire at least the average number of resources typically used. This reduces acquisitions during the routine execution of the application. User requirements, along with system analysis, help to determine the average number of resources to be acquired. It is important to remember that too many eagerly-acquired resources can be a liability, as they lead to additional resource contention, and should therefore be avoided. See also the Eager Acquisition (53) pattern.

4   *Define a resource interface.* Provide an interface that all pooled resources need to implement. The interface facilitates the maintenance of a collection of resources.

➥   For example, an interface in Java might look like:

```
public interface Resource {}                                    ❏
```

An implementation of the Resource interface maintains context information that is used to determine whether to evict the resource, as well as when to evict it. The context information includes timestamps and usage counts.

➥   For example, an implementation of the Resource interface in Java for a Connection class might look like:

```
public class Connection implements Resource
{
    public Connection () {
        // ....
    }
    // ....
    // Maintain context information to be used for eviction
    private Date lastUsage;
    private boolean currentlyUsed;
}                                                               ❏
```

For legacy code integration, where it may not be possible to have the resource implement the Resource interface, an Adapter [GoF95] class can be introduced. The adapter class can implement the Resource interface and then wrap the actual resource. The context information can then be maintained by the adapter class.

➡ Here is what an adapter class in Java for the `Connection` class might look like:

```
public class ConnectionAdapter implements Resource
{
   public ConnectionAdapter (Connection existingCon) {
      connection = existingCon;
   }

   public Connection getConnection () {
      return connection;
   }

   // Maintain context information to be used for eviction
   private Date lastUsage;
   private boolean currentlyUsed;
   private Connection connection;
}                                                               ❑
```

5   *Define a pool interface.* Provide an interface for the acquisition and release of resources by resource users.

➡ For example, an interface in Java might look like:

```
public interface Pool
{
   Resource acquire ();
   void release (Resource resource);
}                                                               ❑
```

An implementation of the `Pool` interface would maintain a collection of `Resource` objects. When a resource user tries to acquire a resource, the resource would be fetched from this collection. Similarly, when the resource user releases the resource, it would be returned back to the collection.

➡ An example of an implementation of the `Pool` interface in Java that manages a collection of `Connection` objects might look like:

```
public class ConnectionPool implements Pool
{
    public Resource acquire () {
        Connection connection = findFreeConnection ();
        if (connection == null) {
            connection = new Connection ();
            connectionPool.add (connection);
        }
        return connection;
    }
```

```
public void release (Resource resource) {
    if (resource instanceof Connection)
        recycleOrEvictConnection ((Connection) resource);
}

// private helper methods

private Connection findFreeConnection () {
    // ...
}

private recycleOrEvictConnection (Connection con) {
    // ...
}

// ...
// Maintain a collection of Connection objects
private java.util.Vector connectionPool;
}
```

The code above shows one way of doing creation, initialization and eviction of connections. Of course, it is also possible to make those operations flexible, for example by using Strategy [GoF95] and Abstract Factory [GoF95].

The following class diagram shows the structure of the above-mentioned classes.

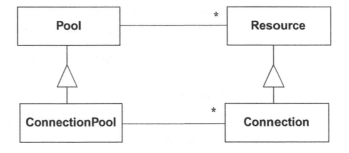

6 *Provide eviction of resources.* A large number of resources in the pool indicate that many unused resources exist, wasting space and degrading performance. To minimize system performance degradation, the pool size should be reduced to a reasonable size by releasing some resources from the pool.

7 *Determine resource recycling semantics.* Resource recycling varies depending on the type of the resource. For example, recycling of a

thread requires cleaning up of its stack and initialization of memory. In the case of recycling objects, Philip Bishop and Nigel Warren offer in their Java Tip [BiWa04a] a way to decompose objects into multiple smaller objects, which are then recycled one by one.

8   *Determine failure strategies.* In the case of any recoverable failure of resource acquisition or release, exceptions and/or error messages should be handled. If it is impossible to recover from a failure, exceptions should be thrown or a 'null' resource, such as a NULL pointer for malloc(), should be handed back to the resource user. In case recycling fails, there are other patterns that can help minimize the impact of failure. For example, the Java Tip [BiWa04a] mentioned above also describes how to recycle broken objects by dividing complex objects into smaller objects. These smaller objects are either recycled, or re-created if broken, then reassembled into the complex object.

Example Resolved   In the case of the Web-based shop example, the database connections are pooled in a connection pool. On every request by the user, the servlet acquires a connection from the connection pool, which it uses to access the database with queries and updates. After access, the connection is released to the connection pool in the context of the current request. As the number of concurrent requests is smaller than the number of current users, fewer connections are needed in total and expensive acquisition cost is avoided.

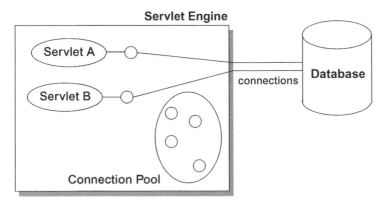

The figure above shows how individual servlets acquire connections from the connection pool to connect to the database. If the connection pool has no connection available and the maximum number of connections is not reached, new connections are created on demand.

Specializations The following specializations reflect applications of this pattern to specific areas such as memory allocations, connection management, or object technology. Some of those specializations have been documented in existing literature.

Connection Pooling [HaBr01]. Connection Pooling is regularly used in scalable frameworks and applications that need to access remote services. Such remote services can be database services, for example via JDBC (Java Database Connectivity), or Web servers, via HTTP.

Thread Pooling [PeSo97]. Thread Pooling is commonly used in environments that are inherently asynchronous. Highly scalable as well as real-time systems use Thread Pooling as their key mechanism for managing multiple threads. Using thread pooling allows such systems to avoid resource exhaustion by running too many threads. A typical thread pool starts with a limited number of eagerly-acquired threads and lazily acquires more threads if it runs short of thread instances.

Component Instance Pooling [VSW02]. Component Instance Pooling is typically used by application servers. Application servers optimize their resource use by pre-instantiating a limited amount of commonly-used components to serve the initial demand quickly. When these components are used up, the application scrver instantiates new components as additional clients request them. If a client stops using a component, the component is put back into the pool.

Pooled Allocation [NoWe00]. In this pattern a pre-allocated pool of memory blocks is recycled when memory blocks are returned. Typically, pooled allocators do not release the memory until system shut-down. Often multiple pools are installed, each with memory blocks of a different size. This avoids wasting of large memory blocks in requests for small blocks.

Object Pool [Gran98]. Object Pool manages the reuse of objects of a particular type that are expensive to create, or for which only a limited number can be created. An Object Pool is different than Pooling, because it assumes that every resource can be represented as an object, whereas Pooling does not make the restriction. The implementation section of Pooling uses objects only because they more easily convey the key idea. Note that in reality resources can be represented by objects. However, the key to note is that those are only representations of resources, not the actual resources. For example, a connection is a resource that need not be represented as an object to make use of the Pooling pattern.

Variants   The following variants describe related patterns that are derived from Pooling by extending or changing the problem and the solution.

Mixed Pool. Resources of different types are mixed in one pool. The interface of the pool might need to be extended to allow resource users to differentiate their requests for resource acquisitions. All resources are managed by the same strategy. The interface has to allow for the acquisition of resources of individual types.

Sub-Pools. In some situations it is advisable to subdivide the pool of resources into multiple smaller pools. For example, in the case of a thread pool, you could partition the thread pool into multiple sub-pools. Each sub-pool could be associated with a specific range of priorities [OMG04b]. This ensures that thread acquisitions for low-priority tasks do not cause resource exhaustion when high-priority tasks need to be executed.

Consequences   There are several **benefits** of using the Pooling pattern:

- *Performance.* The Pooling pattern can improve the performance of an application, since it helps reduce the time spent in costly release and re-acquisition of resources. In cases in which the resource has already been acquired by the resource pool, acquisition by the resource user becomes very fast.

- *Predictability.* The average number of resource acquisitions by the resource user executes in a deterministic time if those resources are acquired eagerly. With a proper eviction strategy in place, most acquisition requests can be served from the pool. As lookup and release of previously-acquired resources is predictable, resource acquisition by the resource user becomes more predictable when compared to always acquiring a resource from the resource provider.

- *Simplicity.* No additional memory management routines need to be invoked by the resource user. The resource user acquires and releases resources either transparently, or directly to and from the resource pool.

- *Stability and scalability.* New resources are created if demand exceeds the available resources. Due to recycling, the resource pool delays resource eviction based on the eviction strategy. This saves costly release and re-acquisition of resources, which increases overall system stability and scalability.

- *Sharing.* Using the pool as a Mediator [GoF95], unused resources can be shared between resource users. This also benefits memory use and can result in an overall reduction in the memory footprint of the application.

The pool does not synchronize access to the resources. Therefore if synchronization is required, it must be provided by the resource user.

There are also some **liabilities** of using the Pooling pattern:

- *Overhead.* The management of resources in a pool consumes a certain amount of CPU cycles. However, these CPU cycles are typically less than the CPU cycles required for release and re-acquisition of the resources.

- *Complexity.* Resource users have to explicitly release resources back to the resource pool. Patterns such as Leasing (149) can be used to address this.

- *Synchronization.* In concurrent environments, acquisition requests to the pool have to be synchronized to avoid race conditions and the possibility of corrupting the associated state.

Known Uses **JDBC connection pooling** [BEA02]. Java Database Connectivity (JDBC) connections are managed using connection pooling. JDBC Specification Version 2 includes a standard mechanism for introducing connection pooling. The management interface is called `javax.sql.DataSource` and provides a factory for pooled connection objects.

COM+ [Ewal01]. The COM+ Services runtime, as part of the Windows operating system, supports object pooling for COM+ objects and .NET applications. .NET applications have to set configuration attributes of the .NET `System.EnterpriseServices` package.

EJB application servers [Iona04] [IBM04a]. Application servers that are based on component technology use Component Instance Pooling to manage the number of component instances efficiently.

Web servers [Apac02]. Web servers have to serve hundreds, if not thousands, of concurrent requests. Most of them are served quickly, so creation of new threads per request is inefficient. Therefore most Web servers use Thread Pooling to efficiently manage the threads. Threads are reused after completing a request.

See Also Flyweight [GoF95] uses sharing to support a large number of objects efficiently. The Flyweight objects can be maintained using Pooling.

This pattern is also known as Resource Pool [BiWa04a].

The Caching pattern (83) is related to Pooling, but Caching is about managing resources with identity. In the case of Caching, the resource user cares about which of the cached resources are returned. In the case of Pooling, the resource user does not care about the identity of the resource, since all resources in the pool are equal.

Credits Thanks to the patterns team at Siemens AG Corporate Technology for their feedback and comments on earlier versions of this pattern. Special thanks to our EuroPLoP 2002 shepherd Uwe Zdun and the writer's workshop participants, Eduardo Fernandez, Titos Saridakis, Peter Sommerlad, and Egon Wuchner, for their valuable feedback.

Coordinator

The *Coordinator* pattern describes how to maintain system consistency by coordinating the completion of tasks involving multiple participants, each of which can include a resource, a resource user and a resource provider. The pattern presents a solution such that in a task involving multiple participants, either the work done by all of the participants is completed or none are. This ensures that the system always stays in a consistent state.

Example   Consider a large-scale system that is distributed over a network of processing nodes. The subsystem deployed on each node comprises of one or more services that need to be updated frequently. Assuming that shutting down the system to update all the services is not a feasible alternative, the most common solution is to implement the Deployer [Stal00] pattern. Using the Deployer pattern, the services deployed in each subsystem can be dynamically updated without requiring the system to be shut down.

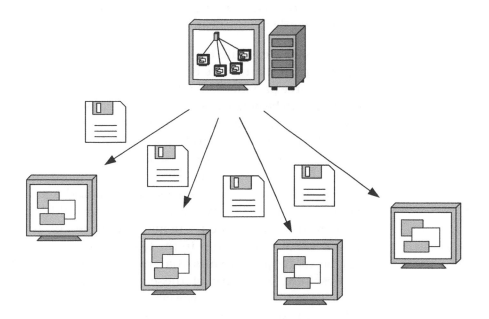

To allow dynamic update of each subsystem requires a software download component to be present on each node. To update the overall system configuration, a central administration component is used that communicates with the software download component on each node. The central component typically sends update requests to each software download component, which then dynamically updates the subsystem deployed on the respective node.

Consider the scenario in which a global update needs to be made to the system configuration. As a result, the central administration component needs to send update requests to multiple software download components. Assume that the first few software download components successfully update their respective subsystems, but that one of the software download components fails to update its subsystem. The result would be that only part of the system would be successfully updated. If the global update requires all subsystems to be successfully updated, such a scenario would leave the system in an inconsistent state. The subsystem that failed to update could be left with an old and incompatible version of the software, making the entire system unusable.

Context   Coordination of multiple participants that work on the same task. The task is divided among the participants, which then work independently to contribute to the total success of the task.

Problem   Many systems execute tasks that involve more than one participant. A participant is an active entity that can include both resource users and resource providers. In addition, in some cases resources, such as services, can be active and therefore directly participate in a task. The participants can be co-located in the same process, or can span multiple processes as well as multiple nodes. Each participant executes part of the task in a sequence. For the task to succeed as a whole, the work performed by each participant must succeed. If a task is successful, the changes made should keep the system in a consistent state. However, consider what would happen if the work performed by one of the participants were to fail. If the work is to be performed at a later stage in the task execution sequence, then there will be many participants that have already completed their work successfully. The work of these participants will have introduced changes to the system. However, the participant that failed will not be able to make the necessary changes to the system. As a result, inconsistent changes will be made to the system. This can lead to unstable and even malfunctioning systems. Partial failure in such systems is therefore worse than total failure.

One possible solution is to introduce point-to-point communication among the participants. The participants could communicate the results of their work to each other and take the steps necessary to keep the system state consistent. However, such a solution would require the participants to be aware of all other participants involved in the task, which is not practical. In addition, such a solution would scale poorly with the number of participants.

To address these problems requires resolution of the following *forces*:

- *Consistency*. A task should either create a new and valid state of a system, or, if any failure occurs, should return all data to its state before the task was started.

- *Atomicity*. In a task involving two or more participants, either the work done by all the participants should be completed, or none should be, even though the participants are independent of one another.

- *Location transparency*. The solution should work in distributed systems, even though distributed systems are more prone to partial failures than total ones.

- *Scalability*. The solution should be scalable with the number of participants without degrading performance significantly.

- *Transparency*. The solution should be transparent to the system user and should require a minimum number of code changes.

Solution   Introduce a coordinator that is responsible for the execution and completion of a task by all the participants. The work performed by each of the participants is split into two parts or phases: *prepare* and *commit*.

In the first phase, the coordinator asks each participant to prepare for the work to be done. This phase must be used by each participant to check for consistency and also to determine if the execution would result in failure. If the prepare phase of a participant does not return successfully, the coordinator stops the execution sequence of the task. The coordinator asks all participants that have successfully completed the prepare phase to abort and restore the state prior to the start of the task. Since none of the participants have made any persistent changes, the system state remains consistent.

If all the participants complete the prepare phase successfully, the coordinator then initiates the commit phase for each of the participants. The participants do the actual work in this phase. Since each participant has indicated in the prepare phase that the work would succeed, the commit phase succeeds, leading to the overall success of the task.

Structure   The following elements form the structure of the Coordinator pattern:

- A *task* is a unit of work that involves multiple participants.

- A *participant* is an active entity that does a part of the work of a task. A participant can include resource users, resource providers, and resources.

- A *coordinator* is an entity that is responsible for coordinating the completion of a task as a whole.

- A *client* is the initiator of a task. The client directs the coordinator to execute a task.

The following CRC cards describe the responsibilities and collaborations of the elements of the Coordinator pattern.

Class	Collaborator
Task	
Responsibility	
• Unit of work	

Class	Collaborator
Participant	• Task
	• Coordinator
Responsibility	
• Does part of the work of a task	
• Registers with the Coordinator	
• Includes resource users, resource providers, and resources	

Class	Collaborator
Coordinator	• Participant
Responsibility	
• Coordinates the consistent completion of a task	

Class	Collaborator
Client	• Coordinator
	• Task
Responsibility	
• Initiates a task	
• Commits a task	

The dependencies between the participants are illustrated in the following class diagram.

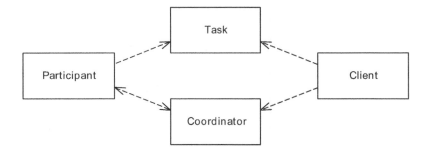

Dynamics There are two main interactions in the Coordinator pattern. The first is between the client and the coordinator, and the second is between the coordinator and the participants.

Scenario I. The interactions start with the client directing the coordinator to begin a task. Following this, all participants involved in the task register with the coordinator. The client then directs the coordinator to commit the task. At this point the coordinator asks each participant to execute the prepare phase. If a participant indicates failure in the prepare phase, the coordinator aborts the entire task. On the other hand, if the prepare phase of all the participants succeeds, the coordinator initiates the commit phase of all the participants.

The following sequence diagram shows a scenario involving two participants in which the prepare phase of both the participants succeeds.

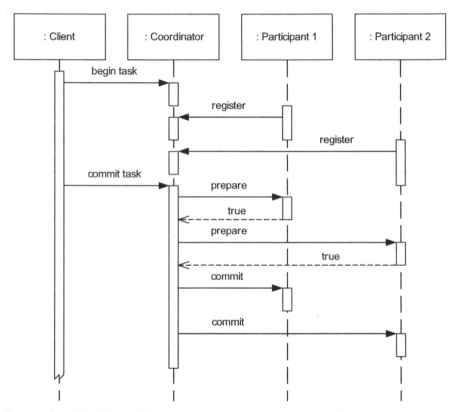

Scenario II. The following sequence diagram shows a scenario involving two participants in which the prepare phase of the second participant fails. The coordinator subsequently aborts the task, asking the first participant that succeeded in the prepare phase to revert any changes that it might have made.

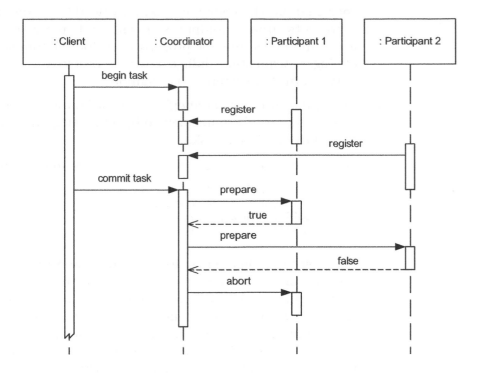

Implementation   There are three steps involved in implementing the Coordinator pattern.

1   *Identify participants.* Any participant whose work needs to be coordinated by the coordinator must first be identified. In the context of resource management, a participant can be a resource user, a resource provider, or a resource itself. A resource user can be a participant if it actively tries to acquire, use, and release multiple resources, and therefore requires coordination. A resource provider can be a participant if it requires coordination when trying to provide one or more resources to resource users. A resource, such as a service, can be a participant if it is active and can therefore directly participate in a task.

In addition, any other entity that uses or manages resources can be regarded as a participant, and therefore would need to be coordinated. For example, in the case of Lazy Acquisition (38), a resource proxy can be regarded as a participant that requires coordination. The resource proxy may need to acquire the resource it represents from multiple sources, and therefore the resource acquisition task must be properly coordinated. Similarly, in the case of Eager Acquisition (53), a provider proxy can be regarded as a participant that requires coordination.

2   *Define the coordination interface.* A coordination interface should be defined that will be implemented by all participants that will execute part of the work of a task.

➥   For example, the `Coordination` interface in Java might look like:

```
public interface Coordination {
   public boolean prepare ();
   public void abort ();
   public void commit ();
}                                                                       ❏
```

The `prepare()` method is used by the coordinator to initiate the prepare phase of each participant. This phase is used by each participant to check for consistency, and also to determine if the execution would result in failure. A return value of `true` indicates that the prepare phase succeeded, and therefore that the commit phase will also succeed. A return value of `false` indicates that the prepare phase failed, and that therefore the participant will not be able to execute the commit phase successfully.

If any of the participants return `false` in the prepare phase, the coordinator will abort the execution of the task. It will call the `abort()` method of each participant that has already returned successfully from the prepare phase. This would indicate to the participants that the task is being aborted and that they should perform any clean-up that is necessary.

3   *Define the coordinator interface.* The coordinator interface should provide the means for a client to begin or terminate a task. In addition, it should allow participants of the task to register. Before the participants can register themselves, they must be able to discover the coordinator. To facilitate this the participants can use the Lookup (21) pattern.

➥   For example, the `Coordinator` interface in Java might look like:

```
public interface Coordinator {
   public void beginTask ();
   public void register (Coordination participant);
```

```
    public boolean commitTask ();
}                                                                      ❏
```

The beginTask() method is used by the client to define the beginning of a task. At this point the coordinator does not do anything. Once a task has begun, the participants of the task then register with the coordinator using the register() method. Once all the participants have registered, the client executes the commitTask() method on the coordinator. This serves as an indicator of two things to the coordinator—firstly, that all participants of the task have registered, and secondly, that the coordinator can begin coordinating the execution of the task by the participants. The coordinator now uses the two-phase commit protocol defined by Coordination interface to ensure that the participants complete the task.

4 *Handle error conditions.* Using the coordinator allows the participants to indicate whether or not the work they are responsible for will succeed. If any participant indicates that its work will not succeed, the coordinator can abort the task without causing any persistent inconsistencies in the system state. If all participants indicate success in the prepare phase, the coordinator goes ahead with the commit phase on all of the participants. However, there is still a possibility that one or more participants may fail in the commit phase, even though their prepare phases completed successfully. This could be, for example, a result of factors beyond the control of the participants, such as a connection being disconnected. To handle such error conditions, participants may optionally maintain state information prior to executing their part of the task. If the commit on one of the participants fails, the coordinator can call a rollback() method on all of the remaining committed participants. This would give the participants a chance to restore their state prior to the execution of the task. Note, however, that such functionality requires state information to be maintained and can be expensive. For more details on this, please see Three-phase Commit in the *Variants* section.

Example Resolved   Consider the example of a distributed system with multiple nodes. To allow dynamic update of the entire system, each subsystem contains a software download component. To update the overall system configuration, a central administration component is used that communicates with the software download component on each node.

Using the Coordinator pattern, the task that needs to be executed is therefore the updating of the entire system. The central administration component is the client controlling the execution of the task. Each software download component acts as a participant of the task and implements the Coordination interface. The sub-tasks that the participants perform correspond to the update of the respective subsystems.

```
public class SwDownload implements Coordination {
    // Flag indicating current state
    private boolean downloading = false;

    public boolean prepare () {
        // Mark start of software downloading
        downloading = true;

        // Check if our state is consistent and
        // whether a software update can take place
        if (!this.validateState ())
            return false;

        // Now download the software but do not commit
        // the update. If download fails, return false.
        // ....
    }

    public void abort () {
        // Do not install the downloaded software.
        downloading = false;
    }

    public void commit () {
        // Commit/Install the downloaded software.
        // ...
        downloading = false;
    }
}
```

A coordinator is introduced that will be used by the central administration component to begin and commit the task. Once the task has begun, all the software download components are registered with the coordinator. This can be done by the software download components themselves, or by the central administration component—see the *Variants* section. When all the participants are registered, the central administration component asks the coordinator to begin the task of updating the entire system.

```
public class CentralAdministrator {
    // Assume we have a reference to the coordinator
    Coordinator coordinator;

    public void updateSoftware () {
        // Ask the coordinator to begin the task
        coordinator.beginTask ();

        // Assume we have a list of sub-components stored
        // in an ArrayList. We now need to iterate over
        // this list and register all the sub-components
        // with the coordinator
        ArrayList components = getComponents ();
        for (Iterator i= components.iterator(); i.hasNext();) {
            Coordination swDownload = (Coordination) i.next();
            // Register the sub-component
            coordinator.register (swDownload);
        }
        // Now tell the coordinator to start the actual task
        coordinator.commitTask ();
    }
}
```

When the coordinator has been asked to commit the task, it will begin the two-phase commit protocol. The coordinator first initiates the prepare phase of each software download component. During this phase each software download component checks for consistency and also determine whether the execution of the update would result in failure. Each software download component then downloads the software update, but does not install it. If an error occurs while downloading the software, the prepare phase for that software download component returns failure.

If any of the software download components does not return success in the prepare phase, the coordinator terminates the execution of the task. The coordinator then asks any software download components that succeeded in the prepare phase to abort. No changes are made in any of the subsystems, and therefore the system state remains consistent.

If all the software download components return successfully from the prepare phase, the coordinator initiates the commit phase. Each software download component installs the downloaded software and updates its respective subsystem during this phase. Since each software download component indicated in the prepare phase that the update would succeed, the commit phase succeeds, leading to the overall success of the system update.

```java
public class SWCoordinator implements Coordinator {
    // Flag indicating if a task is in progress. Note that
    // this simple version only handles one task at a time.
    boolean taskInProgress = false;

    // List of registered participants
    private ArrayList list = new ArrayList ();

    public void register (Coordination participant) {
        if (!taskInProgress)
            return;
        if (!list.contains (participant))
            list.add (participant);
    }

    public void beginTask () {
        taskInProgress = true;
    }

    public boolean commitTask () {
        if (!taskInProgress)
            return false;

        // Keep track of participants that complete prepare
        // phase successfully
        ArrayList prepareCompleted = new ArrayList ();

        // Iterate over registered participants
        // and use 2-phase commit
        for (Iterator i= list.iterator() ;i.hasNext() ;) {
            Coordination participant = (Coordination) i.next();
            boolean success = participant.prepare ();

            if (success)
                prepareCompleted.add (participant);
            else {
                // Ask all participants that have completed
                // prepare phase successfully to abort.
                for (Iterator iter = prepareCompleted.iterator();
                        iter.hasNext();) {
                    Coordination p = (Coordination) iter.next();
                    p.abort ();
                } // end for
                list.clear ();
                taskInProgress = false;
                return false;
            } // end else
        } // end for
```

```
                              // If we reach here, it means prepare phase of all
                              // participants completed successfully. Now invoke
                              // commit phase and assume it will succeed.
                              for (Iterator i= list.iterator() ;i.hasNext() ;) {
                                  Coordination participant = (Coordination) i.next();
                                  participant.commit ();
                              } // end for
                              list.clear ();
                              taskInProgress = false;
                              return true;
                          }
                      }
```

Note that exception handling has been left out of the code presented in this section for the sake of brevity. If an exception is thrown during the prepare phase, it should typically be regarded as failure and the entire task aborted. If an exception is thrown during the commit phase, the changes made to the system should be rolled back—see Three-Phase-Commit in the *Variants* section.

Variants   *Third-Party Registration.* The registration of the participants with the coordinator need not be done by the participants themselves. It can be done by a third party, including the client. This is useful if the client needs to control who the participants in a task should be.

Participant Adapter. A participant of a task need not implement the coordination interface directly. Instead, the object can be contained inside an Adapter [GoF95], which then implements the coordination interface. The coordinator will invoke the prepare() method on the adapter object, which will then be responsible for performing consistency checks and determining whether the task would succeed. When the coordinator invokes the commit() method on the adapter object, the adapter object delegates the request to the actual object. This variant makes it easier to integrate legacy code without requiring existing classes to implement the coordination interface.

Three-phase Commit. To handle the possibility of failure in the commit phase, a third phase can be introduced to supplement the two-phase commit protocol. Each participant needs to maintain state information prior to executing its part of the task. If the commit on one of the participants fails, the coordinator executes the third phase by invoking a rollback() method on all the committed participants. This gives the participants a chance to restore their state prior to the execution of the task. If the commit phase of all the participants succeeds, the coordinator executes the third phase, but invokes a different method, `clear()`, on all the participants. This method allows the participants to discard the state they were maintaining in case of failure of the commit phase.

Consequences   There are several **benefits** of using the Coordinator pattern:

- *Atomicity*. The Coordinator pattern ensures that in a task involving two or more participants, either the work done by all of the participants is completed, or none is. The prepare phase ensures that all participants will be able to complete their work. If any participant returns failure during the prepare phase, the task is not executed, ensuring that no work is done by any of the participants.

- *Consistency*. The Coordinator pattern ensures that the system state remains consistent. If a task executes successfully, it creates a new and valid state of the system. On the other hand, if any failure occurs, the Coordinator pattern ensures that all data is returned to its state before the task was started. Since each task is considered to be atomic, either all participants complete their work, or no participants do any work. In both cases, the end result leaves the system in a consistent state.

- *Scalability*. The solution is scalable with the number of participants. Increasing the number of participants does not affect the execution of a task. With an increase in the number of participants, the likelihood of a failure of one of the participants increases. However, using the pattern, such a failure can be detected in the prepare phase, ensuring that the system stays in a consistent state.

- *Transparency*. Using the Coordinator pattern is transparent to the user, since two-phase the execution of a task is not visible to the user.

There are some **liabilities** of using the Coordinator pattern:

- *Overhead*. The Coordinator pattern requires that each task be split into two phases, resulting in the execution sequence involving all the participants being repeated twice. If the participants are distributed, this implies a doubling of the number of remote calls. This in turn can result in a potential of loss of transparency.

- *Additional responsibility.* The Coordinator pattern imposes additional responsibility on the participants by requiring them to register with the Coordinator. If the participants are distributed, the registration process in turn results in the participants making remote calls.

Known Uses   **Java Authentication and Authorization Service (JAAS)** [Sun04e]. The Login Context of the JAAS implements the Coordinator pattern. JAAS supports the notion of dynamically-configurable stacked login modules that perform authentication. To guarantee that either all login modules succeed, or none succeed, the login context performs the authentication steps in two phases. In the first phase, or the 'login' phase, the login context invokes the configured login modules and instructs each to attempt only the authentication process. If all the necessary login modules successfully pass this phase, the login context then enters the second phase and invokes the configured login modules again, instructing each to formally 'commit' the authentication process. During this phase, each login module associates the relevant authenticated principals and credentials with the subject. If either the first phase or the second phase fails, the login context invokes the configured login modules and instructs each to abort the entire authentication attempt. Each login module then cleans up any relevant state it has associated with the authentication attempt.

Transaction services. Many transaction models and software implement the Coordinator pattern. The Object Transaction Service (OTS) [OMG04e] is a distributed transaction processing service specified by the Object Management Group (OMG). One of the principal interfaces provided by the specification is that of a coordinator that is responsible for coordinating distributed transactions. Many implementations of the OTS specification are available, including ITS from Inprise, Orbix 6 from Iona [Iona04], and ArjunaTS from Arjuna Solutions Ltd.

Java Transaction Service (JTS) [Sun04d] implements the Java mapping of the OMG OTS specification. JTS includes a Transaction Manager that plays the role of coordinator. The JTS Transaction

Manager is responsible for coordinating database transactions. The participants in these transactions implement transaction-protected resources, such as relational databases, and are called 'resource managers'.

Distributed Transaction Coordinator (DTC) [Ewal01] as part of the Microsoft COM+ Services is a transaction server implementing the Coordinator pattern.

Databases [GaRe93]. Databases make extensive use of the Coordinator pattern and the two-phase commit protocol. If, for example, a database update operation involves several dependent tables, and the computer system fails when the database update is only partially completed, using two-phase commit would ensure that the database is not left in an inconsistent or an inoperable state.

Software installation [Zero04b] [FIK04]. Most software installation programs implement the Coordinator pattern. In the prepare phase, checks are performed to ensure that the installation task would execute smoothly. This includes, for example, checking for necessary hard disk space and memory. If the prepare phase succeeds, the commit phase executes the installation of the software. This becomes especially important in distributed software installation.

Real-world example I. A real-world example of the Coordinator pattern is a priest conducting a marriage ceremony. The priest is the coordinator while the bride and groom are the participants. In the prepare phase, the priest first asks the bride and groom, 'Do you take this person to be your spouse?' Only if they both respond 'I do' does the priest commit them to marriage.

Real-world example II. Another real-world example could be a purchasing deal between two parties managed by a broker, who plays the role of a coordinator. In the prepare phase, the broker ensures that the first party puts an item to sell on the table, while the other party brings the money they are ready to offer for the item. If both parties are satisfied with what the other has to offer, the broker initiates the commit phase in which they exchange the money for the item.

See Also   The Command Processor [POSA1] pattern describes techniques for remembering and undoing a sequence of operations. It can be used as a means of encapsulating sub-tasks to be performed by the participants.

The Master-Slave [POSA1] pattern models the partitioning of work into sub-tasks and coordinating them. A master component distributes the work to slave components and computes a final result from the results returned by the slaves. Master-Slave is different than Coordinator, as it uses a 'divide and conquer' strategy followed by the integration of results, whereas Coordinator is about the consistency of state achieved after each sub-task. The Coordinator pattern can extend the Master-Slave pattern to ensure for consistency before the results of the sub-tasks are integrated.

Credits   Thanks to the patterns team at Siemens AG Corporate Technology, to our EuroPLoP 2002 shepherd, Kevlin Henney, and the writer's workshop participants, Eduardo Fernandez, Titos Saridakis, Peter Sommerlad, and Egon Wuchner, for their valuable feedback and comments.

Resource Lifecycle Manager

The *Resource Lifecycle Manager* pattern decouples the management of the lifecycle of resources from their use by introducing a separate Resource Lifecycle Manager, whose sole responsibility is to manage and maintain the resources of an application.

Example Consider a distributed system that needs to service thousands of clients. As a consequence, thousands of network connections are established between the clients and the server, as shown in the figure below.

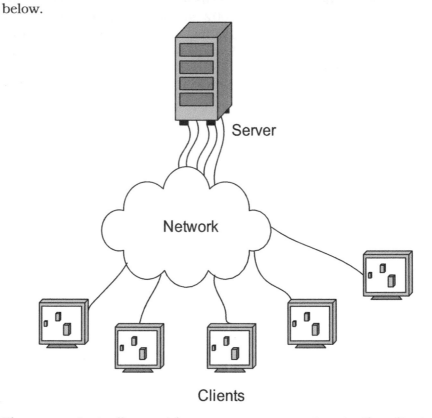

The server typically provides one or more services to the clients. A client invokes a request on the server using its connection, and the response to the synchronous invocation on the remote service is sent back via the same connection as a result. If the request needs to be decoupled from the response and some form of asynchronous communication is required between the client and the server, then the server would need to open a new connection to the client and use it to initiate a call-back to the client. For example, the server may use a call-back to notify a client about events in the service.

Maintaining thousands of network connections becomes even more complex in the case of real-time systems for which stringent QoS requirements exist. As a result, the server connection policies are typically quite complex. Connections might be associated with properties, such as the priority of requests to use the connection.

As connections depend on multiple low-level resources, they should be freed when no longer needed to ensure system stability. As a result, complex lifecycle scenarios for each connection must be managed by the application. This complexity in managing the lifecycles of connections can affect the core functionality of the application, and as a consequence can make its business logic hard to understand and maintain due to the entangled connection-management code.

Context Large and complex systems that require simplified management of the lifecycle of their resources.

Problem Building large-scale systems is challenging. Making large-scale systems robust and scalable is even more challenging. The most important aspect of making large-scale systems robust and scalable is the way in which resources are managed. Resources in systems can be of many different types, such as network connections, threads, synchronization primitives, servants and so on. Network connections represent communication channels between client applications and distributed application services. Managing them efficiently requires the ability to determine when to establish connections and when to release them. Threads are especially important in large-scale systems, since they provide asynchronous behavior between different parts of an application, for example decoupling UI interaction from typical client functionality and service provisioning. However, managing threads effectively can be quite challenging, since it involves close monitoring of their execution, and the ability to determine when to create new threads or destroy threads that are no longer needed. Similarly, synchronization primitives such as locks and tokens are typically needed to synchronize the asynchronous parts of an application and to allow for their internal coordination and interaction. However, when and how these synchronization primitives are created and released is both important and very challenging to implement.

Solving the problem of managing the lifecycle of resources in an effective and efficient manner requires resolution of the following *forces*:

• *Availability.* The number of available resources typically does not grow at the same rate as the size of the overall system. In large systems, therefore, managing resources efficiently and effectively is important to ensure that they are available when needed by users.

• *Scalability.* As systems become large, the number of resources that need to be managed also grows, and can become much more difficult to manage directly by the users.

• *Complexity.* Large systems typically have complex interdependencies between resources that can be very difficult to track. Maintaining and tracking these interdependencies is important to allow proper and timely release of resources when they are no longer needed.

• *Performance.* Many optimizations are typically made to ensure that large systems don't face any performance bottlenecks. However, providing such optimizations can be quite complex if performed by individual resource users.

• *Stability.* If resource users have to manage resource lifecycle issues, they might forget to free resources, leading to system instability in the long term. In addition, it should be possible to control the acquisition of resources, to ensure that there is no starvation of available resources at the system level, also leading to instability.

• *Interdependencies.* In complex systems resources of the same or different types might depend on each other. This means that the lifecycle of resources are interdependent and need to be managed appropriately.

- *Flexibility.* Management of the resource lifecycle should be flexible, allowing support for different strategies. A strategy should provide a hook to allow configuration of resource management behavior.

- *Transparency.* Resource lifecycle management should be transparent to the resource user. In particular, the resource user should not have to deal with any of the complexities of managing resources.

Solution Separate resource usage from resource management. Introduce a separate Resource Lifecycle Manager (RLM) whose sole responsibility is to manage and maintain the resources of a resource user.

Resource users can use the RLM to retrieve and get access to specific resources. If a resource that is requested by a resource user does not yet exist, the RLM can initiate its creation. In addition, the RLM allows users to request explicit creation of resources.

An RLM has knowledge of current resource use and can therefore reject a request for resource acquisition from a resource user. For example, if the system is running low on available memory, then the RLM can reject a resource user's request to allocate memory.

The RLM also controls the disposal of the resources it manages, either transparently for the resource users or at their explicit request. The RLM maintains its resources on the basis of appropriate policies that take into account available computing resources such as memory, connections, and file handles.

An RLM can be responsible for a single type of resource, or for multiple types of resource. If interdependencies between resources exist, the RLMs for individual resources have to work in concert. That means that they have to maintain dependencies between resources. This can be done by a central RLM having the full responsibility over individual as well as dependent resources, or by a separate RLM that only deals with the interdependencies, while leaving the management of resources of the same type to resource-specific RLMs. In strongly-layered architectures a cascade of RLMs can be used, such that an RLM is present at every abstraction level, for example at the OS, framework, and application levels.

Structure   The following participants form the structure of the Resource Lifecycle Manager pattern:

- A *resource user* acquires and uses resources.

- A *resource* is an entity such as a network connection or a thread.

- A *resource lifecycle manager* manages the lifecycle of resources, including their creation/acquisition, reuse, and destruction.

- A *resource provider*, such as an operating system, owns and manages resources. The resource provider might itself be a resource lifecycle manager at the same or different abstraction level.

The following CRC cards describe the responsibilities and collaborations of the participants.

Class **Resource User**	*Collaborator*
Responsibility	• Resource
• Acquires and uses resources.	• Resource Lifecycle Manager
• Releases unused resources to the resource lifecycle manager.	

Class **Resource**	*Collaborator*
Responsibility	
• Represents a reusable entity, such as memory or a thread.	
• Is acquired from the resource provider by the resource lifecycle manager.	

Class **Resource Lifecycle Manager**	*Collaborator*
Responsibility	• Resource
• Coordinates lifecycle of resources including creation/acquisition, reuse, and destruction.	• Resource Provider

Class **Resource Provider**	*Collaborator*
Responsibility	• Resource
• Owns and manages several resources.	

The following class diagram illustrates the structure of the Resource Lifecycle Manager pattern.

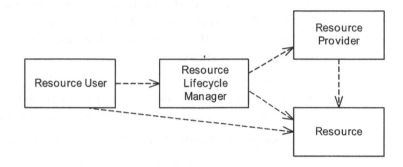

Dynamics The interactions between the participants are shown in the following sketch.

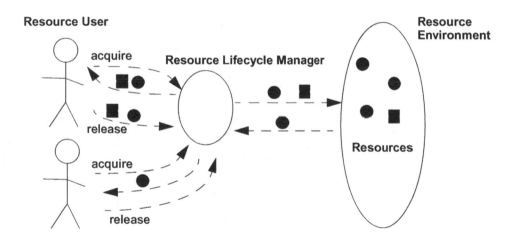

Scenario I. The dynamics of the pattern consists of the following activities: first, the system starts and initializes the RLM. The resource user needs a resource, and therefore tries to acquire the resource from the RLM. The RLM accepts the acquisition request and acquires the resource according to the resource-acquisition strategy. The resource is therefore passed to the user, which now uses it, accessing the resource.

When the resource is no longer used by the user, it hands it back to the RLM. The RLM checks dependencies of the resource on other resources and decides either to recycle the resource or to evict it.

These steps are illustrated in the following sequence diagram.

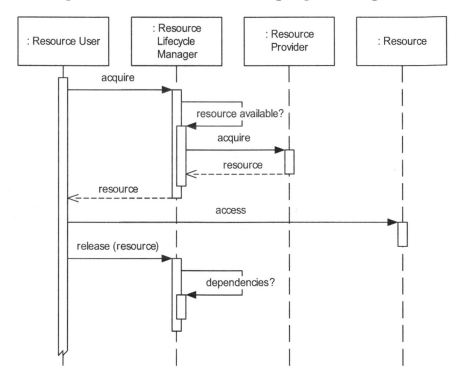

Scenario II. When a resource of the same type needs to be accessed again, the resource user can acquire it from the RLM again. The RLM can now apply Pooling (97) and Caching (83) as optimizations to avoid expensive acquisitions from the resource provider. See the sequence diagram below.

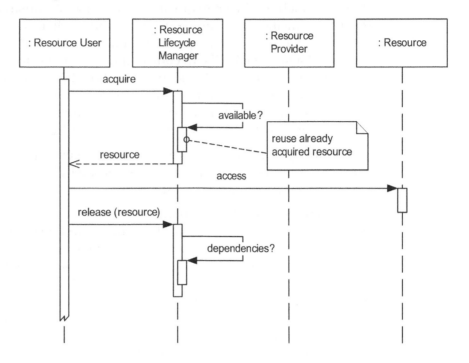

Implementation   Seven steps are involved in implementing the Resource Lifecycle Manager pattern.

1   *Determine resources that need to be managed.* A developer needs to first identify all resources whose lifecycle needs to be managed. Since resources can be of many different types, an application can provide multiple RLMs for different types of resource, for example an RLM for handling computing resources such as processes, threads, file handles, and connections, and another for maintaining application components. On the other hand, a single RLM can also handle resources of different types. Such a solution can be effective when complex interdependencies also need to be maintained among different types of resource (see also implementation step 4). If only a single instance of an RLM is needed, it should be implemented as a Singleton [GoF95].

2   *Define resource creation and acquisition semantics.* A developer needs to determine how resources will be created or acquired by the RLM.

This includes determination both of when resources will be created or acquired, as well as how resources will be created or acquired. Patterns such as Eager Acquisition (53), Lazy Acquisition (38), and Partial Acquisition (66) can be used to control when resources will be acquired, while patterns such as Factory Method [GoF95] and Abstract Factory [GoF95] can control how resources are created. Note that resources are typically acquired by the RLM so that it can have full control over the lifecycle of those resources. However, it may also be the case that certain resources are not acquired or created by the RLM, but may still need to be managed by the RLM.

To ensure system stability, the RLM may reject acquisition requests from resource users for various reasons, including the situation in which available resources become scarce.

An implementation of the Pooling (97) pattern can manage resources that are typically created up-front during the initialization of the RLM, using either Eager Acquisition or Partial Acquisition. Eager Acquisition acquires a resource completely and before it is ever accessed—thus the resource is usable immediately after its acquisition. However, it can take a long time to fully create or acquire large resources. Partial Acquisition can help reduce up-front acquisition time by performing step-wise resource acquisition. Using Lazy Acquisition, the entire acquisition of a resource is deferred until it is actually accessed.

3   *Define resource management semantics.* One of the principal responsibilities of the RLM is to manage resources efficiently and effectively. Frequent acquisition and release of resources can be expensive, so the RLM typically uses patterns such as Caching (83) and Pooling to optimize the management of resources. Pooling can be used to keep a fixed number of resources continuously available. This strategy is particularly useful for managing resources such as threads and connections, because the users of these resources typically do not rely on their identity on re-acquisition. Caching, in contrast, is advisable if resources must keep their identity.

➡   For example, Caching (83) is mostly applied for stateful application components involved in a task, because they must keep their state and hence their identity. Once the tasks are completed, the components are not needed until the same tasks are again executed. To avoid degrading the quality of service of an application, it can therefore be helpful to remove unused components temporarily from memory, so that the space and the computing resources they occupy become available for components that are in use. The Passivation [VSW02] pattern describes passivation and re-activation of components. Using both Caching and Passivation patterns together can help to limit total resource consumption. ❏

4   *Handle resource dependencies.* In many applications resources are dependent on each other. The first step therefore is to isolate the different resource lifecycles into separate RLMs to ease maintenance. However, optimizations based on dependent resources will be hard to apply.

   ➥   In the example above, dependent resources can include application services that have been accessed via a specific connection. In real-time environments, servants implementing the application services are often directly associated with prioritized connections from clients, so that priorities can be obeyed end-to-end. The removal of any such connection therefore influences the behavior of the servant, including its used resources. The servant might become inaccessible if dependent connections are evicted. Thus an RLM with a common responsibility should be considered for managing connections, servants, and their interdependencies.   ❏

5   The exact applicability of such an RLM, as well as its implementation, is heavily dependent on the application context as well as on the types of resource. One possible solution is to group interdependent resources into a given context. The creation of multiple dependent resources can be controlled by the Builder [GoF95] pattern. Such a grouping can be used to control resource acquisition, access and release of interdependent resources. For example, a strategy can be configured that ensures that if a resource is released, all its dependent resources in the group are also automatically released.

6   *Define resource release semantics.* When resources are no longer needed they should be automatically released by the RLM. Patterns such as Leasing (149) and Evictor (168) can be used to control when and how resources are released. An Evictor allows for a controlled removal of less-frequently used resources from the cache. To prevent any release of resources that are still referenced, an RLM can use the Leasing pattern, allowing it to specify the time for which the resources will be available to resource users. Once this expires, the resources

can be safely and automatically released by the RLM. Additionally, a Garbage Collector [JoLi96] can be used to identify unused resources—resources that are not referenced by any resource user or other resource—and evict them. For safe eviction of resources, consider using a Disposal Method [Henn03].

7   *Define resource access semantics.* Resources that have been created or acquired need to be easily accessible. The RLM can use patterns such as Lookup (21) to allow easy access to resources.

8   *Configure strategies.* For each of the above steps, the RLM should allow the configuration of different strategies for controlling how the lifecycle of resources is managed. For example, if a resource is expensive, it should be acquired as late as possible using Lazy Acquisition and released as early as possible using Evictor. Measurement of the expense of a resource is application dependent. For example, a resource can be considered expensive if it consumes a large amount of memory, or is a contentious resource with high demand among resource users. On the other hand, a resource that is relatively less expensive and is used frequently should be acquired early using Eager Acquisition and retained through the lifetime of the application. In dynamic environments, reflection [POSA1] mechanisms can be employed to adapt configuration strategies according to the environment. When dependencies between resources have to be managed, use the Coordinator (111) pattern to synchronize their release.

Example Resolved   Introduce a component that is responsible for the resource lifecycle management and hence free the application from this responsibility.

This decouples the management of connections from the business logic of the application.

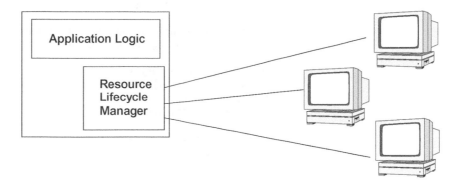

The resource lifecycle manager is introduced in the client and server parts of the distributed application. The clients then use the resource lifecycle manager to request new connections to the server. Once these connections are given to the clients, their lifecycle is managed by the resource lifecycle manager.

In the following paragraphs a concrete implementation of the resource lifecycle manager is presented. The ResourceLifecycleManager class provides the primary interface for the Resource Lifecycle Manager pattern. Using this class one can acquire and release resources of different types. The ResourceLifecycleManager makes use of multiple resource pools to manage the lifecycle of resources. If a resource is not found in the appropriate pool, a factory is used to create the resource. Once a resource has been created, it must be added to a resource group by the resource user to allow it to be properly managed. It is assumed that each resource belongs to at least one group. Note that for the sake of brevity, all error and exception handling has been left out of the code.

```
public class ResourceLifecycleManager {

    public ResourceLifecycleManager () {
        // Create and set up all the appropriate pools and
        // factories
    }

    public Resource acquire (ResourceType type) {

        Pool pool = (Pool) resourcePools.get (type);
        if (pool != null) {
            Resource resource = pool.acquire ();
            if (resource != null)
```

```
                return resource;
        }
        // The Resource pool did not have a resource, so try
        // creating one using the appropriate factory.

        ResourceFactory factory =
            (ResourceFactory) resourceFactories.get (type);
        if (factory != null)
            return factory.create();

        // Handle error... no resource available
        return null;
    }

    public void release (Resource resource) {
        ResourceGroup group = this.findGroup (resource);
        if (group != null)
            group.release ();
    }

    // Set the factory for the type of resource
    public void setFactory (ResourceType type,
                            ResourceFactory factory) {
        resourceFactories.put (type, factory);
    }

    // ... (group related methods)
}
```

The acquire() method tries to acquire a resource of the given type. The method first finds the resource pool corresponding to the given type. It tries to fetch the resource from the pool if possible. If a resource is not available in the pool, the method finds the appropriate factory for the resource type and uses it to create the resource. Note that it is up to the factory to be configured with different strategies and policies to determine when the resource is actually created or acquired.

The release() method releases the resource as well as any dependent resources. The dependent resources are those that belong to the ResourceGroup to which the resource belongs. The ResourceLifecycleManager internally uses the Coordinator (111) pattern to ensure either that all resources are released or none are. Each resource acts as a participant in the two-phase protocol initiated by the ResourceLifecycleManager, which acts as the coordinator.

For all group-related functionality, the following set of methods is offered by the ResourceLifecycleManager class.

```
public ResourceLifecycleManager {

    // ... (already described methods)

    public ResourceGroup createGroup (String groupID,
                                        Resource resources []) {
        ResourceGroup group = new ResourceGroup (groupID);
        for (int i = 0; i < resources.length; i++) {
            Resource resource = resources[i];
            group.add (resource, r.type ());
        }
        return group;
    }

    public void addResourceToGroup (Resource resource,
                                    ResourceGroup group) {
        group.add (resource, resource.type ());
    }

    public boolean release (ResourceGroup group) {
        // Iterate over all resources in the group and release
        // them according to the Coordinator pattern
        // ...
    }

    private ResourceGroup findGroup(Resource resource) {
        // Find the group to which this resource belongs
    }
)
```

The createGroup() method creates a group identified by a group ID
and adds resources to it. The addResourceToGroup() method delegates
the addition of resources to a method of the ResourceGroup class. Every
resource to be managed has to implement the Resource interface.

```
public interface Resource {

    // Called before the resource is evicted
    public boolean beforeEviction ();

    // Return the type of the resource
    public ResourceType type ();
}
```

The hook method [Pree94] beforeEviction() is called before the
resource is evicted. A resource should first determine if it is in a state
to allow itself to be evicted. If it is not, this method should return false
and the resource will not be evicted. Otherwise, the resource should
do any necessary cleanup before it gets evicted and should return

true. A `Connection` resource implements the `Resource` interface as follows:

```
public class Connection implements Resource {

    public void authenticate(SecurityToken token) {
        // ...
    }

    public boolean beforeEviction () {
        if (!consistentState)
            return false;
        // Release any other resources and clean up
        // ...
        return true;
    }

    public ResourceType type() {
        return ResourceType.CONNECTION;
    }

    private boolean consistentState;
}
```

The hook method `beforeEviction()` first checks whether the resource can be evicted. For this it uses the Boolean flag `consistentState`, which indicates whether the resource is in a state to be evicted. In our example, the connection can be authenticated using a security token. The security token also implements the `Resource` interface, and is represented as secondary resource on which the connection depends.

An application that uses authenticated connections and wants to delegate the lifecycle management of both resources would use the `ResourceLifecycleManager` as follows:

```
ResourceLifecycleManager rlm =
    new ResourceLifecycleManager();

Connection connection = null;
SecurityToken token = null;

// Acquire the resources
connection =
    (Connection) rlm.acquire(ResourceType.CONNECTION);

token =
    (SecurityToken) rlm.acquire(ResourceType.SECURITY_TOKEN);

Resource resources [] = new Resource [2];
resources[0] = connection;
```

```
resources[1] = token;

// Put the resources in a group so they can be
// managed properly
ResourceGroup group =
  rlm.createGroup ("xyz123", resources);

// Use the resources ...
connection.authenticate (token);

// ...

// Release all the resources by releasing the group
rlm.release (group);
```

This code provides interface methods explicitly for group-related resources. If the application is not to be burdened with the additional responsibility of group management, a Wrapper Facade [POSA2] can be used to hide the complexity.

Consequences   There are several **benefits** of using this pattern:

- *Efficiency.* The management of resources by individual users can be inefficient. The Resource Lifecycle Manager pattern allows coordinated and centralized lifecycle management of resources. This in turn allows for better application of optimizations and a reduction in overall complexity.

- *Scalability.* Using the Resource Lifecycle Manager pattern allows for more efficient management of resources, allowing applications to make better use of available resources, which in turn allows higher application load.

- *Performance.* The Resource Lifecycle Manager pattern can ensure that various levels of optimizations are enabled to achieve maximum performance from the system. By analyzing resource use and availability, it can use different strategies to optimize system performance.

- *Transparency.* The Resource Lifecycle Manager pattern makes management of resources transparent to resource users. Different strategies can be configured to control resource creation and acquisition, management and release. By decoupling resource usage from resource management, the RLM reduces complexity of use and thereby makes the life of a resource user easier.

- *Stability.* The Resource Lifecycle Manager pattern can ensure that a resource is allocated to a user only when a sufficient number of resources are available. This can help make the system more stable by avoiding situations in which a resource user can acquire resources from the system directly, causing resource starvation.

- *Control.* The Resource Lifecycle Manager pattern allows better control over the management of interdependent resources. By maintaining and tracking interdependencies among resources, the RLM allows proper and timely release of resources when they are no longer needed

There are some **liabilities** of using this pattern:

- *Single point of failure.* A bug or error in the RLM can lead to the failure of large parts of the application. Redundancy concepts help only partly, as complexity is further increased and the performance is further constrained.

- *Flexibility.* When individual resource instances need special treatment, the Resource Lifecycle Manager pattern might be too inflexible.

Known Uses **Component container**. A container manages the lifecycle of application components and provides application-independent services. Further, it manages the lifecycle of resources used by the components (see also Container and Managed Resource patterns in [VSW02]). Container functionality is offered by many technologies, including J2EE Enterprise JavaBeans (EJB) [Sun04b], CORBA Component Model (CCM) [OMG04d], and COM+ [Ewal01]. All implement an RLM. Similarly, Java 2 Connector Architecture (JCA) [Sun04i] defines a framework for integrating a user-defined RLM with an EJB-based RLM.

Remoting middleware. Middleware technologies such as CORBA [OMG04a] and .NET Remoting [Ramm02] implement an RLM at multiple levels. Middleware ensures the proper lifecycle management of resources such as connections, threads, synchronization primitives, and servants implementing the remote services.

Current developments such as Ice [Zero04a] prove that CORBA and .NET are not the sole examples for middleware frameworks that implement RLM functionality. RLM is a proven concept in all middleware frameworks.

Grid computing [BBL02] [Grid04]. Grid computing is about sharing and aggregation of distributed resources such as processing time, storage, and information. A grid consists of multiple computers linked together as one system. Participating computers that offer resources in the grid have to manage their local resources by some means. Often a resource lifecycle manager is used to make the resources in a grid available and fulfill local as well as distributed requests to those resources.

See Also The Object Lifetime Manager [LGS01] pattern is specialized for the management of singleton objects as resources in operating systems that do not support static destructors properly, such as real-time operating systems.

The Garbage Collector [JoLi96] pattern is specialized for the eviction of unused objects and their associated resources. Garbage collection is therefore not a complete RLM, as it does not deal with creation, allocation or acquisition of resources.

The Pooling (97) pattern focuses specifically on the recycling of resources, and does cover the complete lifecycle of resources

The Caching (83) pattern is specialized for avoiding expensive acquisitions and associated initialization of resources.

The Manager [Somm98] pattern focuses on the management of objects, rather than on general resource management.

The Abstract Manager [Lieb01] pattern focuses on the management of business objects in enterprise systems, rather than on general resource management.

The Resource Exchanger [SaCa96] pattern describes how resources are shared between resource users. It uses a generator, such as a network driver, and an acceptor, such as a server. The generator initially acquires the resource, which is then exchanged with the acceptor. This sets the resource to a state that is read later by the generator. The pattern keeps resource utilization stable by using the resource exchanger to manage the resources generated by the resource generator.

Credits   Thanks to our EuroPLoP 2003 shepherd Ed Fernandez and the writer's workshop participants, Frank Buschmann, Kevlin Henney, Wolfgang Herzner, Klaus Marquart, Allan O'Callaghan, and Markus Völter.

4 Resource Release

Timely release of resources that are no longer being used is essential in maintaining system stability and avoiding cases of resource exhaustion. Optimizing the release of resources is beneficial, as system performance and scalability depend directly on it. If reusable resources have to be acquired repeatedly, overhead is incurred. If the resources are not freed when no longer needed, it can lead to resource starvation. This in turn can lead to system instability and degrade scalability of the system.

Releasing resources explicitly can be tedious and sometimes error-prone. Both the Leasing (149) pattern and the Evictor (168) pattern address resource release by ensuring that acquired reusable resources are released in a timely manner. The Leasing pattern simplifies resource release by associating time-based leases with resources when they are acquired. The resources are automatically released when the leases expire and are not renewed. The Evictor pattern deals with determining *when* to release resources and *which* resources to release. The patterns together help to optimize the number of acquired resources at any point in time.

Leasing

The *Leasing* pattern simplifies resource release by associating time-based leases with resources when they are acquired. The resources are automatically released when the leases expire and are not renewed.

Example   Consider a system consisting of several distributed objects implemented using CORBA [OMG04a]. To allow clients to access these distributed objects, the server containing the objects publishes the references to the objects in a lookup service (21) such as a CORBA Naming Service [OMG04c]. Clients can then query the lookup service to obtain references to the objects. For example, consider a distributed quoter service object registered with the CORBA Naming Service. The quoter service provides stock quotes to any clients that connect to it. A client queries the Naming Service, obtains a reference to the quoter service, then communicates directly with the quoter service to obtain stock quotes.

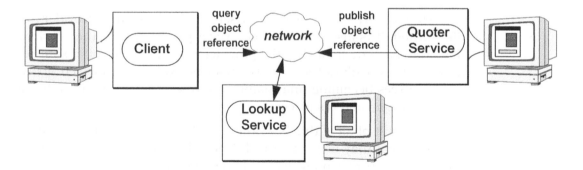

Consider what would happen if the server containing the quoter service were to crash and never come back up. The quoter service would no longer be available, but its reference would never be removed from the Naming Service. This can create two problems. First, clients would still be able to obtain a reference for the quoter service from the Naming Service. However, the reference would be invalid, and therefore any requests sent by the clients would typically result in an exception being thrown. Secondly, lacking any explicit means to remove the invalid object reference, unused resources such as invalid object references would build up at the lookup service over a period of time.

Context   Systems where resource use needs to be controlled to allow timely release of unused resources.

Problem   Highly robust and scalable systems must manage resources efficiently. A resource can be of many types, including local as well as distributed services, database sessions and security tokens. In a typical use case, a resource user retrieves the interface of a resource provider and then asks the provider for one or more resources. Assuming that the provider grants the resource, the resource user can then start using the resources. Over a period of time, however, the resource user may no longer require some of these resources. Unless the resource user explicitly terminates its relationship with the provider and releases the resources, the unused resources will continue to be consumed needlessly. This in turn can have a degrading effect on the performance of both the resource user and provider. It can also affect resource availability for other resource users.

In systems in which the resource user and the resource provider are distributed, it is also possible that over a period of time the provider machine may crash, or that the provider may no longer offer some of its resources. Unless the resource user is explicitly informed about the resources becoming unavailable, the resource user may continue to reference invalid resources.

The net result of all of this is a build-up of resources on the resource user side that may never get freed. One solution to this problem is to use some kind of monitoring tool that periodically checks a user's resource use as well as the state of the resources used by the resource user. The tool can then recommend to the resource user possible resources that can be freed. However, this solution is both tedious and error-prone. In addition, a monitoring tool may hinder performance.

To solve this problem in an effective and efficient manner requires resolution of the following *forces*:

- *Simplicity.* The management of resources for a resource user should be simple, by making it optional for the resource user to explicitly release the resources it no longer needs.

- *Availability.* Resources not used by a resource user, or no longer available, should be freed as soon as possible to make them available to new resource users. For example, resources associated with a network connection should be released once the connection is broken.

- *Optimality.* The system load caused by unused resources must be minimized.

- *Actuality.* A resource user should not use an obsolete version of a resource when a new version becomes available.

Solution   Introduce a lease for every resource that is used by a resource user. A lease is granted by a grantor and is obtained by a holder. A lease grantor is typically the resource provider, while a lease holder is typically the resource user. A lease specifies a time duration for which the resource user can use the resource.

If the resource is held by the resource user, then once the time duration elapses, the lease is said to have expired and the corresponding resource is freed by the resource user. On the other hand, if the resource is held by the resource provider and the resource user holds a reference to the resource, then on lease expiration the resource reference becomes invalid and is released by the resource user. In addition, the resource provider can also release the resource.

While a lease is active, the lease holder can cancel it, in which case the corresponding resource is also freed. Before a lease expires, the lease holder can apply to renew the lease from the lease grantor. If the lease is renewed, the corresponding resource continues to be available.

Structure The following participants form the structure of the Leasing pattern:

- A *resource* provides some type of functionality or service.

- A *lease* provides a notion of time that can be associated with the availability of a resource.

- A *grantor* grants a lease for a resource. The grantor of the lease is typically identical to the resource provider.

- A *holder* obtains a lease for a resource. The holder of the lease is typically identical to the resource user.

The following CRC cards describe the responsibilities and collaborations of the participants.

Class Resource	*Collaborator*	*Class* Lease	*Collaborator*
Responsibility • Represents a reusable entity, such as a connection or a service.		*Responsibility* • Specifies a time period for which a resource is available.	

Class Grantor	*Collaborator* • Holder • Lease • Resource	*Class* Holder	*Collaborator* • Resource • Lease • Grantor
Responsibility • Grants a lease on a resource to the holder.		*Responsibility* • Obtains and maintains a lease. • Uses a resource. • (Optionally) renews the lease.	

The dependencies between the participants of the Leasing pattern are shown in the following class diagram.

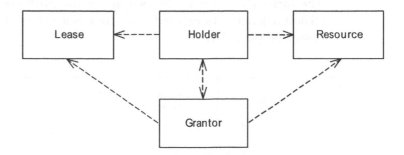

Dynamics In the following sequence diagrams the grantor of the lease is the same as the resource provider, and the holder of the lease is the same as the resource user.

Scenario I. In the first step the resource user acquires the resource from the resource provider. In this step, the lease is created and the duration of the lease is negotiated between the lease requestor and the lease grantor. The resource user is returned the resource and a corresponding lease. From that point on, the resource user can access the resource.

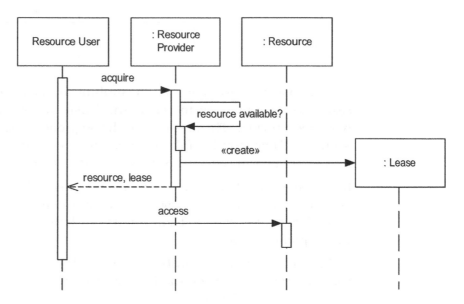

Scenario II. The following sequence diagram shows the scenario in which a lease has expired and the resource user is informed by the resource provider.

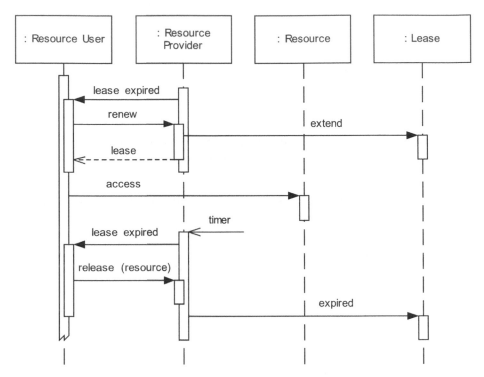

In response, the resource user has multiple options. For example, the resource user may try to renew the lease by interacting with the resource provider. The first part of the sequence diagram shows this scenario. Alternatively, if the lease is an active entity, it may be able to initiate its own renewal. See the *Variants* section for more details.

If the lease no longer needs to be renewed, the timeout can be accepted by the resource user, and consequently the resource user can release the resource. This scenario is shown in the second part of the sequence diagram.

If the lease is an active entity, it may be able to initiate the resource release process by using the Evictor (168) pattern. See the *Variants* section for more details.

Scenario III. In the case in which the resource is held by the resource provider and the resource user holds only a reference to the resource provider, the interactions on lease expiration are slightly different. When the lease expires, the resource user only needs to release the reference to the resource, whereas the actual resource is released by the resource provider. The following sequence diagram illustrates this.

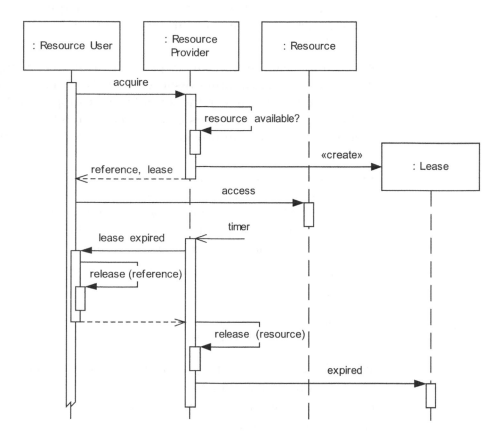

Implementation   Four steps are involved in implementing the Leasing pattern.

   1   *Determine resources with which to associate leases.* A lease should be associated with any resource whose availability is time-based. This includes resources that are short-lived, resources that are not used continuously. and resources that are updated frequently with newer versions.

2   *Determine lease creation policies.* A lease is created by the lease grantor for every resource used. If a resource can be shared by multiple resource users, multiple leases will be created for the resource. A lease can be created by the lease grantor using a factory, as described by Abstract Factory [GoF95]. Lease creation requires specification of the duration for which the lease is to be granted. The duration may depend on the type of resource, the requested duration and the policies of the lease grantor. The lease requestor and the lease grantor may negotiate the duration for which the lease should be granted.

A resource user may want to pass the resource, along with the associated lease, to another resource user. The lease creation policies can be used to specify whether or not this is supported. If a resource and its corresponding leases can be passed to other resource users, then the lease needs to provide operations allowing its ownership to be changed.

3   *Provide lease holder functionality.* Each lease holder must implement a notification interface that can be used by the lease grantor to notify the lease holder of lease expiry. When the resource user acquires a resource and the corresponding lease from the lease grantor, it will register this interface with the lease grantor.

➡   Such an interface in C++ might look like:

```
class LeaseHolder
{
public:
    void lease_expired (Lease &lease) = 0;
};
```

The lease_expired() method is a call-back method that is used by the lease grantor to notify the lease holder of a lease that has expired. In the implementation of this method, the resource user can release the resource whose lease has expired.   ❑

4   *Provide lease grantor functionality.* Once a lease has been created, the grantor needs to maintain a mapping between the lease and the corresponding resource. This allows the grantor to keep track of the time for which the resource is being used, and to determine the resources that are still available for which new leases can be granted.

In addition, to support the notification of resource users, a mapping of the lease to the corresponding resource user is necessary. The

Observer [GoF95] pattern describes how to implement such notifications.

5   *Determine lease responsibility.* If a lease can be renewed, it is necessary to determine who is responsible for renewing it. If the lease is an active entity, it may automatically renew itself, or the renewal process may require re-negotiation between the grantor and the holder. A re-negotiation of the lease may result in new policies for the lease, including the duration for which the lease is renewed.

6   *Determine lease expiration policies.* Once a lease expires and is not renewed, the resource associated with it needs to be released. This can be done automatically, for example by using the Evictor (168) pattern, or may require some intervention on the part of the resource user. Similarly, the lease grantor needs to remove the mapping between the lease, the resource and the resource user. Typically, the lease contains some kind of Asynchronous Completion Token [POSA2] with information about the holder that it uses to allow proper clean-up in the grantor when the lease expires.

Example Resolved   Consider the example in which a distributed quoter service object needs to be available to CORBA clients. The server containing the quoter service object registers the object with a CORBA Naming Service. The Naming Service is therefore a resource provider, while the resource is the service object reference that is registered with the Naming Service. The server containing the quoter service object is the resource user. The server and the Naming Service negotiate the lease details, including the duration for which the quoter service object reference needs to be registered, as well as policies regarding renewal of the lease. Once these negotiations are completed, the Naming Service registers the quoter service object reference with it and creates a lease of the agreed duration. The Naming Service is the lease grantor, while the server is the lease holder.

While the lease has not expired, the Naming Service keeps the quoter service object reference and makes it available to any clients that request it. Once the lease expires, the server may need to explicitly renew the lease, to indicate a continued interest in keeping the quoter service object reference available to clients. If the server does not renew the lease, the Naming Service automatically removes the quoter service object reference and releases any additional resources associated with it.

The C++ code below shows how a server can register a quoter service object reference with the Naming Service. In this example, the LookupService provides a Wrapper Facade [POSA2] around the Naming Service, so that the standard interface of the CORBA Naming Service need not be changed. The LookupService serves as a lease grantor.

To publish the quoter service, the application binds the hosted quoter object with the lookup service. When the leasing time is accepted a valid lease is returned. The lease can be renewed via the Lease interface before its expiration. When the lease expires the registered object of the type LeaseHolder is notified by the lease.

```cpp
int main (int argc, char* argv[])
{
  // First initialize the ORB
  CORBA::ORB_var orb = CORBA::ORB_init (argc, argv);

  // Create a quoter service
  quoter_Impl *quoter_impl = new quoter_Impl;

  // Get the CORBA object reference of it
  quoter_var quoter = quoter_impl->_this ();

  // Create a holder callback object
  LeaseHolder_Impl *lease_holder_impl =
      new LeaseHolder_Impl;

  // Get the CORBA object reference of it
  LeaseHolder_var lease_holder = lease_holder_impl->_this ();

  // Get hold of the lookup service which is also the lease grantor
  CORBA::Object_var obj =
      orb->resolve_initial_references("LookupService");

  // Cast from CORBA::Object
  LookupService_var lookup_service = LookupService::_narrow (obj);

  TimeBase::TimeT duration = 120; // seconds

  CosNaming::Name name;
  name.length (1);
  name[0].id = "quoter ";

  Lease_var lease;
  try
  {
```

```
                            // Publish the quoter service by registering the object
                            // reference of the quoter object with the lookup service
                            lease = lookup_service->bind (name, quoter , duration,
                                                          lease_holder);
                        }
                        catch (InvalidDuration &)
                        {
                            // Try with a shorter lease duration or give up.
                        }

                        // Do other things
                        // ...

                        // Renew lease if still interested in publishing the
                        // quoter service

                        duration = 180; // seconds
                        lease->renew (duration);

                        return 0;
                    }
```

The following code shows how the LookupService_Impl class wraps the CORBA Naming Service. After checking for an acceptable duration and creating a corresponding lease, the actual binding is delegated to the standard Naming Service. Note that the Reactor [POSA2] pattern is used for the notion of timers. The LookupService_Impl class therefore implements not only the LookupService interface, but also the Event_Handler interface. This allows the lease to register itself with the reactor to receive timeouts on lease expiration.

```
        class LookupService_Impl :
            public POA_LookupService, Event_Handler {
        public:
            LookupService_Impl () {};
            ~LookupService_Impl () {};

            Lease_ptr bind (const CosNaming::Name &name,
                            CORBA::Object_ptr object,
                            TimeBase::TimeT duration,
                            LeaseHolder_ptr lease_holder)
                throw (InvalidDuration)
            {
                if (this->duration_is_acceptable (duration))
                {
                    // Create a new lease
                    Lease_Impl *lease_impl =
                        new Lease_Impl (current_time () + duration,
                                        this->_this(), name, lease_holder);
```

```
                    // Get the CORBA object reference
                    Lease_var lease = lease_impl->_this ();

                    reactor_->register_timer (duration, this, lease);

                    // Delegate binding to actual Naming Service
                    name_service_->bind (name, object);

                    return lease;
                }
                else
                {
                    // Reject the bind request
                    throw InvalidDuration();
                }
        }

        void cancel_lease (Lease_ptr lease)
        {
            CosNaming::Name_var name = lease->get_name ();

            // Delegate to the Naming Service
            name_service_->unbind (name);

            // Cancel timer with the reactor
            reactor_->unregister_timer (this, lease);
        }

        TimeBase::TimeT prolong_lease (Lease_ptr lease,

            TimeBase::TimeT duration)
            throw InvalidDuration()
        {
            if (this->duration_is_acceptable (duration))
            {
                // Reschedule the timer with the reactor for the
                // new duration of the lease
                reactor_->unregister_timer (this, lease);
                reactor_->register_timer (duration, this, lease);
            }
            else // Reject the bind request
            {
                throw (InvalidDuration());
            }
        }

        // The lease is used as Asynchronous Completion Token [POSA2]
        void on_timer_expire (Lease_ptr lease)
        {
            LeaseHolder_var lease_holder =
                lease->get_lease_holder ();
```

```
                        // Notify lease holder of lease expriation
                        lease_holder->lease_expired (lease);

                        if (lease->get_remaining_time () <= 0)
                        {
                            // If the lease did not get renewed by the lease holder
                            lease->expired ();
                            CosNaming::Name_var name = lease->get_name ();
                            name_service_->unbind (name);
                        }
                    }
                }

                //...
            };
```

The following code shows how a lease could be implemented. The
lease will be created by the lookup service. It maintains the
association between the name used to register and the lease holder.

```
            class Lease_Impl : public POA_Lease
            {
            public:
                Lease_Impl (TimeBase::TimeT expiration_time,
                            LookupService_ptr lookup_service,
                            const CosNaming::Name &name,
                            LeaseHolder_ptr lease_holder)
                  : lookup_service_ ( LookupService::_duplicate (lookup_service)),
                    lease_holder_ (LeaseHolder::_duplicate (lease_holder)),
                    expiration_time_ (expiration_time),
                    name_ (name),
                    valid_lease_ (TRUE)
                {
                }

                // Renew the lease for the given time
                void renew (TimeBase::TimeT duration)
                    throw (InvalidDuration)
                {
                    TimeBase::TimeT accepted_duration =
                        lookup_service_->prolong_lease (this->_this (), duration);

                    if (accepted_duration != 0)
                    {
                        expiration_time_ = current_time () + accepted_duration;
                        valid_lease_ = TRUE;
                    }
                }

                TimeBase::TimeT get_remaining_time ()
                {
```

```
            if (valid_lease_)
                return expiration_time_-current_time ();
            else
                return 0;
    }

    void expired ()
    {
        valid_lease_ = FALSE;
    }

    LeaseHolder_ptr get_lease_holder ()
    {
        return LeaseHolder::_duplicate (lease_holder_);
    }

    CosNaming::Name *get_name ()
    {
        return &name_;
    }

    //...
};
```

An object of the LeaseHolder_Impl class is handed over to the lookup
service on registration of the quoter object. It will receive a notifciation
when the lease expires. It can prolong the lease, or prepare to have
the registration of the quoter object removed from the Lookup service.

```
class LeaseHolder_Impl : public POA_LeaseHolder
{
public:
    void lease_expired (Lease_ptr lease)
    {
        // prolong the lease
        TimeBase::TimeT new_duration = 240; // seconds
        lease->renew (new_duration);

        // or remove the binding of the quoter
        // object from the lookup service
    }
    //...
};
```

Variants   Specific lease creation and expiration policies can yield various
variants of the Leasing pattern.

Active Lease. When the lease is an active entity, the lease can take
over the responsibility for notifying the lease holder of lease

expiration. It can either release the resource directly, or use Evictor (168) to trigger the release of the resource.

Auto-renewable Lease. An active lease may be created with a policy to automatically renew itself when it expires. In this case the lease maintains enough information about the holder and the grantor to renew itself. Automatic renewals with short lease durations are preferable to a single, longer, lease, since each lease renewal offers the opportunity for the lease holder to update the resource it holds if the resource has changed. A further variation on this is to limit the number of automatic renewals based on some negotiation between the lease grantor and the lease holder.

Leasing Delegate. The renewal of a lease need not be done automatically by the lease or the lease holder—it can be done by a separate object. This frees the lease holder from the responsibility of renewing leases when they expire.

Non-expiring Lease. A lease may be created with no expiration. In this case, the holder must cancel the lease explicitly when it no longer needs the resource associated with the lease. This variant, however, loses many of the benefits of using the Leasing pattern, but allows integration of legacy systems in which the notion of leasing cannot be introduced easily.

Self-reminding Leases. Callbacks can be used to inform lease holders about expiring leases, to give them a chance to renew them. This can help lease holders who do not want to, or are not capable of, determining when a lease will expire.

Invalidating Leases. The Leasing pattern allows invalid resources such as object references to be released in a timely manner. The pattern can be extended using Invalidation [YBS99] to allow invalid resources to be released explicitly. If a resource becomes invalid, the resource provider can send an invalidation signal to the lease grantor, which can then propagate the signal to all the lease holders. The lease holders can then cancel the leases, allowing the resource to be released. Note that Invalidation can result in additional complexity and dependencies between the resource provider, the lease grantor, and the lease holders. It should therefore only be used when it is not sufficient to wait for the lease duration to expire, and is instead necessary to release resources as soon as they become invalid.

Consequences   There are several **benefits** of using the Leasing pattern:

- *Simplicity.* The Leasing pattern simplifies the management of resources for the resource user. Once the lease on a resource expires and is not renewed by the resource user, the resource can be automatically released.

- *Efficiency of use.* A resource provider can control resource use more efficiently through time-based leases. By bounding resource use to a time-based lease, the resource provider can ensure that unused resources are not wasted by releasing them as soon as possible, allowing them to be granted to new resource users. This can lead to minimization of the overall system load caused by unused resources.

- *Versioning.* The Leasing pattern allows older versions of resources to be replaced with newer versions with relative ease. The resource provider can supply the resource user with a new version of a resource at the time of lease renewal.

- *Enhanced system stability.* The Leasing pattern helps to increase system stability by ensuring that resource users do not access invalid resources. In addition, the Leasing pattern helps to reduce wastage of unused resources, and therefore helps to avoid shortage of resources.

There are some **liabilities** of using the Leasing pattern:

- *Additional overhead.* The Leasing pattern requires an additional object, a lease, to be created for every resource that is granted by a resource provider to a resource user. Creating a pool of lease objects and reusing them with different resource allocations can help to simplify this problem. In addition, on lease expiry, the lease grantor needs to send a notification to the resource user, adding additional overhead.

- *Additional application logic.* The Leasing pattern requires the application logic to support the concept of leases as the glue between the resource providers and resource users. Application architects therefore need to keep in mind that resources are not unlimited, and that they are not available all the time. Putting repetitious leasing code into a framework alleviates the coding complexity.

- *Timer watchdog.* Both the resource provider and the resource user need to be able to determine when a lease will expire. This requires support for some kind of a timer mechanism, which may not be available in some legacy systems. If however the legacy systems are event-based applications, they can be made timer-aware with very little overhead.

Known Uses

Jini [Sun04c]. Sun's Jini technology makes extensive use of the Leasing pattern by using it in two ways. First, it couples each service with a lease object that specifies the duration of time for which a client can use that service. Once the lease expires and is not renewed by the client, the service corresponding to the lease object is no longer available to the client. Second, it associates a lease object with each registration of a service with the Jini lookup service. If a lease expires and the corresponding service does not renew the lease, the service is removed from the lookup service.

.NET Remoting [Ramm02]. Remote objects in .NET Remoting are managed by the Leasing Distributed Garbage Collector. Leases can be renewed in three ways: firstly, the lease is renewed implicitly on every new request. Secondly, clients and servers can explicitly renew the lease using the Renew() method on the ILease interface. Remote objects can influence their leasing-based lifecycle management by implementing the ILease interface. Thirdly, the remote objects can also transfer lease management to a lease provider—a 'sponsor'—which has to implement the ISponsor interface. When a lease expires, the sponsor is asked for an extension to the lease. Leases are most useful for client-activated objects, as singletons are typically configured to live forever.

Software licenses [Macr04]. A software license can be regarded as a lease between the software and the user. A user may obtain a license for using a particular software. The license itself may be obtained, for example, from a license server, and is usually for a set period of time. Once the period of time expires, the user must renew the license or else the software can no longer be used.

Dynamic Host Configuration Protocol [DHCP04]. The purpose of DHCP is to enable individual computers on an IP network to extract their configuration settings from a DHCP server. The motivation behind this is to reduce the work necessary to administer a large IP network. The most significant piece of information distributed in this manner is the IP address. In that context a DHCP lease is the time that the DHCP server grants permission to the DHCP client to use a particular IP address. The lease time is typically set by the system administrator. Note that DHCP clients themselves monitor when a lease expires—they are not triggered by the DHCP server.

File caching. Some network file systems such as SODA [KoMa95] use leases as extensions to traditional protocols such as NFS in order to assure the consistency of cached file blocks in distributed file systems, achieving improvements in performance and scalability.

Magazine/newspaper subscriptions. A real-world known use of the Leasing pattern is magazine and newspaper subscriptions. In this case, the subscription represents the lease, which usually expires after a set period of time. The subscription must be renewed by the subscriber or the subscription terminates. In some cases, the subscriber may set up automatic renewal, for example by providing bank account information or credit card information.

Web-based e-mail accounts. Many Web-based e-mail accounts, for example MSN Hotmail [MSN04] or GMX [GMX04], become inactive automatically if not used for a certain period of time. In this case, the time duration can be regarded as a lease whose renewal requires use of the e-mail account.

See Also   The most common implementation of the Leasing pattern relies on event-based callbacks to signal lease expiration. An event-based application typically uses one or more event dispatchers or Reactors [POSA2], such as the Windows Message Queue, InterViews' Dispatcher [LiCa87], or the ACE Reactor [Schm02] [Schm03a]. Event dispatchers typically provide an interface to register event handlers, such as timer handlers that are called on timer expiration.

In applications that do not contain an event loop, the Active Object [POSA2] pattern can be used to substitute timer handling. The Active Object has its own thread of control and can either instrument the OS or run its event loop to signal leases via callbacks on timer expiry.

To make leasing transparent to the resource user, the Proxy [GoF95] [POSA2] pattern can be employed. The resource proxy can handle lease renewals, policy negotiations, and lease cancellations that would otherwise normally be done by the user. CORBA Smart Proxies

[Schm04] provide the appropriate abstraction in CORBA, while Smart Pointer is the counterpart to this in C++.

For concurrent resources, a resource provider has to manage multiple resource users holding leases to the same resource. Reference counting [Henn01] is a typical solution for keeping track of the event for which no leases are held by any resource user and the resource can be evicted.

Credits
Thanks to our shepherd Irfan Pyarali and the writer's workshop participants at PLoP 2000, Ralph Johnson, Rani Pinchuk, Dirk Riehle, Yonat Sharon, Michel Tilman, Hallvard Traetteberg, and Martijn van Welie.

Evictor

The *Evictor* pattern describes how and when to release resources to optimize resource management. The pattern allows different strategies to be configured to determine automatically which resources should be released, as well as when those resources should be released.

Example Consider a network management system that is responsible for managing several network elements. These network elements are typically represented as a topology tree. A topology tree provides a virtual hierarchical representation of the key elements of the network infrastructure. The network management system allows a user to view such a tree, as well as to get details about one or more network elements. Depending on the type of the network element, its details may correspond to a large amount of data. For example, the details of a complex network element may include information about its state as well as the state of its components.

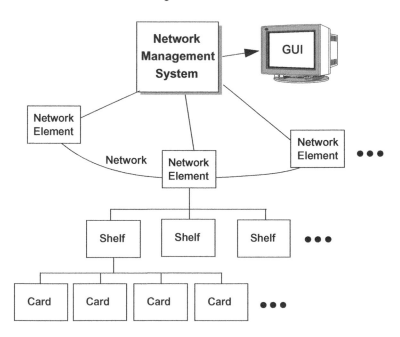

The topology tree is typically constructed at application start-up or when the user asks to view the tree of network elements, or some time in between. Similarly, the details of all the network elements can be fetched as the tree is constructed, or can be deferred until the user requests it. Regardless of when the details of the network elements are brought into memory, keeping these details in memory over time can be quite expensive. If the details of a network element are never accessed by the user again, they will consume valuable resources in the form of memory. On the other hand, the user may request the details of the same network elements, and therefore keeping the details in memory can improve performance. If the details of a network element that is frequently accessed by a user are not cached, it can lead to expensive calls to the real network element to get its details. This in turn can degrade system performance.

The relevant questions are: when is the right time to release resources, and which resources should be released?

Context   Systems in which the release of resources needs to be controlled to ensure their efficient management.

Problem   Highly robust and scalable systems must manage resources efficiently. Over time, an application acquires many resources, some of which are only used once. If an application keeps on acquiring resources without ever releasing them, it will lead to performance degradation and system instability. To avoid this, the application may immediately release resources after using them. But the application may need to use the same resources again, which would require re-acquisition of those resources. However, re-acquisition of resources can itself be expensive, and should therefore be avoided by keeping frequently used resources in memory.

To address these conflicting requirements of resource management requires the resolution of the following *forces*:

- *Optimality*. The frequency of use of a resource should influence the lifecycle of a resource.

- *Configurability*. Resource release should be determined by parameters such as type of resource, available memory and CPU load.

- *Transparency*. The solution should be transparent to the resource user.

Solution   Monitor the use of a resource and control its lifecycle using some form of strategy such as Least Recently Used (LRU) or Least Frequently Used (LFU). Each time a resource is used, it is marked by the application. A resource that is not recently used or not frequently used does not get marked. Periodically or on demand the application selects the resources that are not marked and releases or evicts them. Resources that are marked continue to stay in memory, since they are used frequently.

Alternatively, other strategies can be used to determine which resources to evict. For example, for memory-constrained applications, the size of resources can be used to determine which resource(s) to evict. In such case, a high-memory consuming resource may be evicted even if it has been used recently.

Structure   The following participants form the structure of the Evictor pattern:

- A *resource user* uses a resource, and can include an application or an operating system.

- A *resource* is an entity such as a service that provides some type of functionality.

- An *evictor* evicts resources based on one or more eviction strategies.

- An *eviction strategy* describes the criteria that should be used to determine whether or not a resource should be evicted.

The following CRC cards describe the responsibilities and collaborations of the participants.

Class **Resource User**	Collaborator • Resource	Class **Resource**	Collaborator
Responsibility • Acquires and uses a resource.		Responsibility • Represents a reusable entity, such as memory or a thread.	

Class **Evictor**	Collaborator • Resource • Eviction Strategy	Class **Eviction Strategy**	Collaborator
Responsibility • Evicts resources based on one or more eviction strategies		Responsibility • Describes criteria to use to determine which resource to evict.	

The participants of the Evictor pattern form the following class diagram.

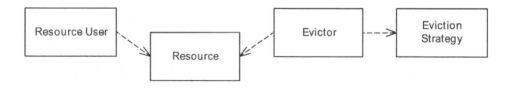

Dynamics The resource user first acquires the resource. Depending on the resource, the resource user registers it with the Evictor. The Evictor monitors the resource from then on. When the Evictor detects that a resource should be evicted according to its eviction strategy, it queries the resource to see if it can be evicted. If the resource can be evicted, it is given a chance to clean up, and is then removed.

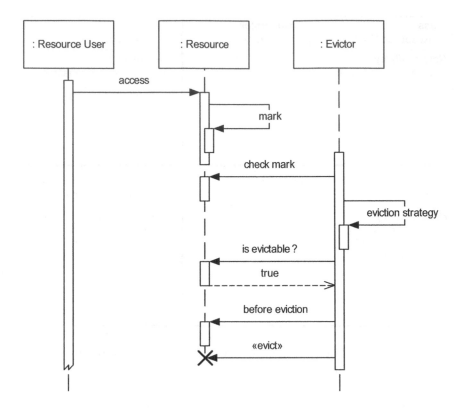

The sequence of steps in most implementations stays the same. Some variations can occur when, for example, resources can not be marked, and as a result the Evictor has to intercept requests to resources to get statistical information on which to base its eviction strategies.

Implementation   Four steps are involved in implementing the Evictor pattern.

1   *Define the eviction interface.* An eviction interface should be defined that will be implemented by all resources able to be evicted.

➡   For example, the eviction interface in Java might look like:

```
public interface EvictionInterface {
   public boolean isEvictable ();
   public Object info ();
   public void beforeEviction ();
}
```

The method isEvictable() can be used to determine whether an object is evictable—see step 2 for details. The info() method is used by the Evictor to extract strategy-specific information from the object, to determine whether or not to evict it—see step 4 for details. The beforeEviction() method serves as a hook method [Pree94] that can be called by the Evictor before it evicts an object. This gives the object a chance to release any resources it may have acquired.

For example, the EJB Session Bean [Sun04b] and Entity Bean interfaces include a method called ejbPassivate() that is called just before an entity or a session bean is evicted. This gives the bean a chance to release any acquired resources. ❑

2   *Determine evictable resources.* The developer must determine which resources can and should be evicted. For example, resources that are always required by an application, or those that can not be re-acquired, should not be evicted. Any resource that can be evicted must implement the eviction interface. Prior to evicting the resource, the application should call the interface, giving the resource a chance to do any necessary clean-up, including persisting any necessary state.

➡   In the Java interface described above, the application can use the method isEvictable() to indicate whether a resource can be evicted. If the method returns true, the resource is considered by the Evictor as a possible candidate for eviction. If the method returns false, the Evictor ignores the resource. ❑

3   *Determine an eviction strategy.* Based on application requirements, different eviction strategies can be used to determine when to evict resources, as well as which of the evictable resources to evict. Some of the common strategies used to determine which resources to evict include Least Recently Used (LRU) and Least Frequently Used (LFU).

In addition, a user-defined strategy can be used that may take different parameters. For example, an eviction strategy may take into account how expensive it is to re-acquire an evicted resource. Using such a strategy, resources that are less expensive to re-acquire may be evicted, even if they have been more frequently used when compared to resources that are more expensive to re-acquire.

4   *Define the use of eviction in the system.* The business logic of evicting resources needs to be added to the Evictor. This includes determining

how and when resources should be evicted, as well as actually marking resources to be evicted. Typically, the Evictor exists as a separate object or component in the application and is configured with the necessary eviction strategy by the application. For example, an application may choose to evict resources only when available memory goes below a specific threshold. A different application might implement a more proactive policy and could periodically evict resources even if memory does not go below a threshold.

An Evictor can use the Interceptor [POSA2] pattern to intercept user access to an object. The Interceptor can mark the object as being recently used in a manner that is completely transparent to the resource user. Periodically or on demand, the Evictor will typically query all evictable objects to determine which object(s), if any, to evict. In the Java interface described above, the Evictor will invoke the info() method on each object and use the information it receives, in the context of the eviction strategy, to determine whether or not to evict the object. For the actual eviction a Disposal Method [Henn03], sometimes also referred to as Explicit Termination Method [Bloc01], can be used. The Disposal Method pattern describes how classes should provide an explicit method to allow them to be cleaned up before being evicted.

Example Resolved

Consider the example of a network management system that is responsible for managing a network of several network elements. The details of the network elements can be fetched at system start-up or when the resource user makes a request for them. Without a priori knowledge of a user's intentions, resource use needs to be optimized so that only those network elements that are frequently accessed by the resource user are kept in memory. The eviction strategy used for this example is therefore to evict network elements that have not been accessed by the resource user for a threshold amount of time.

Each network element needs to implement the Eviction interface:

```
public class NetworkElement implements EvictionInterface {
    private NetworkElementComponent [] components;
    private Date lastAccess;

    public boolean isEvictable () {
        // Assume all network elements can be evicted
        return true;
    }
```

```
        public Object info () {
            // Return the date/time of last access, which
            // will then be used by the Evictor to determine
            // whether or not to evict us
            return lastAccess;
        }

        public void beforeEviction () {
            // First, release all resources currently held

            // Now, call beforeEviction() on all network element
            // components to give them a chance to release
            // necessary resources
            for (int i = 0; i < components.length; i++) {
                components[i].beforeEviction ();
            }
        }
        // ... other network element operations ...
    }
```

Similarly, all network element components and sub-components need to implement the Eviction interface, so that they can recursively release any resources when they are evicted.

The Evictor can be implemented as an object that runs in its own thread of control. This allows it to periodically check if there are any network elements that have not been accessed for a threshold time.

```
    public class Evictor implements Runnable {
        private NetworkElement [] nes;
        public Evictor () {
            new Thread(this).start();
        }

        public void run() {
            // For simplicity, we run forever
            while(true) {
                // Sleep for configured amount of time
                try {
                    Thread.sleep(pollTime);
                }
                catch(InterruptedException e) { break; }

                // Assume "threshold" contains the date/time such
                // that any network element accessed before it will
                // be evicted

                // Go through all the network elements and see
                // which ones to evict
                for(int i = 0; i < nes.length; i++) {
```

```
                        NetworkElement ne = (NetworkElement)nes[i];
                        if (ne.isEvictable()) {
                            Date d = (Date) ne.info();
                            if (d.before(threshold)) {
                                ne.beforeEviction ();
                                // Now remove the network element
                                // application-specifically
                            }
                        }
                    }
                }
            }
        }
```

Note that the information returned by the `info()` method and the way in which the Evictor interprets the information is application-specific, and can be tailored according to the eviction strategy that needs to be deployed.

Variants   *Deferred Eviction.* The process of evicting one or more objects can be refined into a two-step process. Instead of removing the objects immediately, they can be first put into some kind of a FIFO queue. When the queue is full the object at the head of the queue is evicted. The queue therefore serves as an intermediate holder of objects to be evicted. thereby giving the objects a 'second chance' in a similar way to Caching. If any of the objects are accessed prior to being removed from the queue, they need not incur the cost of creation and initialization. This variant, of course, incurs the cost of maintaining a queue, and also the resources associated with keeping the evicted objects in the queue.

Evictor with Object Pool. An object pool can be used to hold evicted objects. In this variant, when an object is evicted, instead of removing it from memory completely, it simply loses its identity and becomes an anonymous object. This anonymous object is then added to the object pool provided that it is not full. If the object pool is full, the object is removed from memory. When a new object needs to be created, an anonymous object from the queue can be dequeued and given a new identity. This reduces the cost of object creation. The size of the object pool should be set according to available memory. For more details, refer to the Pooling (97) pattern.

Eviction Wrapper. An object that is evictable need not implement the Eviction interface directly. Instead, the object can be contained inside a Wrapper Facade [POSA2] that then implements the Eviction interface. The Evictor will invoke the beforeEviction() method on the wrapper object, which in turn is responsible for evicting the actual object. This variant makes it easier to integrate legacy code without requiring existing classes to implement the Eviction interface. An example of this variant is the use of reference objects as wrapper objects in Java. See the *Known Uses* section for further details of this example.

Consequences There are several **benefits** of using the Evictor pattern:

- *Scalability.* The Evictor pattern allows an application to keep an upper bound on the number of resources that are being used, and that are hence in memory at any given time. This allows an application to scale without impacting total memory consumption.

- *Low memory footprint.* The Evictor pattern allows an application to control, via configurable strategies, which resources should be kept in memory and which resources should be released. By keeping only the most essential resources in memory, an application can be kept lean as well as more efficient.

- *Transparency.* Using the Evictor pattern makes resource release completely transparent to the resource user.

- *Stability.* The Evictor pattern reduces the probability of resource exhaustion and thus increases the stability of an application.

There are some **liabilities** of using the Evictor pattern:

- *Overhead.* The Evictor pattern requires additional business logic to determine which resources to evict, and to implement the eviction strategy. In addition, the actual eviction of resources can incur a significant execution overhead.

- *Re-acquisition penalty.* If an evicted resource is required again, the resource needs to be re-acquired. This can be expensive and can hinder application performance. The probability of this happening can be reduced by fine-tuning the strategy used by the Evictor to determine which resources to evict.

Known Uses **Enterprise JavaBeans (EJB)** [Sun04b]. The EJB specification defines an activation and deactivation mechanism that can be used by the container to swap beans out from memory to secondary storage, freeing memory for other beans that need to be activated. The bean instances must implement the ejbPassivate() method and release any acquired resources. This method is called by the container immediately before swapping out the bean.

.NET [Rich02]. The Common Language Runtime (CLR) of .NET uses a garbage collector internally to release unused objects. The garbage collector categorizes objects in three generations, depending on the lifetime of the object. If an object wants to be informed before it is completely evicted, it must implement the Finalize() method. .NET suggests the use of a Disposal Method [Henn03] Dispose(), which clients should use to release objects explicitly.

Java [Sun04a]. The release of JDK 1.2 introduced the concept of reference objects that can be used to evict an object when heap memory is running low or when the object is no longer being used. A program can use a reference object to maintain a reference to another object in such a way that the latter may still be reclaimed by the garbage collector when memory is running low. In addition, the Reference Objects API defines a data structure called a reference queue, into which the Garbage Collector [NoWe00] places the reference object prior to evicting it. An application can use the reference queue to take necessary action when specific objects become softly, weakly, or phantomly reachable and hence ready to be evicted.

CORBA [OMG04a]. To manage memory consumption in an application, a Servant Manager typically keeps an upper bound on the total number of instantiated servants. If the number of servants reaches a specified limit, the Servant Manager can evict an instantiated servant before instantiating a servant for the current request [HeVi99].

Paging [Tane01]. Most operating systems that support virtual memory make use of the concept of paging. The memory used by a process is partitioned into pages. When the OS runs short of memory, unused pages are evicted from memory and paged out to disk. When a page is accessed again, the OS copies the required page from disk into main memory. This allows the OS to keep an upper bound on the total number of pages in main memory. Paging is different than swapping: swapping evicts all pages of a process at once, while paging evicts only individual pages.

See Also   The Leasing pattern (149) describes how the use of resources can be bounded by time, allowing unused resources to be released automatically. The Lazy Acquisition (38) pattern describes how resources can be (re-)acquired at the latest possible time during system run-time in order to optimize resource usage.

The Resource Exchanger [SaCa96] pattern describes how to reduce a server's load in allocating and managing resources. While the Evictor pattern deals with releasing resources to optimize memory management, the Resource Exchanger pattern deals with exchanging resources to minimize resource allocation overhead.

Credits   Thanks to the patterns team at Siemens AG Corporate Technology and to our PLoP 2001 shepherd, John Vlissides, for their feedback and valuable comments.

5 Guidelines for Applying Resource Management

"See first that the design is wise and just:
that ascertained, pursue it resolutely;
do not for one repulse forego the purpose
that you resolved to effect."

William Shakespeare

The resource management pattern language presented in this book addresses domain-independent non-functional requirements of software systems. The pattern language can be applied to almost any domain and can be very effective in resolving resource management problems in that domain. Yet every domain has its own specific and recurring set of problems and forces that most applications of that domain need to resolve. Identifying a set of problems and forces that need to be addressed for an application is typically done during the application's design. While several solutions for a particular problem may be possible, finding a solution that also promotes effective resource management can require extra effort. This is where the resource management pattern language described in this book can prove most useful.

To best apply the resource management pattern language in a particular domain and for a specific application, follow these steps:

1 *Identify key components.* One of the most important steps in applying resource management effectively is to first identify the key components of the system. The key components of a system are those that consume the most expensive resources or the greatest number of resources. A resource can be expensive if it is rare, or if it is costly to acquire and/or release, or if it can lead to contention among resource users. Identifying key components typically requires domain expertise and/or an insight into the system architecture and design. A common strategy is first to analyze both the functional and non-functional requirements of the system that can have a bearing on system resources. Using these requirements as a baseline, the components that address the requirements should then be further analyzed. The key components of a system can be both critical and non-critical to the functioning of the system.

Often analysis of the system architecture alone does not reveal all the key components—an analysis of the run-time behavior of the system is also required. For performance measurement and stability analysis, therefore, use system profiling to identify intensive resource use. Also identify expensive resources and the components that use them.

2 *Identify the context.* The problem and forces of an application typically describe the initial context in which a pattern can be applied. The application of a pattern transforms the initial context into a new context, called the resulting context. The resulting context typically sets the stage for a new set of forces and requirements, leading to the applicability of additional patterns. The initial context of the application should be identified and used

when applying the resource management pattern language to each of the key components.

Consider Lazy Acquisition. The pattern is applicable to initial contexts where there is a large time lag between resource acquisition and resource use. The resulting context after applying the pattern is that resources are acquired as late as possible, up to directly before their use, minimizing the number of acquired resources. The resulting context also contains the liability that late resource acquisitions can introduce performance penalties at run-time.

3 *Identify 'hot spots'.* All the hot spots should be identified for each key component. A hot spot is a part of a component that can have an impact on one of the following aspects of the component: resource consumption, performance, scalability, and stability. In the case of increased resource consumption, as a first step all components that consume resources dynamically should be declared as possible hot spots until the root causes of the increased resource consumption have been identified.

Typically there should be a close relationship between the forces that need to be resolved and the hot spot categories identified. The identification of hot spots can be difficult, since all parts of the system cannot be declared 'hot'—there are always parts that are more critical than others. Different views of the components often reveal new information about possible hot spots. Use multiple evaluation and profiling methods to better and more completely localize hot spots.

4 *Apply patterns.* For each hot spot that is identified, apply one or more patterns from the resource management pattern language based on the category and context to which the hot spot belongs. Applying the pattern should yield a new context that may resolve the initial set of forces sufficiently. However, it is possible that some forces remain unresolved or additional forces are added. In this case, additional patterns from the pattern language should be applied.

These guidelines are applied in the case studies described in the following two chapters. The key components of the systems are identified along with the most critical forces of the systems. The resolution of hot spots is then described in the solution sections of each case study.

6 Case Study: Ad Hoc Networking

"Walking on water and developing software from a specification are easy if both are frozen."

Edward V Berard

A few years ago Sun Microsystems introduced a new technology called Jini [Sun04c]. Jini offers a platform-independent 'plug and play' technology, and supports ad hoc networking by allowing a service to be added to a network without requiring any pre-planning, installation, or human intervention. Ad hoc networking is based on the principle of spontaneous addition, discovery, and use of services in a network. The services can be of many types, such as simple time services, PowerPoint presentation services, or MP3 player services. Once a service has been registered on a network, Jini allows other services and users to discover the new service. The ability to do all this in a transparent manner without manual intervention embodies the basic principle of 'plug and play' technology.

The area of ad hoc networking is still attracting a lot of research and development. Recently, some research was completed on how the concept of Jini could be implemented in C++. Instead of Java byte code, JinACE [KiJa04] ships platform-dependent shared libraries across the network. Similarly, in addition to Jini, various technologies such as UPnP [UPnP04], and Microsoft .NET [Rich02] are built around the concept of ad hoc networking.

While all the ad hoc networking technologies are either platform- or language-dependent, they share a common underlying architecture. Given this common architecture, the requirements of resource management are similar among these systems. As resources are continuously added and removed from an ad hoc network, managing these resources in an efficient manner becomes very important.

6.1   Overview

Assume that you want to build an ad hoc networking solution for your company. The solution should enable you to distribute and acquire applications transparently across your network in the form of distributed services. Most ad hoc networks are typically comprised of mobile devices running some kind of software that accesses distributed services. In fact, the next generation of mobile phones are increasingly providing runtime environments [Sun04j] [Symb03] that allow services to be loaded dynamically and executed.

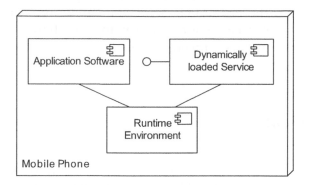

Since mobile devices have limited resources, such as memory and processing power, the software of the mobile clients needs to have a small memory footprint [NoWe00].

As an example, assume your network is a mobile network and your clients are mobile phones. The services can be of many different types such as:

- A stock quote service that delivers real time stock quotes.

- A news service that delivers the latest news, customized according to user preferences.

- An advertisement service that delivers advertisements according to user preferences and location.

In all these cases, the services themselves would reside on the mobile phone and would be responsible for communicating with back-end providers and obtaining the necessary information. However, since mobile phones have limited processing power and memory, it will not be possible to host several such services simultaneously. Therefore, to save resources within the mobile phone, services need to be loaded on demand and removed when no longer needed.

If a service needs to be loaded on demand, there must be a mechanism for finding the service dynamically—the service should be available on the network such that the mobile phone can easily find it. Once the mobile phone finds a service, it should be able to download and install it without requiring any user interaction.

Over time, if the user no longer needs or uses one or more services, there should be a mechanism for removing those services to conserve scarce resources of the mobile phone. This again should not require any user involvement.

6.2 Motivation

The limited resources and highly dynamic behavior of the clients require flexible resource management.

Devices such as mobile phones that form part of an ad hoc network are typically constrained by memory, processing power, and storage. Such devices can use different services when they are part of the network. A device that uses a service is called the *client* of the service. Each service, when installed, consumes some resources. If a device were to install all services up front, much overhead would be incurred and a lot of resources would be consumed unnecessarily. On the other hand, some devices may require highly deterministic behavior, and therefore mandate installation of services up front.

Over time a device may no longer require some of the services it has acquired. Unless the device terminates its relationship with the service provider explicitly and releases the services, along with the corresponding resources, the unused resources will continue to be needlessly consumed. This in turn can have a degrading effect on performance of both the device and the provider, as swapping or other memory management activities might occur. In addition, it can also affect service availability for other devices.

The following forces, derived from the requirements above, are characteristic of the ad hoc networking domain:

- *Efficiency*. Unnecessary service acquisitions should be avoided, as the acquisitions themselves are potentially expensive. In addition, the system load caused by unused services must be minimized.

- *Simplicity*. The management of services used by a client should be simple, by making it optional for the client to release explicitly the services it no longer needs.

- *Availability.* Services not used by a client, or no longer available, should be freed as soon as possible to make them available to new clients.

- *Adaptation.* The frequency of use of a service should influence the lifecycle of a service. Service release is determined by parameters such as available memory and CPU load.

- *Actuality.* A device should not use an obsolete version of a service when a new version becomes available.

- *Transparency.* The solution should be transparent to clients. The solution should incur minimum execution overhead and software development complexity.

These forces extend the forces mentioned in Chapter 1. The next sections describe how these forces can be resolved using the resource management pattern language.

6.3   Solution

To address the above forces, the solution that is typically implemented by ad hoc networks can be described using the resource management pattern language.

Every ad hoc network comprises the following key components:

- *Service.* A service is published so that it can be discovered and used by clients in the ad hoc network.

- *Lookup service.* A lookup service is used by service providers that register services, and by clients to discover the services.

- *Client.* A client, such as a mobile device, is an entity that makes use of a service. The client finds a service using the lookup service.

- *Service provider.* A service provider is an entity that provides a service for clients by registering the service, or only part of it, with the lookup service.

The above four components are responsible for the key interactions in applying the resource management pattern language to the domain of ad hoc networking. Their dependencies are illustrated by the following diagram.

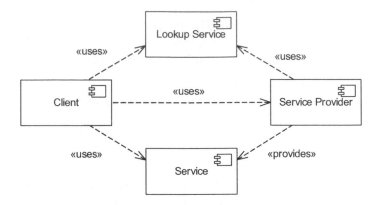

Consider the stock quoter application for mobile phones, described earlier. The quoter application consists of:

- The *stock exchange* as service provider, running on a back-end server machine.

- The *quoter service* as service, running on a back-end server machine.

- The *application software* of the mobile phone, acting as a client.

- The *quoter proxy* as front-end client software, to be downloaded on the mobile phone for accessing the back-end quoter service and query for stock quotes.

- The *directory* of services as lookup service.

The following figure shows the deployment of the quoter example.

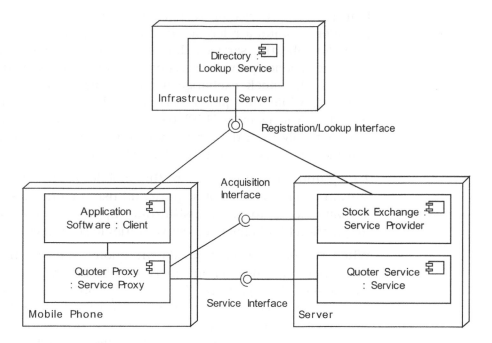

In the first step, the stock exchange creates and registers the stock quoter service with the directory, as illustrated in the following sequence diagram.

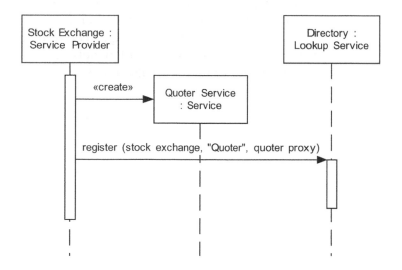

During the process of registration, the stock exchange service provider submits a reference to itself along with a set of properties that describe the services that it provides. In addition, the stock exchange service provider registers the quoter proxy with the lookup service. The stock exchange service provider acts as a resource provider, while the quoter service is the actual resource that it provides. The Leasing (149) pattern is used to remove references automatically from the directory to service providers that no longer provide any services, and therefore whose leases have expired.

To optimize resource use in the mobile phone, the application software will typically not acquire and use the quoter service until it actually needs to. This just-in-time approach described by Lazy Acquisition (38) helps to conserve valuable resources for the client.

When the phone user requests the quoter service, the application software of the mobile phone queries the directory, which implements the Lookup (21) pattern. The directory provides a reference to a quoter proxy, along with a reference to the stock exchange service provider that hosts the quoter service that corresponds to the quoter proxy. A reference to the stock exchange is needed by the quoter proxy to allow it to communicate with the quoter service implementation, which is located at the stock exchange service provider. Therefore, after installing the quoter proxy, the application software provides the reference of the stock exchange service provider to the quoter proxy. Using that reference, the quoter proxy accesses the service at the stock exchange. The quoter proxy becomes part of the application software, which acts as a client. These steps are shown in the sequence diagram below.

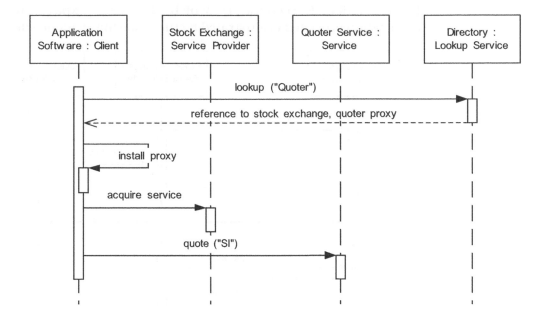

Prior to finding a service through the directory, the application software of the mobile phone must find the directory itself. Finding the directory, registration of services, and the lookup of services is well documented by Lookup (21). The download of the client proxy from the lookup service is specific to this scenario.

Once the mobile phone finds a service, it acquires a lease to gain access to the service. A lease is a grant of guaranteed access for a specific time. Each lease is negotiated between the client and the service provider. The Leasing (149) pattern describes this, along with different variations that can be supported.

Once a lease has been acquired, the mobile phone uses the service directly. This typically requires loading of a service or part of a service into the mobile phone's address space. To optimize resource use, this is typically done as late as possible, as and when required. Lazy Acquisition (38) describes how this is done.

When the lease for the service expires, or the service is no longer needed, the mobile phone will stop using the service, and the association of the service with the client along with its corresponding resources will be evicted. This resource management is described by

Evictor (168). A scenario in which the lease expires and the association is evicted is illustrated by the following sequence diagram.

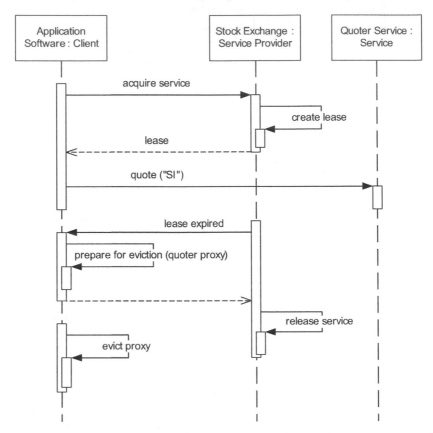

The application software of the mobile phone first acquires the service, then accesses it via the quoter proxy to query a quote. If the quoter service is not used regularly, the lease with the stock exchange—the service provider—expires, and the application software is informed. The quoter proxy is typically registered with an evictor. When the quoter proxy is not used for a predefined time, the evictor selects it and finally evicts it from memory. At that point, the service is released automatically by the stock exchange.

Going back to a more general view of ad hoc networking, the following figure shows the participants and how they relate with the patterns of the pattern language.

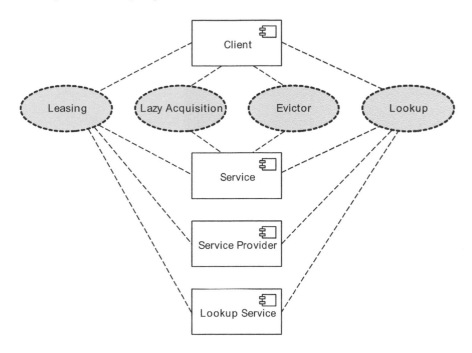

The picture shows that Evictor is used by clients to evict services. Lazy Acquisition is used during the client's acquisition of a service. The Lookup pattern is used first by a service provider to register a service with the lookup service, then by a client to look up a service from the lookup service. Finally, Leasing is used by the service provider for registrations at the lookup service and by clients to lease services from service providers.

In addition to the resource management patterns described in this book, additional patterns can be useful to address the requirements of ad hoc networking systems. For example, Pick & Verify [Wisc00] can be used by a client to randomly pick a service from a pool of services, to handle situations in which it is impossible to determine up front which services are available for use. Similarly, if the services are moving and hence the references to them are changing over time, Locate & Track [Cohe00] can help to keep track of the location changes.

7 Case Study: Mobile Network

"I have always wished
that my computer would be
as easy to use as my telephone.
My wish has come true.
I no longer know how to use my telephone."

Bjarne Stroustrup

This chapter describes a domain-specific example and shows how the patterns presented in Chapter 2, *Resource Acquisition*, Chapter 3, *Resource Lifecycle*, and Chapter 4, *Resource Release*, can be applied to the resource management requirements of a domain. The example presented is a telecommunications system for mobile phones. As described in Chapter 5, we follow the steps by first identifying the hot spots in the system. Since there is a close relationship between the hot spots and the forces that must be resolved, we apply the resource management pattern language to directly address the forces.

This chapter first presents an overview of some of the key concepts of the domain. It then goes into details and tries to identify the forces specific to the domain that need to be addressed. Using the patterns presented in the previous chapters, the forces are addressed and a solution presented using the resource management pattern language.

7.1   Overview

A mobile network includes all the network elements necessary to accept a call from a mobile phone and forward the call to the core telecommunication network.

The protocols and the deployment of responsibilities among the network elements involved are defined by the Universal Mobile Telecommunications System (UMTS) standard [3GPP04], sometimes also referred to by the term '3rd-generation' (3G) mobile communication system. UMTS is expected to replace existing technologies, such as the Global System for Mobile Communications (GSM) in Europe, within the next few years. The architecture we describe in this chapter has been derived from real projects developing software for UMTS.

A mobile network typically consists of three different types of network elements [LoLa01]: base stations (also referred to as NodeB), Radio Network Controllers, and Operation and Maintenance Centers (OMC). In addition, several other network elements play an important role in the functioning of the network and are represented as part of a core network. These elements include a registry of home locations, a registry of visitor locations, and various gateways to external communication networks. However, for the purpose of the case study, we focus primarily on the three main network elements, namely base stations, Radio Network Controllers, and Operation and Maintenance

Centers. The responsibilities of each of these three network elements are described below.

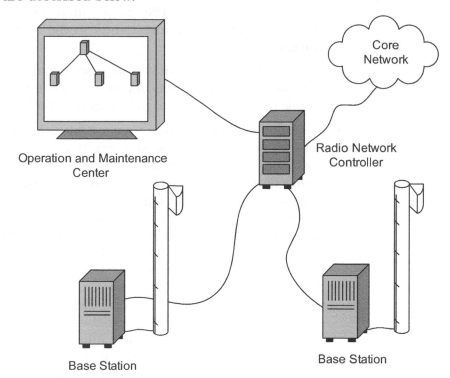

* *Base stations.* Basc stations are responsible for communicating with mobile phones, and have one or more antennas associated with them. The antennas are used to transmit digitized voice via radio signals. The base station forwards a call from a mobile phone to the Radio Network Controller, which forwards it to another base station if the call recipient is a mobile phone, or to the core network if the call recipient is a land-line phone. The base station is operated and maintained by the Operation and Maintenance Center, which controls the configuration of almost every hardware and software element in the network.

  Base stations consist of embedded computers and are distributed over wide geographical areas. They are required to be highly reliable to minimize the need for repair.

* *Radio Network Controllers* (RNC). RNCs mediate calls between base stations, other RNCs and the core network, depending on where

the caller and the call recipient are located. For this, it communicates with the call processing component in other network elements. The RNC is operated and maintained by the Operation and Maintenance Center in the same way as the base stations.

RNCs are high-performance enterprise systems running on general purpose operating systems. As they are a central component in the mobile network, they need to be highly reliable.

- *Operation and Maintenance Center* (OMC). The OMC manages the network of RNCs and base stations. While RNCs are contacted for operation and maintenance through direct connections, the connections to base stations are routed via the RNC. The OMC is responsible for monitoring the proper functioning of network elements and for allowing human operators to intervene when necessary. Besides the local maintenance terminals for base stations and RNCs, the OMC is the only network element in the mobile network that has a user interface. Typically the OMC is implemented as a software system distributed over multiple processes on multiple nodes. This includes a subsystem responsible for managing the network topology, a subsystem responsible for hosting database information about the topology, and a subsystem handling the user interface of the OMC and interacting with the network elements. The OMC is responsible for handling all operations on the network topology, such as rearrangements and optimizations.

These three types of network elements work closely together. The base stations stay in contact with each mobile phone by regularly exchanging information over a common channel, so that each party is prepared for call establishment.

When the user of the mobile phone dials a number, the mobile phone requests a call to be established with the network via a common channel to the base station. The mobile phone sends a data packet with the phone number of the party to be reached, together with additional information.

At this stage the RNC decides whether a connection should be established with the core network, which it does if the called party is a stationary phone or can only be reached via the core network. If the called party is another mobile phone reachable by the same RNC via a second base station, the RNC determines that the call should be forwarded to another base station. After checking with the core network for billing and verification purposes, the RNC establishes a connection. The following figure illustrates the scenario in which a call is established with a land-line phone.

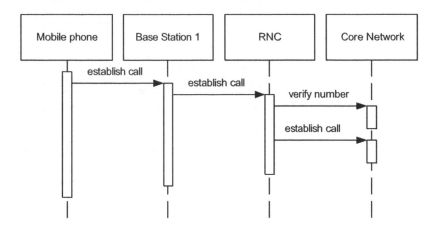

When the base station detects that the radio signal of a mobile phone is too weak, it selects another base station with a stronger radio signal from the mobile phone. The first base station hands over the voice connection to the second base station in a single transaction, ensuring that the connection between the RNC and the mobile phone stays intact. The handover of the connection from one base station to the next is usually so transparent that the user of the mobile phone does not notice it, even if in a train travelling at 200km/h. The scenario for call handover is illustrated in the following sequence diagram.

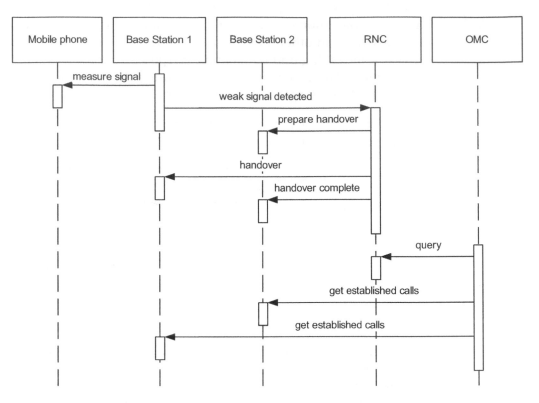

Both base stations and RNCs have to be designed in such as way to guarantee end-to-end quality of service for call establishment and handover, even with many concurrent users.

7.2 Motivation

Since the three types of network elements of the mobile network perform very different tasks, they have different hardware and software architectures. As a result, the requirements are quite distinct for the various network elements. However, they still have many forces in common.

- *Scalability.* One of the main difficulties in the design and implementation of a mobile network is the handling of dozens, if not hundreds, of network elements. Since every network element needs to be represented in software, highly sophisticated resource management techniques are required. The mobile network must be scalable to support additional network elements and additional antennas, as well as additional mobile phones. As a result, efficient resource management is important for handling the additional communication and coordination that is required.

- *Reliability.* The systems in the mobile network have to be highly reliable, as any downtime can impact mobile service to a large number of customers, and can have both serious financial and non-financial ramifications for the provider.

  In addition, if a network element is no longer reachable due to either a software or hardware failure, it can be very expensive for a service technician to fix the problem in the field.

- *Quality of Service* (QoS). The mobile network system must comply with several QoS constraints. These include well-defined and predictable start-up time, response time to new connection requests, and seamless handover of voice connections between base stations. To ensure that these constraints are met, they need to be addressed at all levels of the software architecture.

- *Performance.* The mobile network must meet stringent performance requirements. This can include handling a minimum number of call establishments per second, as well as minimum number of handovers per second between base stations. In addition, every system in the mobile network is usually required to handle a specific number of concurrent calls. The individual network elements of the mobile network should also have a short and constant start-up time. The system response times must be short to ensure subscriber satisfaction.

- *Distribution.* The operation and maintenance software of the mobile network is distributed among multiple machines. The OMC performs general supervision of all network elements while local Operation and Maintenance (O&M) units in the base stations and RNCs monitor their internal state, sending only filtered failure information to the OMC. The complexity of the overall system stems from the inherent distribution defined by geography.

- *Failure handling.* The mobile network must handle many different types of errors and failures. Failures in base stations and RNCs, whether from hardware, software, or connections, should be logged and sent to the OMC. Base stations typically reboot if contact to the OMC is lost due to local failures, so that they can be monitored again. Since the service offered by RNCs must be uninterruptible, the RNCs must cope with failures differently. The RNCs are typically protected against hardware failure by redundant mechanisms.

7.3 Solution

This section describes how the resource management pattern language can be used to address the above forces. The solution describes the architecture of the base station and OMC, and shows how the resource management pattern language can be used to address both the functional and non-functional requirements of these components. The RNC architecture is similar to that of a base station with respect to the distribution of functionality across multiple CPU boards and the separation between O&M and call processing. It is controlled by the OMC similarly to the base stations. This leads to a similar use of the patterns, so the description of the RNC architecture is therefore omitted. The forces presented above are addressed as the architecture of the network elements is explained.

While the example presented here is specific to the telecommunication domain, it is important to understand that the patterns and the pattern language are independent of any domain. They can be effectively applied to many different domains to resolve forces that are common among the domains. The goal is to take a 'problem-oriented' approach by applying the patterns and pattern language to solve a set of problems.

The Base Station Architecture

The architecture of the base station is split into two key functional units: the Call Processing (CP) unit and the Operation & Maintenance (O&M) unit.

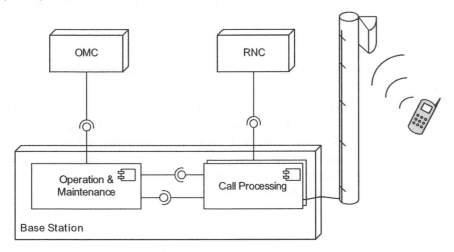

Call Processing Unit

The Call Processing [Hanm01] unit of a base station is typically split across multiple CPU boards. This is because the performance of a single CPU is insufficient to handle a large volume of calls. Multiple CPU boards also provide redundancy, ensuring that a single hardware failure does not lead to a complete loss of the base station. A central, but redundant, CPU board is responsible for coordination of the other CPU boards, while the remainder of the CPU boards are responsible for the actual radio connections. Physically, each CPU board is connected with every other CPU board via an internal communication network.

Call processing includes the following responsibilities:

- *Voice connection management.* The base station acts as the mediator of a connection that must be established between a mobile phone and the RNC.

- *Internal connection management.* The internal CPU boards that must communicate to achieve a voice connection have to be provisioned. The connections between the CPU boards have to be established and resource conflicts avoided.

- *Quality monitoring.* If the communication signal from a mobile phone becomes too weak, the base station must inform the RNC, so that it searches for a base station with a stronger signal.

In summary, call processing encompasses everything that is related to managing connection establishment, handover, and connection termination between a mobile phone and the core network.

Operation & Maintenance Unit

The Operation & Maintenance (O&M) [Hanm02] unit of a base station represents all hardware elements and selected software elements as a tree of 'managed objects'. A managed object can range from an integrated chip to a complete CPU board. The local O&M unit is responsible for monitoring and configuring all hardware and software elements, so that the Call Processing unit can focus solely on its task and not be distracted by resource management issues.The following figure shows a simplified managed object tree, consisting of hierarchically-organized managed objects.

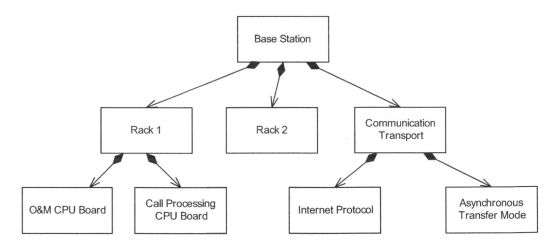

The logic for the O&M unit is split between a local part, implemented by the base station, and a remote part, implemented by the OMC. The tree representation of the managed objects, as shown in the figure above, is accessible remotely by the OMC. This allows the OMC to perform O&M operations on the base station that controls the corresponding (hardware) counterparts of the managed objects.

A base station's O&M unit registers its interface with the OMC in order to be managed and to report errors. Commands arriving at the

O&M interface from the OMC are mainly handled by a CPU board specifically dedicated to O&M.

It is interesting to note that the base station can work independently from the OMC, so it does not have to be connected all the time.

The Base Station Functional Specification

This section describes the resource hot spots in the architecture of the base station. The resource management pattern language is a valuable reference for addressing these hot spots, by resolving many of the functional and non-functional requirements.

Flexible Application Discovery

To make configuration and administration of the applications running at the base station easier, they are implemented as components. This means that every application is cohesive of itself, has well-defined service interfaces and is reusable. Service interfaces describe the syntax and semantics of the individual application's interactions.

Application components typically include Operation and Maintenance, Call Processing, Connection Management, and Start-up Management.

To increase reliability, the applications running on the CPU boards run in multiple processes. When started, the applications connect to each other with their inter-process communication. In order to connect to each other, how can the applications find each other's service interfaces?

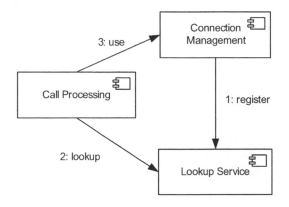

Every service interface is associated with a reference, to allow for flexible and late binding between the applications. References uniquely identify a specific interface of a component. Since the applications are not linked statically, how can they be linked later?

Lookup (21) helps to address these problems in an elegant way. Every application registers its service interfaces with a lookup service. In addition, every application queries for the references of service interfaces to which it needs to connect. Each application, therefore, plays the role of a resource provider, while the service interface is the resource provided by the application.

Note that the lookup service itself is a component that needs to be bootstrapped before any access can be made to it. To address this, the lookup service is typically configured statically.

Connection Management

Since connections from the base station to the OMC are neither reliable nor fixed, and since maintenance can also be done by a local maintenance terminal (such as a notebook computer) connected to the same O&M interface, valuable resources are wasted by broken and lost connections.

This problem is addressed by Evictor (168). An instance of the Evictor component is used, where all connections are registered. The Evictor component is responsible for either actively or passively verifying that currently unused connections are recycled. It is also used to reclaim connections using a least-recently-used strategy, so that resource consumption is always minimized. Minimizing resource consumption is important, as the service providers cannot afford to send a technician into the field to reset the base station after resource exhaustion.

High Performance

The base station has to meet high performance requirements when new voice channels need to be established. Since connection requests can involve multiple CPU boards, those CPU boards have to coordinate among themselves. This can involve data copying, and allocation of new entries in containers that track the association of connection IDs to physical transport resources. Dynamic memory allocations and synchronization are among the most expensive operations on computer systems. Execution of expensive operations in the critical path of voice connection establishment must be avoided.

Eager Acquisition (53) is used to avoid executing expensive resource acquisitions, such as memory allocations, during performance-critical run-time. Eager Acquisition suggests moving the expensive resource acquisitions to earlier stages of program execution. Application start-up is often not so critical—although it must happen quickly, it does not matter if it takes a few micro- or milliseconds longer. On the other hand, such delays are unacceptable during call establishment.

Operation and maintenance of the base station is performed mainly by a dedicated CPU board, but the hardware and software elements of all CPU boards have to be represented in the OMC. The dedicated CPU board typically invokes maintenance and status operations remotely on the other CPU boards. The status information includes properties such as the number of connections in use, the number of transmission failures, or the failure rate on specific connections. The execution of these status operations can involve long delays if many need to be performed. How can the time required to access properties on remote CPU boards be reduced?

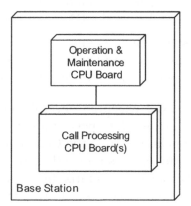

Caching (83) allows the execution between the CPU boards to be better decoupled. Data that is needed from other CPU boards by the dedicated CPU board is stored temporarily in a cache. Instant access to the properties of another CPU board is especially important for system analysis and optimization. Unintentional use of stale data is a risk, which must be avoided by using special protocols when data changes on CPU boards.

Failure Handling

Communication between the base station and the OMC is established by the OMC, as described in *The OMC Architecture* on page 212. In cases of software updates of the OMC, when a new version of a service interface is offered, or in case of reorganization when a new OMC instance is associated with the base station, the service interface to the original OMC can become invalid. How can the base station ensure that a reference to a service interface that is no longer valid is not used?

Leasing (149) is used to associate a lease with the reference of the OMC service interface. This lease is issued by the OMC and has to be kept active regularly by the base station. The OMC can then prolong the lease as long as it is available. If the OMC becomes unavailable, the reference maintained by the base station becomes invalid. In this case, since the lease will not be renewed by the OMC, the base station marks the reference as invalid and does not use that reference to the OMC. Instead, the base station waits until it is contacted from another OMC instance and a new lease is created. The protocol by which the OMC contacts base stations is described in *Station Discovery and Communication* on page 215. Call processing is not affected during the OMC switchover.

Leasing thus ensures that failures or changes are handled automatically and autonomously. Resources, such as reference to the service interface, are released on time.

Concurrency

The OMC executes several actions at the base station, such as measuring the performance of specific voice communication channels. For this, the O&M component in the base station software typically creates a new thread, since this action can take a long time and other threads must be available to guarantee the responsiveness of the base station. If the OMC invokes multiple long-duration actions, which can easily happen if many measurements have to be performed, several threads are spawned and run in parallel. This can cause thread creation overhead and high system load, potentially endangering the Call Processing unit.

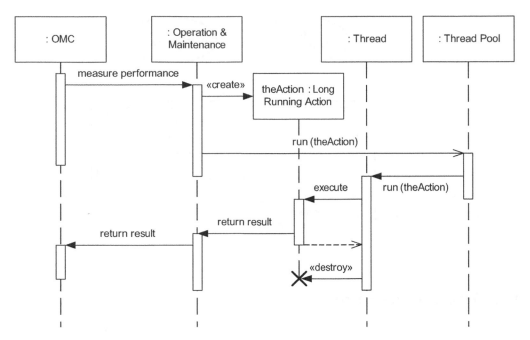

To avoid such overhead and overload situations, Pooling (103) is used. A thread pool manages the threads used for running long-duration actions. The thread pool is configured with a maximum number of threads to be running concurrently. The O&M component delegates the execution of long-duration actions to the thread pool instead of spawning a new thread when an action is triggered. The thread pool internally assigns one of its threads to execute the action. If the maximum number of threads is reached and a new action is triggered, the action is encapsulated in a command, as described in the Command Processor [POSA1] pattern, and is queued for later processing.

Summary   The following figure relates the software components to the patterns used.

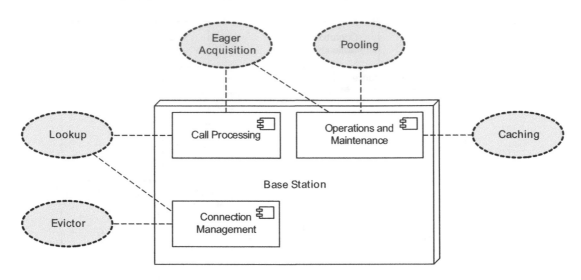

The OMC Architecture

The Operation and Maintenance Center (OMC) is a network management system that is responsible for administration and monitoring of mobile network elements such as base stations and RNCs. It is similar to a network management system for general network elements, consisting of routers and network switches.

To allow administration of the mobile network, the OMC provides a visualization of the network and its elements as a topological tree. The tree subsumes all managed object trees local to the network elements. A graphical interface is more intuitive than a command-line interface (CLI). However, displaying the states of dozens, if not hundreds, of elements graphically, and providing fast interaction with them, requires that the OMC keeps most of the information about the network elements in memory. The graphical user interface, then directly accesses this information

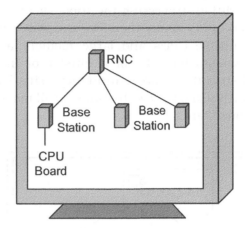

Accessing the network elements to retrieve their state information in real time can be very expensive, since it introduces long delays. Furthermore, if this information needs to be fetched at start-up of the OMC, it would be a long time before the graphical user interface could show enough information to be useful. To avoid the network latency and processing time to retrieve the state of network elements, the OMC stores all network element information in a database. On start-up the memory representation of the managed object is built from the database, and later updated based on the actual physical state of the network elements. State changes of network elements are first updated in memory. If the state changes are critical, they are also persisted immediately, otherwise they are persisted in the background.

The state of all network elements cannot be kept completely in memory because of the huge data volume in large networks. In addition, the OMC functionality of collection of state information from the network elements and the processing of the state information is distributed among multiple nodes that exchange information via a database.

The number of network elements that an OMC typically monitors is in the order of several thousands. Each network element possesses many properties, reflecting the state of its hardware, such as CPU boards and radio antennas, as well as software elements, such as established connections and available memory. It is easy to see that storing all this information persistently requires a large database. In addition, traversing the topological tree requires a lot of processing power. Typically therefore the OMC runs on enterprise servers with multiple CPUs and large memory and disk space. The hardware consists typically of a cluster of machines to support both load distribution and redundancy. This leads to many new challenges, such as how the sub-states on all machines in the cluster can be kept consistent.

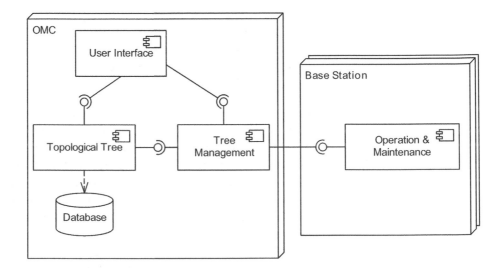

The overall OMC architecture follows the classic Model-View-Controller [POSA1] pattern and can be subdivided into the following key parts:

- *User interface*, to allow interaction of the operator with the network elements (View).

- *Topological tree*, to store network element-specific information in a cache (Model).

- *Tree management*, to allow the user interface to traverse the network elements (Controller).

The topological tree is completely available in the database and in part also in memory. The tree management is responsible for contacting the O&M units of the network elements, such as base stations and RNCs, to retrieve actual data. For some properties, such as the case in which alarms or notifications have been raised, the network elements actively push information to the OMC.

The OMC Functional Specification

This section describes hot spots in the OMC design and how the resource management pattern language resolves them by addressing many of the OMC's functional and non-functional requirements.

Station Discovery and Communication

The OMC is responsible for the operation and maintenance of the base stations and RNCs in the mobile network. For this, it connects remotely to the base stations and RNCs. The networks for communication with the base stations are typically based on TCP/IP, with the base stations identified by IP addresses.

Since a base station is a passive network element, it is not responsible for searching for an OMC and finding its IP address. Instead, the OMC is configured with the IP addresses of all base stations and RNCs. However, knowing the IP address of the network element is not sufficient, since the concrete service interface of the O&M component is unknown.

To solve this, Lookup (21) is used to discover the O&M service interfaces of the network elements. The OMC uses a lookup service to memorize the association between the IP address of a network element and the O&M service interface of that base station. For this, the lookup service uses a specialized bootstrapping protocol based on FTP (file transfer protocol). The lookup service uses the IP address to connect to the network element and recover a file that contains the service interface, for example a stringified CORBA [OMG04a] object reference. This service interface is then memorized in the lookup service's internal table and handed back to the OMC tree management.

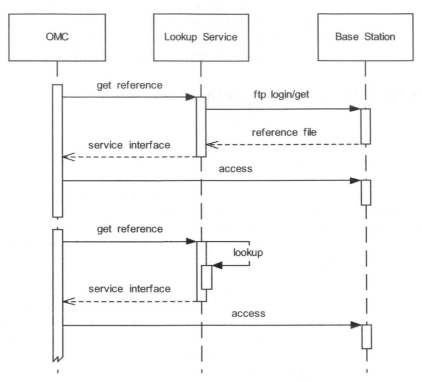

From that point on internal OMC applications can look up the service
interfaces on demand at the lookup service—the initial bootstrapping
via FTP is only necessary when the service interface becomes invalid,
for example due to an upgrade of the station's software. Since such
upgrades are done by the OMC itself, it knows when to trigger the
lookup service to bootstrap the service interfaces.

**Network State
Maintenance**

The OMC represents network elements and their links in a topological
tree. The topological tree is the core of the OMC and plays a key role
in providing the OMC's main functionality. The tree consists of nodes
that   represent   remote   network   elements   connected   via
communication channels.

Since network connections are inherently unreliable, individual
network element state is cached, so that on sudden disconnections
the current state is still available. Using Caching (83) makes available
the base station state that has already been retrieved, even when a
connection to the base station is currently unavailable. To make the

access via the cache as transparent as possible, a Cache Proxy [POSA1] that detects the availability of the base station is used. The proxy directs state queries to the cache automatically when the base station becomes unavailable. To indicate to the operator that the state of the network element is from the cache, the network element is typically highlighted, for example in a different color, to inform the operator about the unavailability. The operator can continue to work, but is also aware that the displayed state might be outdated.

High Performance

Caching (83) not only helps to cover for unavailable network elements, but it can also improve the performance of the user interface.The OMC needs to be highly responsive to user input, such as when selecting network elements and viewing their properties. Quick response times are important, as the operator needs to be able to deploy counter-measures quickly in emergency situations. If the state of the network element has not changed, then Caching can be used to fetch the current state, avoiding the excessive time to query the network element for the system state while ensuring that the state is actual and not outdated.

In addition, the start-up time of an OMC should be relatively short, typically not more than a few minutes. To reduce start-up time, information about the current operator's view of the network, such as the network elements viewed most often, is loaded eagerly to guarantee fast initial access.

Eager Acquisition (53) loads performance-critical resources, such as the state information of the top-level network elements, from the topological tree as soon as possible, typically on start-up. This ensures that resources, such as network element-specific information, can be accessed without delay.

The following sequence diagram illustrates how the cache is filled initially with eagerly-acquired state information about network elements. In the second step, the network elements can be quickly accessed via the cache, avoiding delays for the user.

Care has to be taken to determine what information is loaded at start-up time, since Eager Acquisition can prolong start-up time and waste resources if information is never accessed or accessed only later. To find the optimal balance, it is important to perform system analysis over a period of time. One way to do this is to run the system without

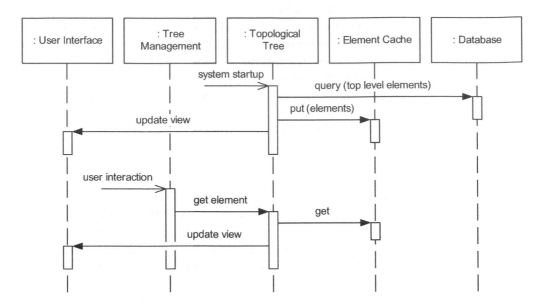

eagerly acquiring any resources and measuring various access times, then optimizing only where it is actually necessary.

On the other hand, some network elements are viewed very seldom. Allocation of memory resources is avoided in these cases, as long as the respective elements are not relevant. To save resources from being used unnecessarily, Lazy Acquisition (38) suggests that resources that are used only seldom are acquired on demand, immediately before the actual access of the resource takes place. In this case, the memory required to hold the managed objects is a resource, reflecting the properties of the network elements in memory. The current state is fetched lazily from the network element. This scenario is illustrated by the interactions in the following sequence diagram.

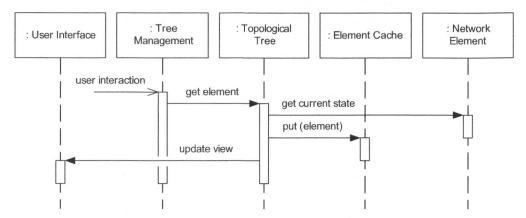

As in the case of Eager Acquisition, system analysis should show where Lazy Acquisition can be used effectively.

High Scalability

The OMC needs to be highly scalable to cope with thousands of network elements. To make the system scalable, it is important that resources are released when they are no longer needed, to allow other users and system components to acquire them. Resources are released, for example, when the operator's view of the topological tree changes.

The managed objects associated with a network element may be extensive. While Caching improves performance and helps to make network element state available even at the time of a disconnect, keeping too much information in memory can also be expensive. The state of managed objects that are not accessed frequently are therefore evicted from memory to free up valuable resources. The Evictor (168) pattern describes how to apply such a mechanism.

Similarly, Partial Acquisition (66) is used to partially acquire the necessary resources. When large alarm logs must be retrieved from a network element, the OMC partially acquires some of the most critical entries from the list of alarm messages, leaving the acquisition of the remaining alarm messages, including the minor ones, until they are required.

When visualizing the network elements, the graphical user interface (GUI) has to mirror the physical network layout. For this, a GUI object is allocated for every network element. When the view of the network changes, potentially new GUI objects need to be allocated. Since the allocation of memory for those GUI objects is an expensive operation, requiring memory consumption and delay, such allocations are avoided.

To avoid the repetitious allocation of memory, the OMC user interface uses Pooling (97) for the GUI objects to create an object pool. This is created with allocations for initial number of GUI objects and adapts its size as the demand increases. When GUI objects go outside the scope of the current view they are released to the object pool.

Maintenance and Upgrade

The network elements monitored by the OMC are typically deployed over long distances and in a wide range of locations, such as on the roofs of buildings, in the field, or in church spires. When new software updates have to be applied to the network elements, it would be too expensive for a technician to drive into the field and manually update the software. Instead, all updates are performed via the O&M interface of the network element. Software changes can also mean changes in protocols or policies, which make it necessary to update all relevant system parts synchronously. How can it be ensured that a software update of dozens or hundreds of network elements is synchronized?

This problem is solved using the Coordinator (111) pattern. The individual O&M components of the network elements act as participants in the overall task of software distribution and update. The role of the coordinator is performed by the OMC. This ensures that the task of updating all the relevant network elements is synchronized. The new software version downloaded to the network elements is only activated when all participating network elements are ready to do so.

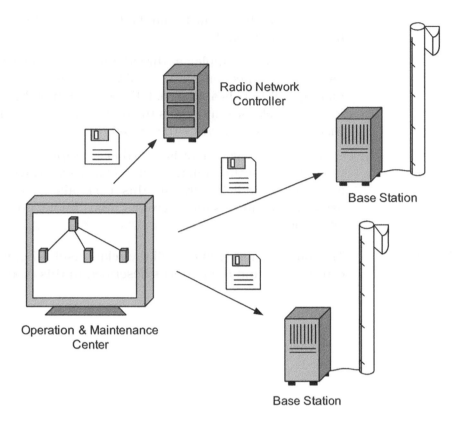

Radio Network Controller

Base Station

Operation & Maintenance Center

Base Station

Complexity   The preceding sections show the wide variety of resources involved in the operation and maintenance of the OMC. The resources often possess strong interdependencies, because resources have to be used in combination to achieve a specific task.

Consider the case of a long-running activity such as a query of the topological tree to find all network elements with a specific property. In this situation a thread operates on multiple managed objects and uses a database connection to fetch its local data. If the thread has to be terminated, all the resources it uses must be released, as well as other resources such as the dynamically-allocated memory for the managed objects and the database connections.

When multiple resources must be coordinated, the Resource Lifecycle Manager (128) is valuable. For every set of related resources, the RLM manages a resource group that instantiates the related resources in the necessary order and releases the resources in the reverse order.

It also remembers how to handle failure situations when a resource becomes unavailable.

In the above example, a thread must first be created, then the database connection, and finally the memory for the relevant managed objects is allocated. If the allocation of the memory fails, the RLM first releases and pools the database connection automatically, then destroys or recycles the thread.

Connection management is a further example of the use of the RLM, in which connections may be closely associated with each other and are useless individually. In this case also, the RLM stores the associations in resource groups that know how to handle this situation.

Summary

The following figure shows all the relationships between the software components and the patterns described in this chapter.

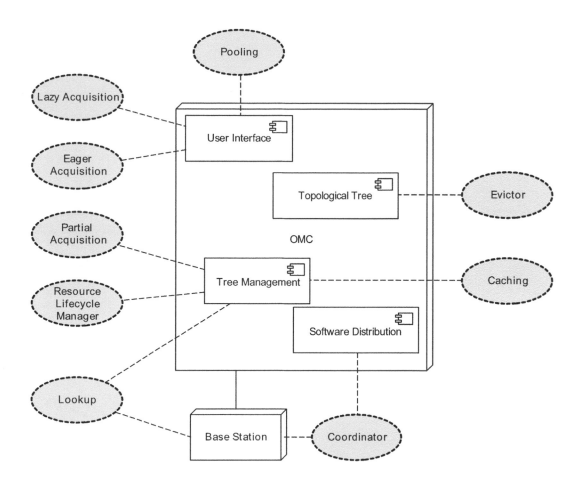

8 The Past, Present, and Future of Patterns

> *"History rarely happens in the right order or at the right time, but the job of a historian is to make it appear as if it did."*
>
> *James Burke*

Konrad Adenauer, Germany's first Chancellor after World War II, once said: *"Was gebe ich um mein Geschwätz von gestern"* ("I don't care about my waffle from yesterday"). Seldom does it happen that you can reflect on your predictions about the future, even less that you have the opportunity to reflect on them twice! Obviously this is a benefit of co-authoring a series of books.

In this chapter, therefore, we revisit our forecasts about the future of patterns that appeared in the second volume of the POSA series, *Patterns for Concurrent and Networked Objects* [POSA2] in 2000. We discuss the directions that patterns have taken in the past four years, analyze where patterns are now, and—with the benefit of hindsight—revise our vision about the future of patterns.

8.1   The Past Four Years at a Glance

In *Patterns for Concurrent and Networked Objects* [POSA2] we predicted how we thought patterns would evolve. Four years later we summarize what actually happened. We reference much of the relevant work during this period, although our list is not exhaustive. Additional references are available at `http://hillside.net/patterns/`.

Patterns

In 2000 we forecast that patterns would be published primarily for the following domains: distributed objects, real-time and embedded systems, mobile systems, business transactions and e-commerce systems, quality of service (QoS) for commercial-off-the-shelf-based distributed systems, reflective middleware, optimization principles, process and organization, and education. We were right in five of these nine areas:

- *Distributed objects.* Most of today's software systems are distributed, especially at the enterprise level. It therefore comes as no surprise that a wealth of patterns and pattern languages have been published in this area. For example, at the recent EuroPLoP and VikingPLoP conferences whole workshops and tracks were dedicated to distributed objects, distributed systems and other distribution aspects [EPLoP01] [EPLoP02] [VPLoP02]. Even more prominently, several good books on the subject have been published. *Server Component Patterns* [VSW02] documents a pattern language that illustrates how to build component-based distributed systems using standard component platforms such as CCM, COM+, and EJB. *Remoting Patterns* [VKZ04] describes a pattern language that explains the basic ingredients of distributed object computing middleware. *Enterprise Solution Patterns Using Microsoft .NET* [TMQH+03] documents how best to employ the .NET technology, and *Core J2EE Patterns: Best Practices and Design Strategies* [ACM01] how to design systems using the J2EE platform.

- *Real-time and embedded systems.* Although the majority of software written today is for embedded applications, surprisingly few patterns have been published in this area—or at least, less than we expected. The PLoP and OOPSLA conferences hosted several workshops on patterns for distributed, real-time, and embedded systems, but only a few of the patterns presented there have made it into the commonly-known pattern vocabulary. The most prominent work in this area is a pattern language for *Time Triggered Embedded Systems* [Pont01].

- *Business transaction and e-commerce systems.* This domain has always been of interest to software developers, reinforced by the growing popularity of the Internet and the Web. The most successful publication in this area is probably the *Enterprise Application Patterns* language [Fowl02]. It describes how to build 3-tier business information systems and places special focus on the design of the database-access layer. A book that focuses solely on persistence aspects is *Database Access Patterns* [Nock03]. Several publications also focus on Internet and Web applications, such as the pattern language for *High-Capacity Internet-Based Systems* [DyLo04] and the pattern language *WU* for Web usability [Grah03].

- *Process.* Process patterns have been popular since the beginning of the pattern movement in software [PLoPD1] [PLoPD2]. This interest has continued and grown over the past four years [EPLoP01] [EPLoP02] [VPLoP02]. In addition to these conference papers, three valuable books on process patterns and process-related patterns have been published: *Object-Oriented Reengineering Patterns* [DDN03], *Domain-Driven Design* [Evans04], and *Configuration Management Patterns* [BeAp02]. All these books tell you about the 'what', the 'when', and the 'why' in their respective areas, and thus provide real value compared to some of the contemporary software development process literature.

- *Education.* There is a small but very active community that publishes pedagogical patterns on its own Web site [Peda04]. This community also runs tracks on education and pedagogy at pattern conferences [EPLoP01] [EPLoP02] [EPLoP03]. All patterns authored by the members of this community deal either with the human side of software development, or with how humans learn or should teach.

Almost no patterns have been published in the other four areas: mobile systems, quality of service for commercial-off-the-shelf-based distributed systems, reflective middleware, and optimization principles. While this may not be surprising for the latter three domains—they are either very narrow or only of limited interest to most developers—there is no reasonable explanation for the lack of visible interest in publishing patterns for mobile systems. Mobility is an important topic in many systems and new projects envision scenarios like 'business traveller', 'mobile office', 'mobile worker', 'enterprise on air', and others. Perhaps there will be more interest in patterns for mobility in the near future so that our prediction of 2000 eventually becomes true.

In addition to our forecast domains, patterns have also been published in many other areas—several of which we probably could have predicted:

- *Resource Management.* Resource management is an important topic, not only for embedded systems. The book you are reading covers the relevant aspects in this domain, from resource acquisition through resource use to resource release.

- *Fault Handling.* Patterns and pattern languages for fault handling were documented before 2000 [ACGH+96], but this area has again gained the attention of pattern authors during the last two years. Many of the up-to-date techniques in this area have been captured in pattern form [Sari02] [Sari03].

- *Security.* Security has become an extremely hot topic in the patterns community. Focus workshops on security patterns were held at several EuroPLoP conferences, and many security patterns were presented in the writer's workshops [EPLoP02] [EPLoP03].

- *Messaging.* Recently a booster in this area has been published: *Enterprise Integration Patterns – Designing, Building, and Deploying Messaging Solutions* [HoWo03]. This book captures all you want and need to know about messaging in pattern form. It is probably one of the most successful pattern work published in the past four years.

- *Human–Computer Interaction.* The interest in patterns for human computer interaction is not new [PLoPD2] [PLoPD3]. Over the past four years, however, it has grown even more. Many interaction patterns have been published at recent pattern conferences [EPLoP02] [EPLoP03] and there is also a Web site for human computer interaction patterns [HCI99]. The first pattern book in this area was *A Pattern Approach To Interaction Design* [Borc01], followed by the pattern language *WU* on Web usability [Grah03].

Despite our failures with some of our predictions, our general forecast on patterns has come true, however, as this summary proves. Only a few general-purpose patterns have been published in the past four years, while the majority of publications were domain-specific patterns. There was only one exception to this rule. We completely underestimated the power of the Gang-of-Four [GoF95]. To be more precise, we did not expect that so much secondary literature on the Gang-of-Four patterns would be published. This literature either translates the Gang-of-Four patterns to other programming languages [Metz02] or explains certain aspects and caveats about them in more depth [ShaTr01] [Henn04].

Pattern Languages

The most important statement we made in our forecast of 2000 was about the growing number and relevance of pattern languages. We predicted three concrete trends—and we are very pleased to see that they all came true:

- New pattern work will primarily be published in the form of pattern languages. In fact, most of the literature that we reference in the previous subsection consists of pattern languages.

- Existing stand-alone patterns, such as those from the Gang-of-Four [GoF95] and *A System of Patterns* [POSA1], will be integrated into current and new pattern languages. The pattern language for distributed computing, which was published in parts at recent EuroPLoP conferences, and which will be included in the fourth volume of the POSA series [POSA4], is probably the most prominent representative of these languages. It consists of more than 100 patterns, most of which are known stand-alone patterns. Another pattern language that integrates many well-known stand-alone patterns is the *Enterprise Application Patterns* language [Fowl02].

- Large, complex, or oversized stand-alone patterns will be decomposed into smaller, more tangible pattern languages. Even this prediction came true. For example, the *Remoting Patterns* [VKZ04] decompose in detail the Broker pattern from *A System of Patterns* [POSA1]. Another pattern from POSA1, Pipes and Filters, is decomposed in *Enterprise Integration Patterns* [HoWo03]. Most recently, several Gang-of-Four patterns [GoF95] were decomposed into societies of smaller patterns [HeBu04].

Experience Reports, Methods, and Tools

Our predictions in this area largely failed. On one hand, some experience reports on the use of patterns were published [Busc03], and a new method for applying patterns was developed [YaAm03]. On the other hand, neither the experience reports nor the *Pattern-Oriented Analysis and Design* method attracted much attention from the patterns community. Their impact is thus very limited, contrary to our predictions for this area.

Pattern Documentation

Little has been published about pattern documentation, so again we failed with our prognoses.

Formalizing Patterns and Pattern Languages

Yet another failure for our predictions—though a totally unexpected one. Formalizing patterns was a popular sport in the late 1990s. Since then, however, it has become quiet in the camp of the pattern formalists. This may be because it became apparent that it is next to impossible to formalize patterns, and that previous approaches to expressing a pattern formally—even though incomplete or very limited—were too complex to be of practical use.

8.2   Where Patterns are Now

This is a very interesting issue. In fact, it is harder to answer than four years ago, and even harder to answer than it was in 1996, when we made our first predictions about the future of patterns [POSA1].

Definitely, patterns are in the mainstream today. Almost every software system includes patterns, often used in isolation to resolve specific problems, sometimes applied holistically to design and implement an entire system on the basis of patterns. The original intention of the patterns community—to spread the word about good software engineering practices—has almost become true.

With respect to domain coverage, we have seen significant progress during the past four years. A decade ago, almost all published patterns were general-purpose: specific domains such as distribution or transaction processing were not addressed at all. Four years ago, the first domain-specific patterns were published, but still only few domains were actually addressed. Today the situation is quite different. Patterns and pattern languages have been published for a variety of domains, including—but not limited to—distribution, concurrency, resource management, transaction processing, messaging, security, fault management, event handling, user interface design, and e-commerce. We are pleased to see this growing interest in documenting experience and best practice in patterns, because it proves the quality and expressiveness of the whole idea.

Regarding the understanding of patterns, we see two camps. Fortunately, the vast majority of software engineers have a much better understanding of patterns than four years ago. Unfortunately, too many members of the software community still stumble into common pitfalls or fall prey to popular misconceptions about patterns. The enormous success of publications *about* patterns, such as the *Design Patterns Java Workbook* [Metz02] and the *Beyond the Gang-of-Four* tutorial [HeBu04], demonstrates this fact and underpins the need for further and more intensive education about what patterns really are.

Last, but not least, the quality of the published patterns and pattern languages has increased significantly. Now that the patterns community can draw on a decade of experience in using and writing patterns, pattern authors are much more experienced in documenting their knowledge in pattern form. Most of the patterns and pattern languages that we reference in the previous section are far more expressive, far more precise, and far more readable than the patterns and pattern languages published in the past.

8.3 Where Will Patterns Go Tomorrow?

Patterns are still as popular in the software community as they were at their beginning: pattern conferences are prospering, talks and tutorials about patterns at other conferences are well attended and received, and a growing number of developers report that they use patterns in their daily work. In other words, patterns are becoming a commodity tool in our treasure chest of software development techniques. It is therefore very likely that patterns will be subject of further research and evolution in the future—to deepen the knowledge and understanding about the concept, to support software engineers in their use of patterns, and to 'patternize' as yet uncovered areas in software development.

Patterns and Pattern Languages

Our main prediction for patterns is that the two main trends from the past four years will continue: authors will focus largely on documenting pattern languages instead of stand-alone patterns, and the majority of all new patterns and pattern languages will be domain-specific rather than general-purpose. Some areas in which we expect patterns and pattern languages to be documented are:

- *Security.* Security has been an important topic for patterns since the beginning of this millennium, but recently key players in the field met at EuroPLoP conferences to work jointly on a more complete coverage of the subject. We therefore not only expect new patterns and pattern languages to be documented in security-related areas such as authentication, authorization, integrity, and confidentiality, we also expect new as well as existing patterns and pattern languages to be integrated to provide a consistent and coherent pattern view for security applications.

- *Fault tolerance and fault management.* Fault tolerance and fault management was a popular topic for pattern authors in the early days of the patterns community [ACGH+96], but for more than five years almost next to nothing was published in this area. It was not until recently that the interest in patterns on this subject grew [Sari02] [Sari03]—probably in correspondence with the growing interest in fault tolerance and fault management in general. It has now been realized and widely acknowledged that quality software, specifically larger-scale and distributed systems, need a proper fault management concept to be truly successful. For this reason we think that, as in the area of security, experts will work on a more in-depth pattern coverage for this area.

- *Distribution.* Distributed systems are, and will continue to be, a major area for pattern authors. Though many distribution topics are already covered by patterns, several blank spots are still left. Peer-to-peer and grid computing, for example, are two hot concepts for which no or only a few patterns exist. However, it will only be a matter of time before we see the first patterns and pattern languages on these and other distribution-related topics being published.

- *Mobility.* Although we failed once with our prediction that mobility will be an area for new patterns and pattern languages, we renew this forecast here. The reason for this is simple: the demand for mobile systems is growing rapidly, and mobile systems are confronted by many challenges that do not arise in non-mobile systems, such as managing low and variable bandwidth and power, or adapting to frequent disruptions in connectivity and service quality. It simply *must be* an exciting area for pattern authors. We therefore expect that experienced mobile systems developers will document their expertise in pattern form to capture the best software development practices in this area.

- *Pervasive Computing.* 'Pervasive', 'ambient', 'ubiquitous', and 'palpable' computing are terms you can hear regularly at conferences and other forums on modern software technology. Yet building such systems is extremely challenging. Not only do several non-trivial domains meet in this discipline, such as embedded systems, real-time systems, and mobile systems, but pervasive systems also come with their own challenges. For example, pervasive systems cannot be maintained and configured centrally via a dedicated administration point, but must instead self-install, self-administer, and self-repair whenever possible. As another example, because the intention behind pervasive systems is to support many activities in our daily life, ranging from home automation to personal health control, they will influence our personal habits both directly and extensively. Pervasive systems are thus required to be designed so that on one hand they are at your service whenever and wherever you need them, but on the other hand respect your privacy and do not try to govern the way you live. Mastering this fine balance between a helping hand and Big Brother requires both technical and social skills. With the growing number of such systems we thus expect that developers will document the solutions to such problems in pattern form.

- *Language-specific idioms.* New programming languages and styles have been developed over the past few years and have gained a certain popularity. Examples of general-purpose languages include Python [MaAs02] and Ruby [ToHu00], AspectJ [Ladd03] as a special-purpose language, and generative programming [CzEi00] as a programming style. Each of these new languages and styles has its own idioms, which distinguish programming in that language or style from programming in others. For C++, Java, C#, and Smalltalk such idioms have already been documented, but this hasn't happened yet for less mainstream languages and styles such as those listed above. We hope that this gap will be filled to advocate a good programming practice for these languages. Whether this will happen or not depends to a great extent on how much attention these languages and styles get from the software community at large. If they remain jargon for a clique of insiders, this will probably not happen, but if a broader community of developers hooks onto them, we can expect such idioms to be collected and published.

- *Process.* Though many areas in software development processes have been described by patterns, some corners are still waiting to be discovered. For example, in the realm of agile processes, disciplines like test-driven development or unit testing have emerged and new insights into project and organizational structures to support agility have been gained. The patterns community has addressed some of these topics occasionally in the past [Cope95], but a thorough pattern coverage has not been provided yet. We therefore expect to see more on process and organizational patterns and pattern languages over the next years.

- *Education.* All major pattern conferences run tracks on patterns for education. It appears as if patterns and pattern languages became the 'standard' vehicle for teachers and consultants to exchange their knowledge about the art of teaching programming and software engineering. Though many pedagogical patterns have been published in the past, workshops on education and teaching held at other conference still suggest a demand for more. We expect this demand to be met.

It is very likely that patterns and pattern languages will also be published for areas other than those listed above, but based on the knowledge and overview we currently have, these appear to be the most promising. Hopefully we will have the opportunity to revisit our forecasts in future to see which of our predictions were fulfilled and which failed.

Theory and Concepts

Today the patterns community has more than a decade of experience in mining, documenting, and applying patterns. Many software systems that intentionally used patterns succeeded, but there are also many failure stories. The time has come to reflect on the past and, with hindsight, adjust and evolve the common understandings about patterns: what are they (really), what properties do they have, what is their purpose, who is their audience, and what are the 'do's and don't's' of using them. Likewise, now that the patterns community is broadly adopting pattern languages, appropriate conceptual underpinnings are needed to avoid misconceptions about, and misapplications of, this pattern organization form.

Such a pattern theory will not be formal—no formalism has yet been discovered to capture their idea—but descriptive. The goal is not to be absolutely precise in a mathematical sense, but to support *understanding* about software development and its best practices.

This understanding is mostly missing in today's world of semi-formalized and tool-supported software engineering. Consequently, and despite all 'support' from formalism and tools, many software development projects still fail. As Kevlin Henney, a renowned member of the patterns community, used to say: "typing has never been the bottleneck in software development, but understanding has".

We therefore expect books and papers on the concept of patterns and pattern languages to be published over the next few years, but the circle of potential authors for such work is—unfortunately—fairly small. It definitely requires expert knowledge of both writing and applying patterns and pattern languages, but only few members of the patterns community can really claim to have 'passed the gate' [Alex79] and have such an intimate familiarity with the concept that they can write the 'Timeless Way of Programming' work that we are all seeking.

Refactoring and Integration

Many patterns have been published in the past decade, and many of them have become part of the design vocabulary of almost every software developer. However, the original descriptions of these patterns do not cover the progress in software development that has been made since their publication. Some patterns, therefore, deserve revision or refactoring to evolve towards the current state of knowledge in design and programming. The patterns community became aware of this and started efforts to refactor some of the best-known patterns to capture what we know about software development today [Metz02] [HeBu04]. We expect to see more of such pattern refactoring in the future, specifically of the patterns published in the classic pattern books.

Another big trend in the patterns community is integration. As I mentioned earlier in this chapter, most publications in the future will be pattern languages. These languages will not only consist of entirely new patterns, but rather will build on existing pattern work. For example, almost all pattern languages published in the recent past somehow connect to the classical patterns from the Gang-of-Four. This not only increases the individual value of older patterns, it also connects the new and the old patterns to a pattern network that spans many pattern languages and many areas of software development. In other words, we will get closer towards one of the original visions of the patterns community: providing a kind of 'grand software architecture handbook'. Although we are still a thousand miles away from achieving this vision, each new pattern language that integrates or builds on existing pattern work is another step on this long journey.

The Gang-of-Four

Although now ten years old, the Gang-of-Four [GoF95] book is still the most influential pattern work. There is no doubt that this book is seminal and has influenced many of us about how we think about software design—but time has not stood still since 1994. Today we know more about patterns and software development in general, and the Gang-of-Four patterns specifically. Consequently, the Gang-of-Four patterns deserve some in-depth explanation and refactoring in both content and conceptual issues.

A number of books and papers have been published about the Gang-of-Four patterns in the past, but still no end to this trend is in sight. We expect that an entire secondary industry will feed the unquenchable demand for ruminations about the Gang-of-Four work. Examples include companions on how to implement the patterns in other programming languages, essays on missing ingredients, alternative solutions, and the proper scope of the patterns, and discussions about whether one or other pattern is not a pattern, or is outdated. The Gang-of-Four: a never-ending story.

8.4   A Brief Note about the Future of Patterns

Although we expect many of the predictions in this chapter to come true—particularly because they are drawn from an in-depth analysis of the past and present—they include a healthy element of uncertainty.

The future of patterns may take directions that we have not imagined today. Therefore consider the forecasts in this chapter as one possible vision among many in the ongoing dialogue on patterns and their future, and not as the prophesies of infallible oracles.

9 Concluding Remarks

*"The sum of human wisdom
is not contained in any one language, and
no single language is capable of expressing all forms
and degrees of human comprehension."*

Ezra Pound

Many of the patterns presented in this book generalize existing patterns to some extent. For example, Pooling (97) has many specific instantiations, such as Thread Pooling and Connection Pooling. One of our goals in writing this book was to find the similarities and differences between such patterns, to ultimately reveal the pattern behind the patterns. The patterns are therefore based not only on our experience, but instead on the experience of many researchers and developers.

As we have tried to show, the patterns presented in this book are not specific to any domain. Managing resources effectively and efficiently is a challenge that spans domains and systems, as well as layers within a system. In identifying patterns in resource management, we have tried to take advantage of our experience in building systems of different sizes in many different domains. Our experience has taken us through building real-time embedded, autonomous, Web-based and large-scale enterprise systems. While the domains and the types of system we built varied greatly, the fundamental problems in resource management were very similar. This provided the stimulus for us to describe the solutions in pattern form that we felt best addressed the problems.

An increasing number of languages and run-time environments support the concept of garbage collection, which allows the run-time system to detect and release memory that is no longer being used automatically. Garbage collection is a specialized instance of the Evictor (168) pattern that embeds logic to support automatic identification of unused resources. By identifying unused resources and releasing them, garbage collection gives much more control and predictability of resource availability to runtime environments. In addition to Java and C# offering implementations of garbage collection in their run-time environments, one can find garbage collection implementation for C++ [Boeh04] as well. A growing demand for the support of automated efficient resource release mechanisms in today's infrastructure environments can be observed, as intermediate code with relaxed rules for explicit release of resources becomes a commodity.

Middleware technologies such as J2EE [Sun04b] and .NET [Rich02], with their JVMs (Java virtual machines) and CLR (common language run-time) respectively, automate much of the previously tedious resource management work that confronts a developer. These technologies employ many of the patterns presented in this book in their infrastructure. Pooling (97) and Caching (83) are used to make EJB containers and JSP and ASP.NET engines efficient. The .NET Data Set makes use of Caching to allow efficient use of database content. Using this pattern, the .NET Data Set avoids expensive accesses to the database by providing the database client with a local copy of relevant data. .NET also makes use of Leasing (149). For example, in .NET Remoting [Ramm02] client-activated remote objects are managed based on leases.

One of the most prominent emerging next-generation technologies is 'grid' computing [Grid03]. Grid computing is about sharing and aggregation of distributed resources, such as processing time, storage and information. A grid consists of multiple computers linked to form a single system. Lookup (21) and Resource Lifecycle Manager (128) fit in well in addressing some of the requirements of grid computing. Both patterns play an important role in linking and managing multiple resources. A grid can be regarded as a large resource management system, in which it is important to manage processor time, memory, network bandwidth, storage, and other types of resource effectively. The overall aim is to schedule the applications that need to use the available resources in the grid environment efficiently and effectively. Some grids, such as Condor [Cond04], use Coordinator (21) to synchronize task submission and task completion. The architectures of available grid computing projects [BBL02] and toolkits vary, but the underlying concepts are the same in most of them. To a large extent, the architecture of a grid computing environment is very similar to that of ad hoc networks and peer-to-peer (P2P) networks. See Chapter 6, *Case Study: Ad Hoc Networking* for more details.

In addition to grid computing, the area of autonomic computing has been gaining popularity recently, with much research being conducted in that area. Modeled on the human body's autonomic nervous system, the goal of an autonomic system is to control the functioning of software without requiring input from the user. An autonomic system manages itself and must therefore also be able to manage its resources in an automated manner. This can pose a new set of requirements and challenges, such as automatic resource reservation, resource allocation and reallocation, and resource movement. An autonomic system needs to anticipate the resources needed while keeping its complexity hidden. In addition, an autonomic system is often regarded as self-healing, with the ability to recover from failures automatically. Again, such behavior and functionality requires effective resource management.

To address the challenges posed by grid computing and autonomic systems, it is likely that our resource management pattern language would need to be extended. While the patterns presented in this book can address a large number of the requirements and forces of these emerging technologies, additional patterns may also be discovered. With this in mind, our contribution here should be regarded only as a start in the search for a much larger resource management pattern language.

We hope that this book is the start of a pattern language for resource management that will grow as knowledge of it spreads and hidden aspects of resource management become visible. We intentionally left out several resource management-related areas, such as the management of resources in fault-tolerance systems [Sari02] [ACGH+96], the influences of load balancing, and the whole area of reference accounting [Henn01].

We are excited how the above-mentioned technologies and resource management-related areas will shape and evolve the pattern language, as awareness of resource management grows in the future.

Referenced Patterns

This section provides brief thumbnail descriptions of the patterns referenced in this book.

Abstract Factory [GoF95] provides an interface for creating families of related or dependent objects without specifying their concrete classes.

Abstract Manager [Lieb01] focuses on the management of business objects in enterprise systems.

Activator [Stal00] helps to implement efficient on-demand activation and deactivation of services that are accessed by multiple clients.

Active Object [POSA2] decouples method execution from method invocation.

Adapter [GoF95] converts the interface of a class into an interface expected by clients. Adapter allows classes to work together that could not do so otherwise because of incompatible interfaces.

Asynchronous Completion Token [POSA2] allows an application efficiently to demultiplex and process the responses of asynchronous operations it invokes on services.

Cache Management [Gran98] focuses on caching objects in Java and on how to combine a cache with the Manager [Somm98] pattern.

Cache Proxy [POSA1] implements caching inside a proxy that represents the data source from which one or multiple clients want to retrieve data.

Comparand [CoHa01] provides a means of interpreting differing objects as being the same in specific contexts. It does this by introducing an instance variable, the comparand, in each class of interest, and using it for comparison. Establishing the 'sameness' of differing objects is necessary when more than one reference refers conceptually to the same object.

Component Configurator [POSA2] allows an application to link and unlink its component implementations at run-time without having to modify, recompile, or statically relink the application.

Command Processor [POSA1] separates the request for a service from its execution. A command processor component manages requests as separate objects, schedules their execution, and provides additional services such as storing request objects for later undo.

Data Transfer Object [Fowl02] carries data, for example other objects or invocation parameters, between remote clients and servers. The encapsulation provided by this pattern reduces the number of remote operations required to transfer such data.

Deployer [Stal00] describes how to configure, deploy, and install software artifacts.

Disposal Method [Henn03] encapsulates the concrete details of object disposal by providing an explicit method for cleaning up objects, instead of abandoning the objects to be garbage collected or terminating them by deletion.

Double-Checked Locking Optimization [POSA2] reduces contention and synchronization overheads when critical sections of code must acquire locks in a thread-safe manner just once during program execution.

Factory Method [GoF95] defines an interface for creating an object, but lets subclasses decide which class to instantiate. Factory Method lets a class defer instantiation to subclasses.

Fixed Allocation [NoWe00] allows memory consumption to be predicted by allocating the necessary memory at program initialization.

Flyweight [GoF95] uses sharing to support large numbers of fine-grained objects efficiently.

Half-Object Plus Protocol [Mesz95] divides the responsibilities of an object into halves and assigns them to two interdependent half-objects when an object is used by two distributed clients. For efficiency reasons, each half-object implements the responsibility that is most used locally. This pattern lets the half-objects coordinate themselves via some protocol.

Interceptor [POSA2] allows services to be added to a framework transparently and triggered automatically when specific events occur.

Lazy Load [Fowl02] defers the loading of data from databases until it is first accessed.

Lazy Optimization [Auer96] optimizes the performance of a piece of software only after the design has been correctly determined.

Lazy Propagator [FeTi97] describes how, in a network of dependent objects, objects can determine when they are affected by the state changes of other objects, and therefore need to update their state.

Lazy State [MoOh97] defers the initialization of the state of an object [GoF95] until the state is accessed.

Manager [Somm98] places functionality that applies to all objects of a class into a separate management object. This separation allows the independent variation of management functionality and its reuse for different object classes.

Master-Slave [POSA1] supports fault tolerance, parallel computation and computational accuracy. A master component distributes work to identical slave components and computes a final result from the results returned by the slaves.

Mediator [GoF95] defines an object that encapsulates the way in which a set of objects interact. Mediator promotes loose coupling by keeping objects from referring to each other explicitly, and allows their interaction to be varied independently.

Memento [GoF95] encapsulates the state of an object in a separate, persistable object.

Model-View-Controller [POSA1] divides an interactive application into three components. The model contains the core functionality and data, the view displays information to the user, and the controller handles user input. The view and controller together comprise the user interface. A change-propagation mechanism ensures consistency between the user interface and the model.

Object Lifetime Manager [LGS01] is specialized for the management of singleton objects in operating systems that do not support static destructors properly, such as real-time operating systems.

Object Pool [Gran98] manages the reuse of objects of a type that is expensive to create, or of which only a limited number can be created.

Page Cache [TMQH+03] improves response times when dynamically-generated Web pages are accessed. A page cache is associated with a Web server that uses it to store accessed pages indexed by their URLs. When the same URL is requested, the Web server queries the cache and returns the cached page instead of dynamically generating its contents again.

Passivation [VSW02] persists and activates memory representations of component instances to and from persistent storage.

Pooled Allocation [NoWe00] pre-allocates a pool of memory blocks, recycling them when returned.

Proxy [GoF95] provides a surrogate or placeholder for another object, to control access to it.

Proactive Resource Allocation [Cros02] anticipates system changes and plans necessary resource allocations ahead of time, with the goal of maintaining system performance even under changed conditions.

Reactor [POSA2] allows event-driven applications to demultiplex and dispatch service requests that are delivered to an application from one or more clients.

Reflection [POSA1] provides a mechanism for changing the structure and behavior of software systems dynamically. A meta level provides information about selected system properties and makes the software self-aware.

Resource Exchanger [SaCa96] reduces a server's load when allocating and using resources by sharing common buffers that are passed between clients and servers.

Singleton [GoF95] ensures a class has only one instance, and provides a global point of access to it.

Sponsor-Selector [Wall97] separates three fundamentally different responsibilities: recommending a resource, selecting among resources, and using a resource.

State [GoF95] allows an object to alter its behavior when its internal state changes.

Strategy [GoF95] encapsulates logic, such as algorithms, into interchangeable classes that are independent of client requests.

Thread-local Memory Pool [Somm02] allows a memory allocator to be created for each thread. This helps to reduce synchronization overheads, since dynamic memory allocations are performed from a thread-local pool of pre-allocated memory.

Thread Pooling [PeSo97] describes how to bound the number of threads used and how to reuse unused threads.

Variable Allocation [NoWe00] optimizes memory consumption by performing memory allocations on demand.

Virtual Proxy [GoF95] loads or constructs the object that the proxy represents on demand.

Wrapper Facade [POSA2] encapsulates the functions and data provided by existing non-object-oriented APIs within more concise, robust, portable, maintainable, and cohesive object-oriented class interfaces.

Notations

Class-Responsibility-Collaborator Cards

Class-Responsibility-Collaborators (CRC) cards [BeCu89] help to identify and specify objects or the components of an application in an informal way, especially in the early phases of software development.

Class Name	Collaborators
	• Partner
	• Components
Responsibility	
• Operations may go across several lines.	

A CRC card describes an entity such as a component, an object or a class of objects. The card consists of three fields that describe the name of the entity, its responsibilities, and the names of other collaborating entities. The use of the term 'class' is historical [Rees92].

UML Class Diagrams

The Unified Modeling Language (UML) [Fowl03] is widely used for analysis and design of software applications. An important type of UML diagram is the class diagram. A class diagram describes the types of objects in a system and the various types of static relationships that exist among them.

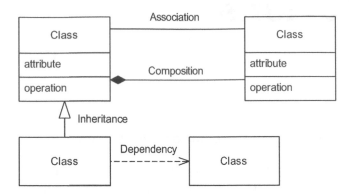

Class. A rectangular box denoting the name of the class and optionally its attributes and operations. Abstract classes' names are labeled in *italics* along with their corresponding abstract methods.

Operation. Operation names are written in the class boxes. They denote the methods of classes. Abstract operations, that is, those that only provide the interface for polymorphism, are denoted by *italics*.

Attributes. Attribute names are written in the class boxes. They denote the instance variables of a class.

Association. A line that connects classes. Associations can be optional or multiple. A number at the end of an association denotes its cardinality. Association of classes is used to show any type of class relationship except aggregation, composition, or inheritance.

Composition. A solid diamond shape at the termination of an association line denotes that the class at the other end of the association is *part* of the class and has the same lifetime.

Dependency. A dependency indicates that a class uses the interface of another class for some purpose.

Realization. A realization represents the relationship between a specification and its implementation.

Inheritance. Inheritance is denoted by a triangle at the top of an association line. The apex of the triangle points to the superclass.

UML Sequence Diagrams

UML sequence diagrams describe how groups of objects collaborate in some behavior [Fowl03].

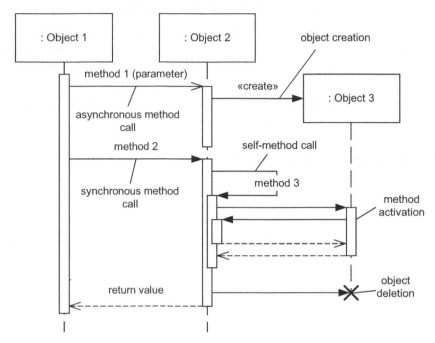

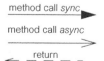

Object. An object or component in a sequence diagram is drawn as a rectangular box. The box is labeled with the name of the component in the pattern. An object that sends or receives method calls in the sequence diagram has a vertical bar attached to the bottom of the box.

Time. Time flows from top to bottom and is represented by a dashed line. The time axis is not scaled.

Method Call. Method calls between objects are denoted by arrows. These arrows are labeled with the method name at the head, if applicable. Synchronous method calls are indicated by solid full-arrowheads, asynchronous method calls by open arrowheads. Returns are indicated by dashed arrows with open arrowheads.

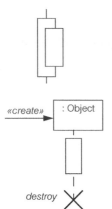

Object Activity. To denote the activity of objects that perform a specific function, procedure or method, rectangular boxes are placed on the vertical bar attached to the object. An object may also invoke self-method calls to activate other methods. This situation is represented by nested boxes offset to the right.

Object Lifecycle. In most cases we assume that all relevant objects already exist, so the corresponding boxes are drawn at the top of the sequence diagram. If a sequence diagram shows object creation, this is denoted by an arrow to a box placed within the sequence diagram. If an object ceases to exist, this is denoted by a cross that terminates the vertical bar.

UML Deployment Diagrams

UML deployment diagrams describe relationships between artifacts, such as components.

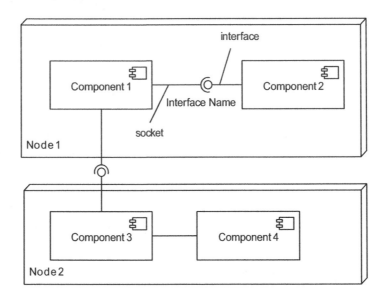

Component. A component is a deployable unit of software. It is differentiated from an object by a small stereotype in the upper right corner.

Interface. An interface describes the syntax and semantics of a component's use. A line and open circle connected to a component is used to indicate an interface. A label associated with the circle represents the interface name.

Socket. Sockets denote the use of a component by another component. Sockets are shown as half-circles that embrace an interface.

Association. An association is shown as a line that connects components. Even though it is recommended that interactions are only through well-defined interfaces, in some cases the interfaces are not of primary concern, so they are replaced by simple associations.

Node. A node represents some run-time environment or hardware on which a software component is running. It is represented as a 3-D box.

Pattern Maps

UML suggests the use of an ellipse to represent a pattern in a diagram. Pattern maps are used to show the relationships between patterns, but also which artifacts, such as components or classes, are involved in a pattern. We have extended this notation to show which non-functional requirements are resolved by a pattern.

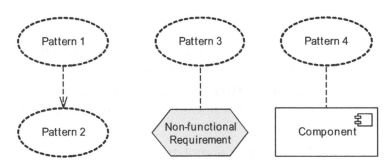

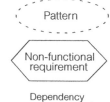

Pattern. The ellipse drawn with a dotted line represents a pattern.

Non-functional Requirement. A non-functional requirement is represented by a shaded hexagonal.

Dependency. A dotted line with an arrow is drawn between two patterns. In the figure above, Pattern 1 applies Pattern 2 to address its forces and solve the problem, respectively. Pattern 2 might be applied optionally, as it is not mandatory for Pattern 1.

Relationship. A dotted line without an arrow connected to a non-functional requirement means that the pattern addresses the non-functional requirement. A dotted line without an arrow connected to a component means that the component is involved in the implementation of the pattern.

Interaction Sketches

In some patterns we use the following informal notation to illustrate the interaction of resource users with other participants in the pattern.

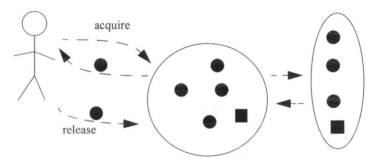

Interaction. An interaction, represented by a dotted arrow, is used to show how various entities interact.

Resource User. A 'matchstick man' represents the resource user, even though a resource user is not necessarily a human in computer systems.

Resource. Different types of resource are represented either as a filled circle or rectangle.

Container. A container holds one or more resources. A container can be a resource environment, or any other participant in the patterns that holds on to one or many resources.

References

[ACGH+96]   M. Adams, J. Coplien, R. Gamoke, R. Hanmer, F. Keeve, and K. Nicodemus: *Fault-Tolerant Telecommunication System Patterns*, in [PLoPD2], 1996

[ACM01]   D. Alur, J. Crupi and D. Malks: *Core J2EE Patterns: Best Practices and Design Strategies*, Prentice Hall, 2001

[Adob04]   Adobe Systems Incorporated, Framemaker, http://www.adobe.com/products/framemaker, 2004

[Alex79]   C. Alexander: *The Timeless Way of Building*, Oxford University Press, 1979

[ALR01]   A. Avizienis, J.-C. Laprie, and B. Randell: *Fundamental Concepts of Dependability*, Research Report N01145, LAAS-CNRS, April 2001

[Apac02]   Apache Group, Tomcat, http://jakarta.apache.org, 2002

[ATT04]   AT&T Corporation, On-line Directory, http://www.anywho.com, 2004

[Auer96]   K. Auer: *Lazy Optimization: Patterns for Efficient Smalltalk Programming*, in [PLoPD2], 1996

[Aust02]   D. Austerberry: *Technology of Video and Audio Streaming*, Focal Press, 2002

[BBL02]   M. Baker, R. Buyya, and D. Laforenza: *Grids and Grid technologies for wide-area distributed computing*, International Journal of Software: Practice and Experience (SPE), Volume 32, Issue 15, Wiley Press, USA, http://www.cs.mu.oz.au/~raj/papers/gridtech.pdf, 2002

[BEA02]   BEA, Weblogic Server, http://www.bea.com/products/weblogic/server, 2002

[BeAp02]   S.P. Berczuk and B. Appelton: *Software Configuration Management Patterns*, Addison-Wesley, 2002

[Beck97]   K. Beck: *Smalltalk Best Practices Patterns*, Prentice Hall, 1996

[BeCu89]   K. Beck and W. Cunningham: *A Laboratory For Teaching Object-Oriented Thinking*, Proceedings of OOPSLA '89, N. Meyrowitz (ed.), special issue of SIGPLAN Notices, Volume 24, Number 10, pp. 1-6, October 1989

[BiWa04a]   P. Bishop and N. Warren: *Recycle broken objects in resource pools*, Java World, http://www.javaworld.com, 2004

[BiWa04b]   P. Bishop and N. Warren: *Lazy Instantiation*, Java World, http://www.javaworld.com, 2004

[Bloc01]   J. Bloch: *Effective Java Programming Language Guide*, Addison-Wesley, 2001

[Boeh04]   H.Boehm: *A garbage collector for C and C++*, Hewlett-Packard, http://www.hpl.hp.com/personal/Hans_Boehm/gc/, 2004

[Boos04]   Boost Library, Memory Pool, http://www.boost.org/libs/pool, 2004

[Borc01]   J. Borchers: *A Pattern Approach to Interaction Design*, John Wiley & Sons, Inc., 2001

[Borl04]   Borland, http://www.borland.com, 2004

[Busc03]   F. Buschmann: *Tutorial: Patterns@Work*, OOPSLA 2003, Anaheim, USA, 2003

[CoHa01]   P. Costanza and A. Haase: *The Comparand Pattern*, Proceedings of the 6th European Conference on Pattern Languages of Programs [EPLoP01], July 2001

[Cohe00]   B. Cohen: *Locate & Track Pattern*, Workshop: The Jini Pattern Language, http://www.posa3.org/workshops/AdHocNetworking, OOPSLA 2000, Minneapolis, USA, 2000

[Cond04]   Condor High Throughput Computing Project, http://www.cs.wisc.edu/condor, 2004

[Cope95]   J.O. Coplien: *A Development Process Generative Pattern Language*, in [PLoPD1], 1995

[Cros02]   J. K. Cross: *Proactive and Reactive Resource Reallocation*, Workshop: Patterns in Distributed and Embedded Real-time Systems, http://www.posa3.org/workshops/RealTimePatterns, OOPSLA 2002, Seattle, USA, 2002

[CzEi00]   K. Czarnecki and U. Eisenecker: *Generative Programming: Methods, Tools, and Applications*, Addison-Wesley, 2000

[DDN03]   S. Demeyer, S. Ducasse, and O. Nierstrasz: *Object-Oriented Reengineering Patterns*, Morgan Kaufmann, 2003

[DHCP04]   DHCP.org, *Resources for DHCP*, http://www.dhcp.org, 2004

[Doug02]   B. P. Douglass: *Real-Time Design Patterns*, Addison-Wesley, 2002

[DyLo04]   P. Dyson and A. Longshaw: *Architecting Enterprise Solutions: Patterns for High-Capability Internet-based Systems*, John Wiley & Sons, Inc., 2004

[EPLoP00]   M. Devos and A. Rüping (eds.): *Proceedings of the 5th European Conference on Pattern Languages of Programs*, 2000, Universitätsverlag Konstanz, 2001

[EPLoP01]   A. Rüping, J. Eckstein, and C. Schwanniger (eds.): *Proceedings of the 6th European Conference on Pattern Languages of Programs*, 2001, Universitätsverlag Konstanz, 2002

[EPLoP02]   A. O'Callaghan, J. Eckstein, and C. Schwanniger (eds.): *Proceedings of the 7th European Conference on Pattern Languages of Programs*, 2002, Universitätsverlag Konstanz, 2003

[EPLoP03]   K. Henney and D. Schütz (eds.): *Proceedings of the 8th European Conference on Pattern Languages of Programs*, 2003, Universitätsverlag Konstanz, 2004

[Evans04]   E. Evans: *Domain-Driven Design: Tackling Complexity in the Heart of Software*, Addison-Wesley, 2004

[EvCa01]   M. Evans and R. A. Caras: *Hamster*, Dorling Kindersley Publishing, 2001

[Ewal01]   T. Ewald: *Transactional COM+: Building Scalable Applications*, Addison-Wesley, 2001

[FeTi97]   P. Feiler and W. Tichy: *Lazy Propagator*, in *Propagator: A Family of Patterns*, Proceedings of TOOLS-23, 1997

[FIK04]   M. Foster, J. Ilgen, N. Kirkwood: *Tivoli Software Installation Service: Planning, Installing, and Using*, IBM RedBooks, http://publib-b.boulder.ibm.com/Redbooks.nsf/RedbookAbstracts/sg246028.html?Open, 2004

[Fowl02]   M. Fowler: *Patterns of Enterprise Application Architecture*, Addison-Wesley, 2002

[Fowl03]   M. Fowler: *UML Distilled*, 3rd edition, Addison-Wesley, 2003

[GKVI+03]   G. Chen, M. Kandemir, N. Vijavkrishnan, M. J. Irwin, B. Mathiske, and M. Wolczko: *Heap Compression for Memory-Constrained Java Environments*, ACM Conference on Object-Oriented Programming, Systems, Languages, and Applications (OOPSLA '03), Anaheim, USA, 2003

[GMX04]   GMX, Mail, Message, More, http://www.gmx.net, 2004

[GoF95]   E. Gamma, R. Helm, R. Johnson, and J. Vlissides: *Design Patterns – Elements of Reusable Object-Oriented Software*, Addison-Wesley, 1995

[GaRe93]   J. Gray and A. Reuter: *Transaction Processing: Concepts and Techniques*, Morgan Kaufmann, 1993

[Grah03]   I. Graham: *A Pattern Language for Web Usability*, Addison-Wesley, 2003

[Gran98]   M. Grand: *Patterns in Java – Volume 1*, John Wiley & Sons, Inc., 1998

[Grid04]   Grid Computing Info Centre, http://www.gridcomputing.com, 2004

[HaBr01]   M. Hall and L. Brown: *Core Web Programming*, Chapter 18: *JDBC and Database Connection Pooling*, Prentice Hall, 2001

[Hanm01]   R. Hanmer: *Call Processing*, Proceedings of PLoP 2001 Conference, 2001

[Hanm02]   R. Hanmer: *Operations and Maintenance*, Proceedings of PLoP 2002 Conference, 2002

[HCI99]   The HCI Patterns Home Page, http://www.hcipatterns.org/, established 1999

[HeBu04]   K. Henney and F. Buschmann: *Beyond the Gang of Four*, Tutorial Notes of the 11th Conference on Object-Oriented-Programming, Munich Germany, 2004

[Henn01]   K. Henney; *C++ Patterns: Reference Accounting*, in [EPLoP01], http://www.curbralan.com, 2001

[Henn03]   K. Henney: *Factory and Disposal Methods*, VikingPLoP 2003, Bergen, Norway, http://www.curbralan.com, 2003

[Henn04]   K. Henney: *One or Many*, available at http://www.curbralan.com, 2003

[HeVi99]   M. Henning and S. Vinoski: *Evictor Pattern*, in *Advanced CORBA Programming with C++*, Addison-Wesley, 1999

[Hill04]   Hillside Group, http://www.hillside.net, 2004

[Hope02]   M. Hope: *Jaune – An ahead of time compiler for small systems*,
               `http://jaune.sourceforge.net`, 2002

[HoSm97]   T. Howes and M. Smith: *LDAP: Programming Directory-Enabled Applications
               with Lightweight Directory Access Protocol*, Macmillan Technical Publishing,
               1997

[HoWo03]   G. Hohpe and B. Woolf: *Enterprise Integration Patterns*, Pearson Education,
               2003

[IBM02]   IBM, *Ahead-Of-Time Compilation*, J9 Java Virtual Machine,
               `http://www.ibm.com/embedded`, 2002

[IBM04a]   IBM, *WebSphere Application Server*, `http://www.ibm.com/websphere`, 2004

[IBM04b]   IBM, *The Eclipse project*, `http://www.eclipse.org`, 2004

[Iona04]   IONA, `http://www.iona.com`, 2004

[IrDA04]   Infrared Data Association (IrDA), `http://www.irda.org`, 2004

[JAP02]   Z. Juhasz, A. Andics, and S. Pota: *Towards a Robust and Fault-Tolerant
               Multicast Discovery Architecture for Global Computing Grids*, in P. Kacsuk, D.
               Kranzlmüller, Zs. Nemeth, J. Volkert (Eds.): *Distributed and Parallel Systems
               – Cluster and Grid Computing*, Proceedings of the 4th Austrian-Hungarian
               Workshop on Distributed and Parallel Systems, Kluwer Academic Publishers,
               The Kluwer International Series in Engineering and Computer Science,
               Volume 706, Linz, Austria, pp. 74-81, 2002

[Jain01]   P. Jain: *Evictor Pattern*, Proceedings of the 8th Conference on Pattern
               Languages of Programs, Allerton Park, Illinois, USA, 2001

[Jain02]   P. Jain: *Coordinator Pattern*, Proceedings of the 7th European Conference on
               Pattern Languages of Programs [EPLoP02], 2002

[JaKi00]   P. Jain and M. Kircher: *Leasing Pattern*, Proceedings of the 7th Conference on
               Pattern Languages of Programs, Allerton Park, Illinois, USA, 2000

[JaKi02]   P. Jain and M. Kircher: *Partial Acquisition*, Proceedings of the 9th Conference
               on Pattern Languages of Programs, Allerton Park, Illinois, USA, 2002

[JoLi96]   R. Jones, and R. Lins: *Garbage Collection: Algorithms for Automatic Dynamic
               Memory Management*, John Wiley & Sons, Inc., 1997

[JXTA04]   JXTA Project, `http://www.jxta.org`, 2004

[KiJa00a]   M. Kircher and P. Jain: *Lookup Pattern*, Proceedings of the 5th European Conference on Pattern Languages of Programs [EPLoP00], 2000

[Kirc01]   M. Kircher: *Lazy Acquisition Pattern*, Proceedings of the 6th European Conference on Pattern Languages of Programs [EPLoP01], 2001

[Kirc02]   M. Kircher: *Eager Acquisition Pattern*, Proceedings of the 7th European Conference on Pattern Languages of Programs [EPLoP02], 2002

[KiJa02]   M. Kircher and P. Jain: *Pooling Pattern*, Proceedings of the 7th European Conference on Pattern Languages of Programs [EPLoP02], 2002

[KiJa03a]   M. Kircher and P. Jain: *Caching Pattern*, Proceedings of the 8th European Conference on Pattern Languages of Programs [EPLoP03], 2003

[KiJa03b]   M. Kircher and P. Jain: *Resource Lifecycle Manager Pattern*, Proceedings of the 8th European Conference on Pattern Languages of Programs [EPLoP03], 2003

[KiJa04]   M. Kircher and P. Jain: *JinACE*, http://www.posa3.org/jinace, 2004

[KiSa92]   J. J. Kistler and M. Satyanarayanan: *Disconnected Operation in the Coda File System*, ACM Transactions on Computer Systems, Volume 10, Issue 1, 1992

[KoMa95]   F. Kon and A. Mandel: *SODA: A Lease-Based Consistent Distributed File System*, Proceedings of the 13th Brazilian Symposium on Computer Networks, 1995

[Ladd03]   R. Laddad: *AspectJ in Action*, Practical Aspect-Oriented Programming, Manning Publications, 2003

[Lapr85]   J.C. Laprie: *Dependability: Basic Concepts and Terminology*, Proceedings of the 15th International Symposium on Fault-Tolerant Computing, 1985

[Lea99]   D. Lea: *Concurrent Programming in Java: Design Principles and Pattern*, Addison-Wesley, 1999

[LiCa87]   M. A. Linton and P. R. Calder: *The Design and Implementation of InterViews*, Proceedings of the USENIX C++ Workshop, November 1987

[LGS01]   D. L. Levine, C. D. Gill, and D. C. Schmidt: *Object Lifetime Manager – A Complementary Pattern for Controlling Object Creation and Destruction*, in *Design Patterns in Communications Software*, Linda Rising, ed., Cambridge University Press, 2001

[Lieb01]   J. Liebenau: *Abstract Manager*, Proceedings of the 8th Conference on Pattern
             Languages of Programs, Allerton Park, Illinois, USA, 2001

[LoLa01]   F. Longoni and A. Laensisalmi: *Radio Access Network Architecture*, in *WDCMA
             for UMTS – Radio Access for Third Generation Mobile Communications*, John
             Wiley & Sons, Inc., 2001

[Luce03]   iMerge, *iMerge Element Manager User's Guide*, Lucent Technologies, 2003

[Lynu04]   LYNUXWORKS, LynxOS, `http://www.lynuxworks.com/rtos`, 2004

[MaAs02]   A. Martelli, D. Ascher: *Python Cookbook*, O'Reilly, 2002

[Macr04]   Macrovision, *FLEXlm Software Licensing System*,
             `http://www.macrovision.com/products/flexlm`, 2004

[Mesz95]   G. Meszaros: *Half-Object Plus Protocol*, in [PLoPD1], 1995

[Metz02]   S.J. Metzker: *Design Patterns Java Workbook*, Addison-Wesley, 2002

[Meye98]   S. Meyers: *Effective C++*, 2nd Edition, Addison-Wesley, 1997

[Micr04]   Microsoft Internet Explorer, `http://www.microsoft.com/windows/ie`, 2004

[MoOh97]   P. Molin and L. Ohlsson: *The Points and Deviations Pattern Language of Fire
             Alarm Systems – Lazy State Pattern*, in [PLoPD3], 1997

[Mozi04]   Mozilla.org, Mozilla Browser, `http://www.mozilla.org/`, 2004

[MSN04]   MSN Hotmail, `http://hotmail.msn.com`, 2004

[Nets04]   Netscape Browser, `http://www.netscape.com`, 2004

[NewM04]   NewMonics Inc., *PERC JVM*, `http://www.newmonics.com/perc/info.shtml`,
             2004

[Newp04]   B. Newport: *Implementing a Data Cache using Readers And Writers*,
             TheServerSide.COM, `http://www.theserverside.com/`, 2004

[Nock03]   C. Nock: *Data Access Patterns: Database Interactions in Object-Oriented
             Applications*, Addison-Wesley, 2003

[NoWe00]   J. Noble and C. Weir: *Variable Allocation Pattern*, in *Small Memory Software:
             Patterns for Systems with Limited Memory*, Addison-Wesley, 2000

[NW088]   M. N. Nelson, B. B. Welch, and J. Ousterhout: *Caching in the Sprite Network Operating System*, ACM Transactions on Computer Systems (TOCS), Volume 6, Issue 1, 1988

[OCI04]   Object Computing Interactive, *The ACE ORB*, `http://www.theaceorb.com`, 2004

[OMG04a]   Object Management Group, *Common Object Request Broker Architecture (CORBA/IIOP)*, `http://www.omg.org/technology`, 2004

[OMG04b]   Object Management Group, *Real-Time CORBA 1.0 Specification*, Chapter 24.15, *Thread pools*, `http://www.omg.org/technology`, 2004

[OMG04c]   Object Management Group, *CORBA Naming Service*, `http://www.omg.org/technology`, 2004

[OMG04d]   Object Management Group, *CORBA Component Model Specification (CCM)*, `http://www.omg.org/technology`, 2004

[OMG04e]   Object Management Group, *Object Transaction Service*, `http://www.omg.org/technology`, 2004

[OMG04f]   Object Management Group, *CORBA Trading Object Service*, `http://www.omg.org/technology`, 2004

[Orac03]   Oracle, *Oracle Application Server: Java Object Cache*, `http://otn.oracle.com/products/ias/joc`, 2003

[Peda04]   Pedagogical Patterns Project, `http://www.pedagogicalpatterns.org`, 2004

[PeSo97]   D. Petriu, G. Somadder: *A Pattern Language For Improving the Capacity of Layered Client/Server Systems with Multi-Threaded Servers*, Proceedings of the 2nd European Conference on Pattern Languages of Programs, Kloster Irsee, Germany, 1997

[PLoPD1]   J.O. Coplien and D.C. Schmidt (eds.): *Pattern Languages of Program Design*, Addison-Wesley, 1995 (a book publishing the reviewed Proceedings of the First International Conference on Pattern Languages of Programming, Monticello, Illinois, 1994)

[PLoPD2]   J.O. Coplien, N. Kerth, and J. Vlissides (eds.): *Pattern Languages of Program Design 2*, Addison-Wesley, 1996 (a book publishing the reviewed Proceedings of the Second International Conference on Pattern Languages of Programming, Monticello, Illinois, 1995)

[PLoPD3]   R.C. Martin, D. Riehle, and F. Buschmann (eds.): *Pattern Languages of Program Design 3*, Addison-Wesley, 1997 (a book publishing selected papers from the Third International Conference on Pattern Languages of Programming, Monticello, Illinois, USA, 1996, the First European Conference on Pattern Languages of Programming, Irsee, Bavaria, Germany, 1996, and the Telecommunication Pattern Workshop at OOPSLA '96, San Jose, California, USA, 1996)

[PLoPD4]   N. Harrison, B. Foote, and H. Rohnert (eds.): *Pattern Languages of Program Design 4*, Addison-Wesley, 1999 (a book publishing selected papers from the Fourth and Fifth International Conference on Pattern Languages of Programming, Monticello, Illinois, USA, 1997 and 1998, and the Second and Third European Conference on Pattern Languages of Programming, Irsee, Bavaria, Germany, 1997 and 1998)

[Pont01]   M. J. Pont: *Patterns for Time-Triggered Embedded Systems: Building Reliable Applications with the 8051 Family of Microcontrollers*, Addison-Wesley, 2001

[POSA1]   F. Buschmann, R. Meunier, H. Rohnert, P. Sommerlad, and M. Stal: *Pattern-Oriented Software Architecture – A System of Patterns*, John Wiley & Sons, Inc., 1996

[POSA2]   D. Schmidt, M. Stal, H. Rohnert, and F. Buschmann: *Pattern-Oriented Software Architecture – Patterns for Concurrent and Distributed Objects*, John Wiley & Sons, Inc., 2000

[POSA4]   F. Buschmann and K. Henney: *Pattern-Oriented Software Architecture – On Patterns and Pattern Languages*, John Wiley & Sons, Inc., to be published 2005

[Pree94]   W. Pree: *Design Patterns for Object-Oriented Software Development*, Addison-Wesley, 1995

[Pryc02]   N. Pryce: *Eager Compilation and Lazy Evaluation*, http://www.doc.ic.ac.uk/~np2/patterns, 2002

[Ramm02]   I. Rammer: *Advanced .NET Remoting*, APress, 2002

[Rees92]   T. Reenskaug: *Intermediate Smalltalk, Practical Design and Implementation*, Tutorial, TOOLS Europe '92, Dortmund, 1992

[Rich02]   J. M. Richter: *Applied Microsoft .NET Framework Programming*, Microsoft Press, 2002

[Risi00]   L. Rising: *The Pattern Almanac 2000*, Addison-Wesley, 2000

[RoDe90]   J. T. Robinson, M. V. Devarakonda: *Data Cache Management Using Frequency-Based Replacement*, In Proceedings of the ACM SIGMETRICS Conference on the Measurement and Modeling of Computer Systems, 1990

[SaCa96]   A. Sane and R. Campbell: *Resource Exchanger*, in [PLoPD2], 1996

[Sari02]   T. Saridakis: *A System of Patterns for Fault Tolerance*, Proceedings of the 7th European Conference on Pattern Languages of Programs [EPLoP02], 2002

[Sari03]   T. Saridakis: *Design Patterns for Fault Containment*, Proceedings of the 8th European Conference on Pattern Languages of Programs [EPLoP03], 2003

[Schm98]   D. C. Schmidt, D. L. Levine, and S. Mungee: *The Design and Performance of Real-Time Object Request Brokers*, Computer Communications, Volume 21, Pages 294-324, Elsevier, 1998

[Schm02]   D. C. Schmidt and S. Huston: *C++ Network Programming: Mastering Complexity with ACE and Patterns*, Addison-Wesley, 2002

[Schm03a]   D. C. Schmidt and S. Huston: *C++ Network Programming: Systematic Reuse with ACE and Frameworks*, Addison-Wesley, 2003

[Schm04]   D. C. Schmidt: *Smart Proxies*, `http://www.cs.wustl.edu/~schmidt/ACE_wrappers/TAO/docs/Smart_Proxies.html`, 2004

[Siem03]   Siemens AG, *UMTS Solutions*, `http://www.siemens.ie/mobile/UMTS`, 2004

[SFHB04]   M. Schumacher, E. Fernandez, D. Hybertson, and F. Buschmann: *Security Patterns*, John Wiley & Sons, Inc., to be published in 2004

[ShaTr01]   A. Shalloway and J.R. Trott: *Design Patterns Explained*, Addison-Wesley, 2001

[Shaw01]   A. C. Shaw: *Real-Time Systems and Software*, John Wiley & Sons, Inc., 2001

[Shif04]   ShiftOne Object Cache, `http://sourceforge.net/projects/jocache`, 2004

[SMFG01]   D. C. Schmidt, S. Mungee, S. Flores-Gaitan, and A.Gokhale: *Software Architectures for Reducing Priority Inversion and Non-determinism in Real-time Object Request Brokers*, Journal of Real-time Systems, Kluwer, Volume 21, Number 2, 2001.

[Smit82]   A. J. Smith: *Cache Memories*, Journal of ACM Computing Surveys, Volume 14 Issue 3, 1982

[Smit85]	A. J. Smith: *Disk Cache – Miss Ratio Analysis and Design Considerations*, ACM Transactions on Computer Systems (TOCS), Volume 3, Issue 3, 1985
[Somm98]	P. Sommerlad: *Manager Pattern*, in [PLoPD3], 1998
[Somm02]	P. Sommerlad: *Performance Patterns*, Proceedings of the 7th European Conference on Pattern Languages of Programs [EPLoP02], 2002
[Squi04]	Squid Web Proxy Cache, `http://www.squid-cache.org`, 2004
[Stal00]	M. Stal: *Activator Pattern*, `http://www.stal.de/articles.html`, 2000
[Stal00]	M. Stal: *Deployer Pattern*, `http://www.stal.de/Downloads/docpatterns.pdf`, 2000
[Stev03]	W. R. Stevens: *Unix Network Programming, Volume 1: The Sockets Networking API*, Third Edition, Prentice Hall, 2003
[Sun04a]	Sun Microsystems, *Java*, `http://java.sun.com/`, 2004
[Sun04b]	Sun Microsystems, *Java2 Enterprise Edition (J2EE)*, `http://java.sun.com/j2ee/`, 2004
[Sun04c]	Sun Microsystems, *Jini*, `http://www.sun.com/jini`, 2004
[Sun04d]	Sun Microsystems, *Java Transaction Service*, `http://java.sun.com/products/jts`, 2004
[Sun04e]	Sun Microsystems, *Java Authentication and Authorization Service*, `http://java.sun.com/products/jaas/`, 2004
[Sun04f]	Sun Microsystems, *Java Naming and Directory Interface*, `http://java.sun.com/products/jndi/`, 2004
[Sun04g]	Sun Microsystems, *Java Remote Method Invocations (RMI)*, `http://java.sun.com/products/jdk/rmi/`, 2004
[Sun04h]	*Solaris 9 Linker and Libraries Guide*, Section on *Lazy Loading of Dynamic Dependencies*, `http://docs.sun.com`, 2004
[Sun04i]	Sun Microsystems, *Java Connector Architecture (JCA)*, `http://java.sun.com/j2ee/connector`, 2004
[Sun04j]	Sun Microsystems, *Mobile Information Device Profile for Java 2 Micro Edition, Version 2.0 – Over The Air User Initiated Provisioning*, `http://java.sun.com/products/midp`, 2004

[Symb03]   Symbian Ltd, *Symbian OS – the mobile operating system*,
                http://www.symbian.com, 2004

[Tane01]   A. S. Tanenbaum: *Modern Operating Systems*, 2nd Edition, Prentice Hall,
                2001

[Tane02]   A. S. Tanenbaum: *Computer Networks*, 4th Edition, Prentice Hall, 2002

[Thom99]   S. Thompson: *Haskell: The Craft of Functional Programming*, 2nd Edition,
                Addison-Wesley, 1999

[TMQH+03]   D. Trowbridge, D. Mancini, D. Quick, G. Hohpe, J. Newkirk, and D. Lavigne:
                Microsoft, *Enterprise Solution Patterns Using Microsoft .NET*,
                http://www.microsoft.com/resources/practices, 2003

[ToHu00]   D. Thomas and A. Hunt: *Programming Ruby: A Pragmatic Programmers Guide*,
                Addison-Wesley, 2000

[TwAl83]   J. Twing and G. Alpharetta: *The Receptionist*, Macmillan McGraw Hill, 1983

[UDDI04]   Universal Description, Discovery, and Integration of Web Services (UDDI),
                http://uddi.org, 2004

[UPnP04]   Universal Plug 'n Play (UPnP) Forum, http://www.upnp.org, 2004

[VBW97]   T. E. Vollmann, W. L. Berry, D. C. Whybark: *Manufacturing Planning and
                Control Systems*, McGraw-Hill Trade, 4th Edition, 1997

[VKZ04]   M. Völter, M. Kircher, and U. Zdun: *Remoting Patterns – Patterns for
                Enterprise, Realtime and Internet Middleware*, John Wiley & Sons, Inc., to be
                published in 2004

[VPLoP02]   P. Hruby and K.E. Sørensen (eds.): *Proceedings of the First Nordic Conference
                on Pattern Languages of Programs 2002*, Microsoft Business Solutions, 2003

[VSW02]   M. Völter, A. Schmid, E. Wolff: *Server Component Patterns – Component
                Infrastructures Illustrated with EJB*, John Wiley & Sons, Inc., 2002

[Wall97]   E. Wallingford: *Sponsor-Selector*, in [PLoPD3], 1997

[Wind04]   Windriver, VxWorks, http://www.windriver.com, 2004

[Wisc00]   M. Wischy: *Pick and Verify Pattern*, Workshop: *The Jini Pattern Language*,
                http://www.posa3.org/workshops/AdHocNetworking,
                OOPSLA 2000, Minneapolis, USA, 2000

[W3C04]   World Wide Web Consortium (W3C), http://www.w3.org, 2004

[YaAm03]   S. Yacoub and H.H. Ammar: *Pattern-Oriented Analysis and Design: Composing Patterns to Design Software Systems*, Addison-Wesley, 2003

[YBS99]   H. Yu, L. Breslau, and S. Shenker: *A Scalable Web Cache Consistency Architecture*, Computer Communication Review, ACM SIGCOMM, Volume 29, Number 4, October 1999

[Zero04a]   ZeroC Inc., *Internet Communication Engine (Ice)*, `http://www.zeroc.com`, 2004

[Zero04b]   Zero G, *InstallAnywhere*, `http://www.zerog.com`, 2004

[3GPP04]   *3rd Generation Partnership Project* (3GPP), `http://www.3gpp.org`, 2004

Acknowledgements

The quotations at the start of each chapter are from the following sources:

Chapter 1: Douglas Adams (1952–2001), from *Mostly Harmless*, Tor Books, 1993, ISBN 0330323113.

Chapter 2: Franklin P. Adams (1881–1960), from *Nods and Becks*, Garden City Publishing, New York, 1946, Second Edition.

Chapter 3: Pindar (518 B.C–438 B.C.).

Chapter 4: Michelangelo Buonarroti (1475–1564) (also attributed to Leonardo da Vinci and Auguste Rodin).

Chapter 5: William Shakespeare (1564–1616).

Chapter 6: Edward V. Berard, from *Life-Cycle Approaches*, White Paper, The Object Agency, http://www.itmweb.com/essay552.htm.

Chapter 7: Bjarne Stroustrup (1950–), quoted at the 2003 International Conference on Intelligent User Interfaces, http://www.iuiconf.org/.

Chapter 8: James Burke (source unknown).

Chapter 9: Ezra Pound (1885–1972), from *The ABC of Reading*, New Directions Publishing, 1960, ISBN 0811201511.

Index of Patterns

Index

Index of Names

Printed and bound by CPI Group (UK) Ltd, Croydon, CR0 4YY

27/10/2024

14580375-0001